ETHNIC POLITICS
IN
NIGERIA

ETHNIC POLITICS
IN
NIGERIA

by

OKWUDIBA NNOLI

Department of Political Science
University of Nigeria
Nsukka

FOURTH DIMENSION PUBLISHERS

First Published 1978 by

Fourth Dimension Publishing Co. Ltd.
179 Zik Avenue,
P.O. Box 553,
Enugu, Nigeria

© Okwudiba Nnoli

ISBN 978 156 008 8

Jacket design by Reno Psaila

*Dedicated to my wife Ebele, and children
Obiora, Ifeyinwa, and Ndukaku.*

PREFACE

This study is motivated by the apparent intractability of the ethnic problem in Nigeria. A cursory glance at the history of ethnicity reveals that as far back as 1936 some Nigerians had warned about the negative effects. Ever since then, many Nigerian patriots, progressives and others have inveighed against it and suggested solutions to it. Some of these solutions have been tried but to no avail. Further examination of the relevant literature indicates that a great deal of intellectual endeavour has been devoted to the ethnic phenomenon.

Yet the basic question remains: why has the ethnic problem persisted and, in many cases, intensified? It was to answer this question and to provide solutions for the difficulty that this study was embarked upon. First, I wrote a paper entitled "Socio-economic Insecurity and Ethnic Politics in Africa," which was presented at the Third Congress of Africanists in Addis Ababa, Ethiopia in December 1973. The positive reception it received by the participants of the Congress, who felt that it represented an important new perspective on the problem encouraged me to work even harder. However, certain criticisms suggested that the study could be strengthened if its theoretical perspective were anchored in some concrete situation. In response to this suggestion I decided to make a concrete study of the Nigerian case.

Since that conference I have written several other papers on the same subject. In the course of writing them, I have revised the Addis Ababa theoretical framework and elaborated its various aspects. In particular, the relationship between class and ethnicity has become clearer to me. This relationship had been badly neglected in the previous works, but it serves as the focal point of this study. Therefore, this book is a culmination of several years of study and reflection on the ethnic question. It reflects my present understanding of the phenomenon and, therefore, an improvement on my previous analyses of it.

Invariably, an analysis of a contemporary social problem elicits the question: what is to be done? I have found that many attempts to answer this question have faltered on two major grounds. First, there is an undue haste to solve the problem. Consequently analysts recommend mere palliatives, possibly because a thoroughgoing solution would take a long time. But these quick remedies often prove sterile. In fact, there is ample evidence that some of them have even exacerbated the situation. Second, the recommendations are rather subjective in nature. They do not emanate logically from analysis. This is essentially the result of the superficiality of analysis, the lack of scientific rigor, and the desire to moralise. It is also the result of unwillingness to face certain solutions which may be detrimental to some cherished vested interests.

In making recommendations I have tried to avoid these pitfalls. Even when others may disagree with my solutions I hope they will at least accept them as the logical end products of the preceding analysis. This acceptance does not have to imply agreement with that analysis. My approach to these recommendations stems from my belief that unless we can identify the major moving forces of a phenomenon and their direction of motion, it is difficult to find solutions to problems posed by that phenomenon. These solutions must be designed to eliminate these forces or, at least, to change their motion to the desired direction. The result may not be what we would otherwise like to see emerge. But such an outcome must represent what needs to be done.

I thank all those who have helped me during the course of this work. The study was begun while I was teaching at the University of Dar-es-Salaam, Tanzania. I am grateful to all those at that institution who helped me in one way or the other to clarify my thinking on the subject. The same applies to my colleagues at the various conferences at which I presented papers on ethnicity. The University of Nigeria provided some funds for part of the research that went into this work. In doing so, it fulfilled its responsibility to promote the search for knowledge. For that I am thankful. Too, I thank all those who have read the manuscript in part or in its entirety and made valuable recommendations. Finally, I wish to thank those who helped with the typing and proof-reading of the manuscript.

OKWUDIBA NNOLI
Nsukka, August 1977

CONTENTS

LIST OF TABLES

LIST OF TABLES

Chapter 1

A THEORETICAL PERSPECTIVE

Tribalism or Ethnicity: Ideology versus Science

It is common to interpret African politics in tribal terms. Tribalism is perceived to be the central unifying concept for the analysis of African life. This perspective was first popularised by colonial anthropologists. It has been internalised to such an extent that even Africans themselves now think of the dynamics of their societies as being dominated by that phenomenon. All this has persisted in spite of the methodological difficulties of applying the concept in scientific analysis, and the obvious failure of analyses based on it to lead to the socioeconomic and political transformation of the various African societies. It is often forgotten that the concepts that prevail in the academic community are not solely of an academic or scientific nature. They usually have an ideological and political character. This is particularly so with the concept of tribalism.

In Africa the concept has a colonial origin and its function was tied to the nature and purpose of colonialism. In Europe in the late nineteenth century, imperialism meant the rule of the powerful monopolies, trusts, combines and cartels controlled by the financial oligarchies of the various European countries, along with the consequent reduction of the market competition which characterised the earlier periods of capitalism. Abroad, for example in Africa, imperialism combined these features with foreign European control of the local apparatus of state. The financial oligarchies organised production to satisfy their needs for profit and capital accumulation as well as to remedy the deficiencies in their production processes at home. Apart from the use of military conquest, African resistance to this material reorganisation and political domination of their societies was attacked from two angles. The one was material, the other ideological. The colonial government changed the material circumstances of the Africans by compelling them to participate in colonial economic activities dominated by the profit motive, through forced labor, taxation, the introduction of new currencies, and the creation of artificial scarcity (via the accumulation of huge surpluses even during times of severe economic depression), low wages, low prices for cash crops, and costly social services. These measures caused the population to leave their former economic activities to enter the new system dominated by alien ownership of the major means of production, distribution and exchange.

At the ideological level, foreign values such as profit motive and individualism were reinforced by the educational system and the new christian churches. These values enabled the Africans to carry on production in the interest of the financial oligarchies. In addition, a myth was necessary to explain the foreign control of the local state, and to ensure foreign domination of production at minimal costs, and with the least possible amount of coercion. The maintenance of peace was essential to gainful colonial activity. The "natives" had to be pacified if sufficient profits were to be accumulated by the financial oligarchies. Colonial racism provided a myth whose primary objective was the complete alienation of the colonised African, enabling a better and more complete domination and control of him.

It was the illegitimacy of the coloniser and oppressor which necessitated the creation of the myth of the inferior "native" as an instrument of domination. Frantz Fanon has observed that the alienated colonised man existed only where there was a dominant culture that reduced him to an inferior status. This was accomplished gradually through the process of his alienation from his culture and tradition, which involved selfhatred or, at least, a profoundly disturbed ambivalence. The rejection of self came as a result of identification with the coloniser and as a result of the acceptance of the latter's image of one's inferior status.[1]

The racism of colonial ideology reflected a Eurocentric devaluation of African culture and a corresponding glorification of the European way of life. The unconditional condemnation of African culture was attended by the unconditional affirmation of the colonisers' world-view: "colonialism is not satisfied merely with holding a people in its grip and emptying the native's brain of all form and content. By a kind of perverted logic, it turns to the past of the oppressed people, and distorts, disfigures and destroys it."[2] The African of precolonial times was portrayed as

1. Irene L. Gendzier, *Frantz Fanon* (London: Wildhouse, 1973), p. 50.
2. Frantz Fanon, *The Wretched of the Earth* (New York: Grove Press, 1966), p. 170.

a primitive savage. His culture was dismissed as characterised essentially by an unreflective adaptation to the environment, operating at varying levels of the Hobbsean state of nature and congenital infantilism.

Tribalism occupied an important place in this racist ideology of colonialism. It was represented as a primitive and barbarous mystique peculiar to the African, the major link between this ahistorical, primitive and barbarous past in which no system of ethics and no principle of conduct were developed, on the one hand, and the "civilising mission" and "white man's burden" of the colonial order on the other. This reactionary racist con-ceptualisation of the African dynamic survived the shifts in the colonisers' metaphysical world-view "from overall negation to singular and specific recognition"[3] of the worth of precolonial African culture. "There is first affirmed the existence of human groups having no culture; then of a hierarchy of cultures; and finally the concept of cultural relativity."[4]

In order to justify this racist view of the African, the colonialists began to categorise African linguistic groups as tribes and to attribute to them differences in culture and way of life. By so doing they distorted the scientific meaning of the word "tribe." As Mamdani has pointed out "there was a time when the word possessed scientific content, when it characterised those social formations that did not possess a state – the communal, classless societies, as for example, the Germanic tribes."[5] Today, however, every single language group in Africa is referred to as a tribe regardless of the nature of its social development. "What is it that makes 2 million Norwegians a people and just as many Baganda a tribe? A few hundred thousand Icelanders a people and 14 million Hausa-Fulani a tribe? There is only one explanation: racism."[6]

Also, the colonialists began to separate these linguistic groups from one another, particularly in residential areas. For example, in Northern Nigeria it was the official British policy to separate the Hausa-Fulani from the Southerners. At first Southern and Northern migrants to Northern cities lived together in harmony

3. Frantz Fanon, *Toward the African Revolution* (New York: Grove Press), p. 31.
4. *Ibid.*
5. Mamood Mamdani, *Politics and Class Formations in Uganda* (New York: Monthly Review, 1976), p. 3.
6. *Ibid.*

3

with their hosts in the native city. This embarrassed the official view that only conflict characterised contact among African tribes. Hence, the migrants were forced to set up abode in Sabongaris. Initially both the Southern and Northern migrants lived in the Sabongaris and got along well, to the embarrassment of the colonialists. Later, the Northern migrants were separated and compelled to live in another section of the city, Tudun Wada.[7] However, in cities like Katsina and Gwandu, where the emirs successfully resisted this policy of "Sabongari," the migrants have continued to live together with their hosts. In fact, colonial confidential reports on the emirs contained a section on their attitude to the Southerners. Those who were favourably disposed to the migrants were reported as "not to be trusted on this question."[8]

An extension of this racism was also evident in the tendency of the coloniser to regard certain African language groups as superior or inferior to others depending on the similarity of their sociopolitical organisation to that of the coloniser, and their progress in the acquisition of colonial socioeconomic fortunes. Thus, for example, the Dogon, some Bambara, and Senufo of Mali; the Bete of Ivory Coast; the pygmies of Zaire; the Masai of East Africa; and the Karamojong of Uganda were regarded as more "primitive" than their compatriots.

As products of socialisation into this colonialist world view, Africans have internalised this discriminatory classification of their countrymen. In his study of the Ivory Coast, Aristide Zolberg observes that both Africans and Europeans widely believed that certain ethnic groups were more progressive, intelligent, or generally more worthy of respect than others.[9] The level and rate of colonial socioeconomic attainments has become a basis for the myth of ethnic superiority.

Thus the ideology of tribalism has taken roots both within and outside Africa. It is clear, however, that what the colonialists referred to as tribalism in Africa is empirically observable in the

---

7. This point was quietly but forcefully made by an Igbo migrant who has lived in Zaria for over sixty years and is now virtually an House citizen. He was very specific about Zaria. He was directly affected by this forced separation of inhabitants. The word "Sabongari" means literally strangers' quarters.

8. Refer to colonial reports on the Emirs located on the Archives in Kaduna.

9. Aristide Zolberg, *Creating Political Order* (Chicago Rand McNally, 1966), p. 69.

anti-Castillian activities of the Basques, Calatans and Galacians of Spain; the animosity of the Swiss against immigrant workers in Switzerland, and the demands of the French-speaking peoples of Berne for political separation from their German-speaking compatriots; South Tyroleans' dissatisfaction with Italian rule; the resurgence of Scottish, Welsh and Irish chauvinism in the United Kingdom; Wallon-Flemish rivalry in Belgium; French Canadian separatism in Canada; racial violence in the United Kingdom and the United States; Croatian separatism in Yugoslavia; and Jewish chauvinism in the Soviet Union. However, ethnicity not tribalism, is the concept associated with this common phenomenon outside Africa. Therefore, ethnicity is a more universal concept for understanding the phenomenon which colonial racism called tribalism.

It is also more scientific. Unlike tribalism, ethnicity is not limited in space. This forces it to act as an abstract mental construct whose characteristics can be more objectively determined. Therefore, it is more dispositional than tribalism in identifying the features that would be exhibited, including hypothetical ones, if certain conditions were fulfilled. Consequently, it offers greater scope for the comparative analysis of data and has a greater capacity for marking out the path by which analysis may move most freely in logical space. It can provide more empirical referents for any theory of which it is a part. Data indicated by it are more amenable to verification and falsification than those indicated by the concept of tribalism. It can therefore explain our subject matter better. Similarly, the concept "ethnic group" has a greater explanatory power than the concept "tribe".

What is ethnicity? It is a social phenomenon associated with interactions among members of different ethnic groups. Ethnic groups are social formations distinguished by the communal character of their boundaries. The relevant communal factor may be language, culture, or both. In Africa, language has clearly been the most crucial variable. As social formations, however ethnic groups are not necessarily homogeneous entities even linguistically and culturally. Minor linguistic and cultural differences often exist within the group, forming the basis for the delineation of sub-ethnic systems. More important still is the possibility of occupational and class differentiation. This is dependent on the level of production in the group, the level of growth of the productive forces, and the consequent extent of the division of labour within the social formation. In this regard different ethnic groups may have a similar pattern of social differentiation.

Ethnocentrism is also associated with the interaction of ethnic groups. It is, therefore, often confused with ethnicity. Although related, the two are quite different phenomena. Ethnocentrism is attitudinal in form and perceptual in content. It represents the subjective dimension of ethnic behaviour. The members of a group are ethnocentric when they are proud of it and consequently are inward-looking. Their attachment to and pride in the group reflect their ethnocentrism. Its attributes are limited to beliefs, group identity, parochial orientation, and group pride.

Ethnicity, on the other hand, includes these attributes but goes beyond them. In other words, it includes but is not limited to ethnocentrism. It is behavioural in form and conflictual in content. First, ethnicity exists only within a political society consisting of diverse ethnic groups. When, as in the case of Somalia, an ethnic group is itself a polity, its relations with other societies and ethnic groups are characterised by nationalism. This is because ethnicity does not involve the demand for sovereign status or the use of the state apparatus on behalf of an ethnic group to the exclusion of others or the incorporation of an ethnic group into a political society. In these cases, nationalism is the relevant social phenomenon. Relations between ethnic groups within the same political system produce ethnicity. Those between ethnic groups which are political systems themselves constitute international relations and are characterised by nationalism. Thus what the colonialists called inter-tribal wars were in fact, international wars fought between independent political entities rather than between different entities within the same political unit.

Second, much more than ethnocentrism, ethnicity is characterised by a common consciousness of being one in relation to the other relevant ethnic groups. This factor more than any other defines the boundary of the group that is relevant for understanding ethnicity at any historical point in time. There is enough evidence in the literature to show that these boundaries have changed over time. During the precolonial times the Yoruba-speaking peoples were organised in kingdoms which fought bitter wars against one another and shared no common consciousness but only a tenuous link in the myth of ancestry. They have since acquired a common identity. Similarly, the precolonial distinction between Olu and Igbo in Igboland has given way to a common Igbo consciousness. In this regard it is probably necessary to make a distinction between the "ethnic group in itself" and the "ethnic group for itself" similar to that Marx made with respect to classes. The former refers to a group marked out by linguistic and/or cultural similarity but without a common consciousness or identity. The latter identifies a group with both linguistic and/or cultural similarity and a common consciousness or identity. It is the latter that is of importance for understanding ethnicity. Under certain conditions, for example the colonial contact situation, the former is transformed into the latter.

The emergence of this common consciousness can be the result of several developments. As in the case of the Jews, it can arise from a long historical association of common struggle to tame nature or against other but hostile groups. It can also arise from inter-ethnic competition for scarce valuable resources. This has been the more common basis of ethnic consciousness in Africa. It has had two dimensions. Mention has already been made of the role of colonial racism in engendering ethnic awareness, sentiment and, consequently, consciousness. But colonial racism served as an instrument in the struggle of the colonialists with the Africans for the scarce local resources. Also in the search for the crumbs from colonial production, competition among Africans created or reinforced common consciousness among the various competing ethnic groups. At times the historical and competitive aspects of this consciousness were linked. There may have been a historical competition among the groups which created and reinforced their varied identity. Contemporary competition among them may have reinforced inherited historical identification. But contemporary competition may create a common consciousness among previously and historically hostile and warring sections of the same ethnic group. It is, therefore, important for understanding ethnicity to know when, and how this common consciousness was brought about.

Third, exclusiveness is an attribute of ethnicity. Ingroup-outgroup boundaries emerge with it and, in time, become marked, more distinct than before, and jealously guarded by the various ethnic groups. Acceptance and rejection on linguistic-cultural grounds characterises social relations. These are expressed inevitably through interethnic discrimination in jobs, housing, admissions into educational institutions, marriages, business transactions or the distribution of social welfare services. This factor of exclusiveness is usually accompanied by nepotism and corruption. Merit is sacrificed on the altar of ethnic chauvinism and solidarity.

Finally, conflict is an important aspect of ethnicity. This is inevitable under conditions of interethnic competition for scarce valuable resources, particularly in societies where inequality is accepted as natural, and wealth is greatly esteemed. The fear of being confined to the bottom of the interethnic ladder of inequality generates divisive and destructive socioeconomic competition which has antisocial effects. It becomes possible for the ingroup to accept the expression of hostility toward the outgroup. Aggressive behaviour may then be used to limit competition in favour of the ingroup. Demonstrations, rioting and various forms of violent agitations become instruments in interethnic relations.

Thus, ethnicity is a very complex phenomenon. Its complexity is not always adequately reflected in sociopolitical thought. The methodological difficulties of studying it may be traced to this complexity. Like any other social phenomenon, ethnicity is not immutable. It alters its form, its place, and its role in the life of society. New elements appear in its content. Its links with other social phenomena change, posing new questions. In our time, for example, ethnicity poses such a threat to the national revolutionary process that special importance ought to be attached to the elucidation of the relationship between the class element and the ethnic element. Also, ethnicity does not exist in a pure form. It is always closely associated with political, juridical, religious and other social views, which constitute its important ingredients as well. It also tends to change its specific historical content and to assume many different forms.

Therefore, the analysis of ethnicity cannot be fruitful unless it is based on a method which is objective, comprehensive, historical, concrete and which defines the most essential connections. An abstract presentation of the question is bound to be sterile. It must be investigated within some definite historical limits, focussed on a particular country, and related to differences between that country and others in the same historical epoch. The study should relate the interactions of different ethnic formations among themselves to the extent to which each has developed its productive forces, the division of labour, production relations and changes in these attributes. This would enable the analyst to determine the real place and role of ethnicity in the life of the society, and to trace its origin, stages of development and future prospects. Any form of community is social in nature and the historical forms of an ethnic community are no exception. The correlation of social nature and ethnic form changes with the succession of socioeconomic formations and the character of ethnic connections. Historical continuity is a feature of the social nature of human community and it is determined, in the final analysis, by the development of the productive forces and the production relations that flow from these forces.

Does Ethnicity Matter?

Of course, ethnicity often intrudes into African politics. In view of the ethnic consciousness that has developed over several generations of the colonial and neocolonial history of Africa, it cannot be otherwise. However, this ethnic ideology in itself needs to be explained. It cannot, therefore, be made a decisive independent variable. Several dangers attend an attempt to explain the ethnic phenomenon in Africa. First, it may succeed in keeping ethnic sentiments aflame by bringing it to the forefront of the consciousness of the reading population. Second, it may generate divisive interethnic controversy. Ethnicity is a very sensitive issue in national politics. Its interpretation may be regarded by some ethnic ideologues as casting an aspersion on their ethnic groups. Others may interpret it as a vindication of their ethnic groups. In either case, the net effect is an unintended growth in ethnic tension.[10] Most important of all is the tendency of such an analysis to overexaggerate the importance of ethnicity in African politics, and to encourage the diversion of research efforts away from other and more important variables. There are other equally, if not more, important variables which must be taken into account in explaining African politics. One of them is the place occupied by actors in the social production process. A focus on it permits us to discern historical trends and to elucidate the direction of social movement.

A focus on ethnicity tends to mask this very significant variable. Archie Mafeje has noted that tribalism is not only an anachronistic misnomer which impedes crosscultural analysis by drawing invidious and highly suspect distinction between Africans

---

10. In Nigeria such a controversy attended the publication of Robert Livine's book *Dreams and Deeds* (Chicago, Illinois: University of Chicago Press, 1966).

9

and other peoples of the world, but that it also oversimplifies, mystifies and obscures the real nature of economic and power relations among Africans themselves and between them and the capitalist world.[11] B. Magubane has convincingly argued that a focus on ethnicity impedes a serious effort to understand African societies because it ignores the ownership of the primary productive forces, the material basis of society, and the nature of the social system.[12] Similarly, Richard Sklar views the focus on ethnicity as obscuring the fact that in Africa, ethnic movements may be created and instigated to action by the new men of power in furtherance of their own special interests which are time and again constitutive interests of emerging social classes. In this way ethnicity becomes a mask for class privileges.[13] For example, tribal historians and analysts tend to focus on tribal migration, tribal warfare, and tribal political institutions. Inevitably they ignore the technological and economic systems that were being developed in different areas, and how such developments or the lack of them were affecting specific social formations, the creation of surplus, and the emergence of internal and inter-African trade. In their analyses of the colonial period, they avoid the fundamental issues of colonial oppression and exploitation, and the resultant economic and social structures that were being created in the colonies by the colonial powers.

There have been very few intelligent analyses of the basic nature of the economic structures of African countries during the post-colonial era, and very little of the determining role of the international context in African life. There is hardly any information or research available in the critical area of ownership of economic undertakings in industry, commerce, agriculture, and real estate, and none of the continuity of the colonial economies in the post-colonial societies. And there is certainly inadequate research on the social and class structure of the African countries. The class structure that inevitably emerged during the colonial period, its continuation, expansion, and consolidation over the past sixteen years have not been sufficiently examined scientifically.

Indeed, there is even hardly any attempt to focus on those

11. Archie Mafeje, "The Ideology of Tribalism," *Journal of Modern African Studies*, Vol. IX, No. 2 (1971), pp. 253–262.
12. B. Magubane, "Pluralism and Conflict Situations in Africa: A New look," *African Social Research*, Vol. VII, No. 2 (June 1969), p. 538.
13. Richard Sklar, "Political Science and Political Integration," *Journal of Modern African Studies* Vol. V, No. 1 (1967), pp. 6–8.

things which are common among ethnic groups, such as elements of history and culture which bind them together or may act as a basis for cooperation and solidarity. The exclusiveness of the ethnic group is stressed. In some cases ethnic intellectuals fabricate ethnic homelands which are much larger than those that existed in pre-colonial times.[14] It is rarely suggested that the various pre-colonial societies evolved over the centuries as the result of successive population contacts in the same area, that various aspects of life are identical across ethnic groups, that there is a great deal of overlap in the activities of the groups even where differences exist, and that what differences there are do not necessarily have to create difficulties in political relations among the groups.

Quite apart from the narrow focus on ethnicity, there is the whole question of what weight should be attached to it as an explanatory variable. The tendency is to point to ethnic contradictions and view these contradictions as the principal ones in African societies. In Africa, ethnic problems are readily apparent and very real. But this is only at the level of mere empirical observation. Ethnic contradictions have an objective basis in the social structure of society. As an element of the ideological superstructure of society, ethnicity rests on, is functional for, and is determined by the infrastructure of society, the mode of production. Ethnic conflicts differ from class conflicts because they are not associated with direct linkages in the production process. In some cases, however, ethnic and class lines coincide.[15] Although a dialectical relationship exists between elements of the superstructure (such as ethnic consciousness) and the production process, it is the latter which generally gives rise to the former and not vice versa. Therefore, the nature of the production process has a higher explanatory capacity than ethnic consciousness which arises from it.

As Karl Marx has clearly demonstrated, social life, including politics, is determined primarily by social production, what is

---

14. P. C. Lloyd, *African in Social Change* (Hammondsworth, England: Penguin, 1967), pp. 288–303.
15. A good example is the relationship between the Indians and Africans in East Africa, and between whites and blacks in white minority regimes. In East Africa, the African peasant met the Asian mainly as a producer and a consumer. The Asian was the trader, the middle man and the creditor. Similarly in South Africa the African met the white as an employee in the service of an employer. See discussion of this issue on page 29.

produced, how it is produced, and how what is produced is distributed. It is characterised by social movement which is a process of natural history governed by laws which are independent of human will and consciousness.[16] Therefore, in any conception of social life the first requirement is to observe this basic fact in all its significance and implications, and to acknowledge its proper importance. The problems posed by ethnicity are magnified out of proportion to their real significance when social reality is conceived in terms of objects of observation isolated from practical human productive activity. Ethnicity is observed as fundamental reality. But the highest point that can be attained by this observation is the description of reality. It cannot be the basis for explaining and changing society.

As an element of the superstructure of society, ethnic consciousness can only be of major significance in the social process to the extent that it is congruent with the production relations which form the infrastructure. Consciousness and productive existence are indeed distinct but they also form a unity. When the two diverge there is false consciousness which, in the long run at least, cannot survive any serious confrontation with objective consciousness based on productive existence. Therefore, the task is to confront ethnic consciousness with class consciousness. The experience of Amilcar Cabral is illuminating:

"you may be surprised to know that we consider the contradictions between the tribes as a secondary one ... Our struggle for national liberation and the work done by our party have shown that this contradiction is really not so important; the Portuguese counted on it a lot but as soon as we organised the liberation struggle properly the contradiction between the tribes proved to be a feeble secondary contradiction."[17]

Thus ethnicity is not a critical variable. It lacks explanatory potency. Its role in African politics, although sometimes considerable, is more apparent than real. Its potential as a force for changing the objective realities of African life is very minimal. However, even this minimal role is unsalutary. Imperialism is an exceedingly reactionary system. It can only be overthrown by the

16. Karl Marx, *A Contribution to the Critique of Political Economy* (London: International Liberal Publishing Company, 1904), preface.
17. Amilcar Cabral, *The Struggle in Guinea* (Cambridge, Mass.: Africa Research Group Reprint, [n.d.]), p. 436.

revolutionary struggle of the oppressed at a high level of political consciousness. By diverting attention away from imperialist exploitation and the resultant distortion of African economic and social structures, ethnicity performs the function of mystification and obscurantism. Consequently, it helps to perpetuate imperialism, and militate against the imperative of revolutionary struggle by hampering the development of a high level of political consciousness by its victims.

Herein lies the justification for studying ethnicity. Its adverse effects on the revolutionary process must be counteracted. This cannot be done without a thorough scientific analysis of the phenomenon itself. Unless reality is fully understood it cannot be transformed in a way that is desirable. Therefore, the necessity for the success of the revolutionary process far outweighs the risks of inflaming ethnic passions attendant on the study of ethnicity. Also, the mystification of social and political processes through the use of the ethnic variable can only be unmasked by confronting such ideological representations with a superior scientific analysis which, while acknowledging the role of the ethnic factor in social life, integrates it into the overall social process and shows its interconnection with other variables, thereby putting its contribution to social praxis in a comparative perspective. The fight against ethnicity is a many-sided and difficult process. Besides utmost vigilance against all intemperate and vague ethnic effusions, it requires thorough and exhaustive study which will enable a successful struggle to be waged against it.

Apart from the need to combat ethnicity there are also the demands of the advancement of knowledge. Ethnicity is a phenomenon associated with interactions among ethnic formations.[18] The latter are themselves social formations. An understanding of the dynamics of their interaction inevitably advances knowledge of social relations which are necessary for social transformation not

18. It has been used in this manner in L. Bloom, "Concerning Ethnic Research," *American Sociological Review*, Vol. XIII, No. 2 (April 1948), pp. 171–177; Daniel Glaser, "The Dynamics of Ethnic Identification," *American Sociological Review*, Vol. XXIII, No. 1 (February 1958), pp. 31–40; M. M. Gordon, *Assimilation in American Life* (New York: Oxford University Press, 1964); P. Hatt, "Classes and Ethnic Attitudes," *American Sociological Review*, Vol. XIII, No 1 Febraury 1948), pp. 36–43. It contrasts, for example, with Van den Berghe's use of it to refer only to groups which are socially defined by cultural differences; cf. P. L. Van den Berghe, *Race and Racism* (New York: Wiley, 1967), pp. 9–11.

only in the area of ethnic relations, but in the field of social relations in general. This leads to social development and, because the latter is closely interdependent with other forms of development, ultimately to economic and political development of the society. This is the duty of all social analyses, to create a better world.

The Inadequacy of Existing Analyses

The most significant and pervasive claim to a theoretical understanding of ethnicity is associated with the "modernisation" school. David Apter expected the charismatic leadership of Kwame Nkrumah to be the crucial integrative mechanism for welding ethnic groups together in Ghana.[19] But he did not and could not explain how the charismatic leader is able to emerge and persist in an ethnically plural society. His view, therefore, had no theoretical value. Similarly, arguments that the emergence of powerful political leaders,[20] strong political movements and parties,[21] and territorial political institutions[22] will act as the instruments and new modes of such integration have proved inadequate. These new mechanisms have failed to arise or succeed.

However, the most dominant theme of this analytical perspective is related to the impact of increased urbanisation, commercialisation, and professionalisation on ethnicity, that modernisation defined in terms of increases in urbanisation, schooling, communication, and transportation facilities will lead to the integration of diverse ethnic groups. Probably based on the dichotomous ideal types of Toennies, Maine, Durkheim, Weber,

19. David Apter, "Political Democracy in the Gold Coast" in Calvin W. Stillman, ed., *Africa in the Modern World* (Chicago: University of Chicago Press, 1955), pp. 55–93.
20. Claude Ake, "Political Integration and Political Stability: A Hypothesis," *World Politics*, Vol. XIX, No. 2 (April 1967), pp. 486–499.
21. J. S. Coleman and Carl G. Rosberg, Jr., *Political Parties and National Integration in Tropical Africa* (Berkeley: University of California Press, 1964). Note especially the introduction and Conclusion.
22. Rene Lemarchand, "Political Clientelism and Ethnicity in Tropical Africa," *American Political Science Review*, Vol. LXVI, No. 1 (March 1972), pp. 68–90; S. N. Eisenstadt, *Modernization: Protest and Change* (Englewood Cliffs, New Jersey.: Prentice Hall, 1966); M. G. Smith, "Social and Cultural Pluralism," *Annals of the New York Academy of Sciences*, Vol. LXXXIII, (January 1960), pp. 762–777; Leo A. Depres, *Cultural Pluralism and Nationalist Politics in British Guyana* (Chicago: University of Chicago Press, 1967); Pierre Van den

and Parsons, its main contemporary influence is Karl Deutsch.[23] Central to this viewpoint is faith in the evolutionary process by which increased functional differentiation would provide new and cross-cutting bases for association. A representative argument is that of Morrison and Stevenson:

"The values associated with modernisation – higher income, education, information and political participation – are increasingly being shared by all members of even the most culturally plural nations, and that to the extent that increasing modernisation is characteristic of new nations the achievement of these values, or the perception that they are being achieved will help to moderate conflicts based on differences in the values of traditional cultures."[24]

On the contrary, after nearly a century of the so-called "modernisation",[25] it has become clear that ethnicity has not only persisted[26] in African and non-African politics but has intensi-

Berghe, "Towards a Sociology for Africa," in Clifford Geertz, ed. *Old Societies and New States* (Glencoe, Illinois: Free Press, 1963) pp. 126–140. Robert E. Ward, "Political Modernization and Political Culture in Japan," *World Politics*, Vol. XV, No. 3 (1963), pp. 569–596.

23. Karl Deutsch, *Nationalsim and Social Communication* (Cambridge, Mass: M.I.T. Press, 1953). Although in 1961 he changed his view and saw social mobilisation as likely to have a negative impact on assimilation, cf. his "Social Mobilization and Political Development," *American Political Science Review*, Vol. LV, No. 3 (September 1961), p. 501, he nevertheless returned to his earlier optimistic view concerning the influence of modernisation on ethnicity, cf. Karl Deutsch, "Nation-Building and National Development: Some Issues of Political Research," in Karl Deutsch and William Foltz, eds., *Nation-Building* (New York: Atherton Press, 1963), pp. 4–5.

24. D. G. Morrison and H. M. Stevenson, "Cultural Pluralism, Modernization and Conflict: An Empirical Analysis of Sources of Political Instability in African Nations," *Canadian Journal of Political Science*, Vol. V, No. 1 (March 1972), p. 90. The following also share the same view: A. L. Epstein, *Politics in an Urban Community* (Manchester: Manchester University Press, 1958); Max Gluckman, "Tribalism in Modern British Central Africa," in I. Wallerstein, ed. *Social Change: The Colonial Situation* (New York: Wiley, 1966), pp. 251–264; Robert Bates, "Approaches to the Study of Ethnicity," *Cahiers d'Études Africaines*, Vol. X, No. 1 (1970), pp. 546–561; Robert Dahl, *Who Governs?* (New Haven from Yale University Press, 1961); James S. Coleman, "The Problem of Political Integration in Emergent Africa," *Western Political Quarterly*, Vol. VIII, No. 1 (March 1955), pp. 34–57.

25. First during the period of colonialism and then in the neocolonial order.

26. The persistence of ethnicity as a theoretical phenomenon has been observed by: Robert Melsen and Howard Wolpe, "Modernization and the Politics of Communalism: A theoretical Perspective," *American Political Science Review*, Vol. LXIV (December 1970), pp. 1112–1130; Michael Parenti,

fied.[27] In fact, Hansen's "Law of the Third Generation" suggests that there is an irresistible tendency toward an increased awareness of ethnicity with the passage of time.[28] Goering's findings support this law. In his sample, 70 per cent of the third generation immigrants in the United States, as opposed to 50 per cent for the first generation and 50 per cent for the second generation thought of themselves in ethnic terms. Thus one component of ethnic consciousness, the awareness or salience of ethnicity, appears most strongly in the third generation.[29]

In an apparent acknowledgement of the bankruptcy of this theoretical perspective a view has developed that ethnicity is an inherent aspect of social change in all culturally heterogeneous societies. This view argues that neither the disappearance nor a significant amelioration of ethnic conflict is possible. It sees the stability of these societies as threatened not by communalism *per*

Footnote 26 continued

"Ethnic Politics and the Persistence of Ethnic Identification," *American Political Science Review*, Vol. LXI (September 1967), pp. 717–726; Raymond Wolfinger, "The Development and Persistence of Ethnic Voting," *American Political Science Review*, Vol. LIX (December 1965), pp. 896–908; John Goering, "The Emergence of Ethnic Interests: A Case of Serendipity," *Social Forces*, Vol. XLIX (March 1971), pp. 348–379; W. S. Bernard, "Interrelationships Between Immigrants and Negroes: A Summary of a Seminar on Integration," *The International Migration Review*, Vol. III (Summer 1969), pp. 47–57; D. Clinel, "Ethnicity: A Neglected Dimension of American History, *The International Migration Review*, Vol. III (Summer 1969), pp. 58–63; N. Glazer and D. Moyiniham, *Beyond the Melting Pot* (Cambridge, Mass: M.I.T. Press, 1963); S. Goldstein and C. Goldshneider, *Jewish American: Three Generations in Jewish Community* (Englewood Cliffs, New Jersey: Prentice Hall, 1968); A Greeley, "Ethnicity as an Influence on Behaviour," *Integrated Education*, Vol. VII, No. 3 (Summer 1969), pp. 33–41.

27. Robert Melsen and Howard Wolpe, *op. cit.*; Meyer Fortes, "The Plural Society in Africa", *The Alfred and Winnifred Hoernk Memorial Lecture, 1968* (Johannesburg, Voelkfrese 1970); Ivor and Rosalind Feierbend and Betty Nevsvold, "Social Change and Political Violence," in Hugh Graham and Ted Gurr, eds., *The History of Violence in America* (New York: Bantam books, 1969), pp. 632–687; J. C. Mitchell, *Tribalism and the Plural Society* (London: Oxford University Press, 1960); C. E. Black, *The Dynamics of Modernization* (New York: Harper and Row, 1966); S. N. Eisenstadt, *op. cit.*; Mancur Olsen, Jr., "Rapid Growth as a Destablizing Force," *Journal of Economic History*, Vol. XXIII No. 4, (December 1963), pp. 529–552.

28. M. L. Hansen, "The Third Generation" in O. Handlin, ed., *Children of the Uprooted* (New York: Harper and Row, 1966).

29. John Goering, *op. cit.*, p. 381. He, however, also found that in spite of this increase in ethnicity with time in America, there is less interethnic hostility with successive generations.

se, but by the failure of national institutions to explicitly recognise and accommodate existing ethnic divisions and interests. And it recommends political arrangements which accord to all communal groups a meaningful role in national life and which are able to keep communal conflicts within manageable bounds.[30] Such a view suggests the inevitability of political instability in Africa.[31]

The failure of the perspective of "modernisation" to explain ethnicity is admitted but its theoretical consequences are not accepted. This failure is not caused by any inherent characteristics of ethnicity but by the inadequacies of the perspective itself. This viewpoint has been unwilling or unable to investigate rigorously the impact of the nature of the socioeconomic and political structures of society on the emergence and persistence of ethnicity. Michael Parenti recognises the role of the nature of the political system in the United States but neglects that of the socioeconomic system.[32] Although economic factors are usually mentioned, most "modernisation" analysts tend to deal with them briefly and then go on to emphasise biocultural factors such as the degree of interethnic racial and cultural differences, ethnocentrism, differences in institutions, the absence of value concensus, and the clarity and rigidity of group definition, or to synthesise or systematise subsets of these.[33]

30. This paraphrase of the viewpoint in question is taken from Robert Melsen and Howard Wolpe, *op. cit.* Others who explicitly share the same view include: C. S. Whitaker, Jr., "A Dysrhythmic Process of Political Change," *World Politics*, Vol. XIX (January 1967), pp. 190–217; Michael Parenti, *op. cit.*; Rene Lemarchand, *op. cit.*

31. On the inevitability of instability in Africa, see Edward Feit, "Military Coups and Political Development: Some Lessons from Ghana and Nigeria," *World Politics*, Vol. XX, No. 1 (January 1968), pp. 179–193; J. O'Connel, "The Inevitability of Instability," *Journal of Modern African Studies*, Vol. V, No. 1 (March 1967), pp. 181–191; Aristide Zolberg, "The Structure of conflict in the New States of Africa," *American Political Science Review*, Vol. LXII, No. 1 (March 1968), 70–78; Aristide Zolberg, "Military Intervenes in the New States of Tropical Africa: Elements of a Comparative Analysis," in Henry Bienen, ed., *The Military Intervenes* (New York: Sage Press 1968), pp. 71–98.

32. Michael Parenti, *op. cit.*, p. 725.

33. Stanley Lieberson, "A Societal Theory of Race and Ethnic Relations," *American Sociological Review*, Vol. XXVI, (December 1961), pp. 902–910; Philip Mason, *Patterns of Dominance* (London: Oxford University Press, 1970). Donald Noel, "A Theory of the Origin of Ethnic Stratification," *Social Problems*, Vol. LXXVI, No. 3 (Fall 1968), pp. 157–172; R. A. Scher-

By focusing on biocultural factors these analysts treat the significant units of social action as though they are innate, as if the socioeconomic organisation of society is static, and the economic structure of society is an indifferent condition of sociopolitical action. Since the nature of the context for the interaction of the various ethnic groups is excluded from analyses, historical changes in it are ignored. Similarities are identified and analogies drawn across the pre-colonial, colonial and post-colonial African societies irrespective of their degree of social differentiation, level of growth of their productive forces, their prevailing relations of production, and the degree of class consciousness of their population. Consequently, as B. Magubane correctly argues, they tend to treat symptoms as underlying causes[34] and to ignore the causative character of the socioeconomic organisation of society.

The tendency of the boundaries of ethnic groups to change indicates that ethnicity is not the primordial force which this analytical perspective suggests. Fredrik Barth observes that this shifting of ethnic boundaries is closely associated with the changes in the set of mutual identification and communications fields in the society.[35] In her study of the San Blas Cuna of Panama, Regina Holloman verifies this shift in ethnic boundaries. But she finds that it is correlated at the macro level with the patterns of access, or lack of them, to political and economic resources, and at the microlevel with the internal structures which simultaneously guarantee rewards adequate to sustain member support of the group and provide for control of change-related deviant behaviour.[36]

Footnote 33 continued

merhorn, *Comparative Ethnic Relations* (New York: Random House, 1970); P. Van den Berghe, "Paternistic versus Competitive Race Relations: An Ideal Type Approach," in Bernard E. Segal, ed., *Racial and Ethnic Relations* (New York: Growell, 1966), pp. 53–69. M. G. Smith, *op. cit.*; Leo Kuper, "Sociology: Some Aspects of Urban Plural Societies," In Robert A. Lystad, ed., *The African World: A Survey of Social Research* (New York: Praeger, 1965) W. Arthur Lewis, *Politics in West Africa* (London: Allen and Unwin, 1965); Clyde Mitchell, *Tribalism and the Plural Society* (London: Oxford University Press, 1960).

34. B. Magubane, "Pluralism and Conflict Situations in Africa: A New Look," *African Social Research*, Vol. VII, No. 2 (June 1969), pp. 529–554.

34. Fredrick Barth, *Ethnic Groups and Boundaries* (Boston: Little, Brown and Co., 1969).

36. Regina E. Holloman, "Ethnic Boundary Maintenance, Readaptation and Societal Evolution in the San Blas Islands of Panama," in Leo A. Despress, ed., *Ethnicity and Resource Competion in Plural Societies* (The Hague: Monton Publishers, 1975), pp. 27–39.

Furnivall's excellent pioneering work on plural societies in tropical colonies which recognises the working of economic forces[37] fails to move further forward in the direction of providing an adequate explanation for ethnicity because of its inverted emphasis on the effects of cultural heterogeneity on the capitalist market situation rather than the effects of the market situation on cultural heterogeneity. Similarly, Gunnar Myrdal provides a useful synthesis in his observation that the interpenetrating and conflicting patterns in a culturally heterogenous society are not culture patterns in the usual sense of the term but value patterns made up of sets of valued activities which further the interests of groups brought together by economic, political, and sociological forces.[38] But Myrdal fails to explain the phenomenon because he de-emphasises the importance of social structures and the impact of the nature of the capitalist organisation of society on the pursuit of these valued activities.

Magubane correctly emphasises the role of social structure in his argument that a serious effort to understand African conflicts cannot ignore the question of the ownership of the primary productive forces. For him this means consideration of the material basis of society, the nature of the social system, the political organisation, the structure of social consciousness, the ideological and socio-psychological orientation of the members of the society, views of the ruling classes and various social groups, and the rivalry between the various groupings within the ruling circles.[39] But he does not go beyond this enumeration to indicate the dynamics of the social structures which yield ethnicity. Others have analysed these structures.[40] However, they ignore the importance of social process and are, therefore, partial in their explanation. A few have sought to integrate social structures and social process,[41] but they wrongly assume ethnicity as given and argue

37. J. S. Furnivall, *Colonial Policy and Practice* (Cambridge: Cambridge University Press, 1943), p. 311.
38. G. Myrdal, *An American Dilemma* (New York: Harper and Row, 1944); G. Myrdal, *Value in Social Theory* (London: Routledge and Kegan Paul, 1958).
39. B. Magubane, *op. cit.*, p. 538.
40. Richard Sklar, "Political Science and National Integration: A Radical Approach," *Journal of Modern African Studies*, Vol. V, No. 1 (1967); Geoffrey Bing, *Reap the Whirlwind: The Account of Kwame Nkrumah's Ghana from 1950–1966* (London: MacGibbon and Kee, 1967); Peter Worseley, *The Third World: A Vital New Force in International Affairs* (London: Weidenfeld and Nicolson, 1967).
41. Oliver Cox, *Caste, Class and Race* (New York: Modern Reader, 1948), pp. 408–422; Marvin Harris, *Patterns of Race in the Americas* (New York:

that ethnic differences in themselves prompt the development of socio-economic stratification which leads to ethnic antagonism. The excellent work of Edna Bonacich challenges this assumption and suggests that economic processes both antedate and postdate ethnic stratification.[42] The theoretical perspective of this book supplements her contention.

The approach of the modernisation school makes an absolute of the ethnic identity and ignores the class factor. On the other hand the ultra-left approach neglects the role of the purely ethnic variable and reduces all analysis to the class factor alone. This sort of vulgar sociology only helps to buttress the ethnic perception of reality. In order to overcome the one-sidedness of these approaches, it is necessary to investigate the inter-connection between the universally human class structures and ethnic elements in the process of history. The close connection between them follows from the fact that the ethnic formation is a historical entity. It encompasses and penetrates all social formations including class-structures, and, in a certain sense, it is a spatial framework for class relations and contradictions.

The ethnic community also represents the continuity of material and spiritual cultures as well as social and everyday forms of communication in the history of definite peoples. It is this fact which makes it possible for class actions to be successfully dressed in ethnic garb, the significance and influence of which should not be overlooked in the analysis of a society's development. Therefore, in order to understand the social place and historical role of ethnicity it is necessary to investigate the connection between the present and past sociopolitical societies to elucidate the historical origins and manifestations of the phenomenon.

Footnote 41 continued

Walker, 1964), pp. 79–94; Gary Becker, *The Economics of Discrimination* (Chicago: University of Chicago Press, 1957); Robert Blau, "Internal Colonialism and Ghetto Revolt," *Social Problems*, Vol. XVI (Spring 1969), pp. 393–408; Michael Reich, "The Economics of Racism," in David M. Gordon, ed., *Problems in Political Economy* (Lexington, Mass.: Health, 1971); J. H. Boeke, *The Structure of Netherlands Indian Economy* (New York: Day Publishers, 1942); Issa Shivji, *The Class Struggle in Tanzania* (Dar es Salaam: Tanzania Publishing House, 1975).

42. Edna Bonacich, "A Theory of Ethnic Antagonism: The Split Labor Market," *American Sociological Review*, Vol. XXXVII, No. 3 (October 1972), pp. 547–559.

Class and Ethnicity

In order to arrive at an adequate theoretical perspective, it is essential to reiterate the fact that ethnicity operates at the level of ideology. Usually, the historical circumstances under which an ideology emerges is important for its understanding. An ideology serves the interests of different classes in society differentially. It is, therefore, important for its understanding to identify the social group whose interests the ideology primarily serves, and from whose point of view it explains reality. In other words we can not fully comprehend the ethnic phenomenon in Africa without an adequate understanding of its historical origin and objective socioeconomic basis. This means that ethnicity would vary from one African country to another depending on the differences in their histories and class structure. Different African countries display different historical patterns and class structures depending on their size, location, the strength and cohesion of their ruling classes, the courage, determination and leadership of the underprivileged, the degree of foreign influence, the pervasiveness and power of the dominant ideology, social custom and tradition, culture, kinship system and form of government. Therefore, ethnicity in Africa can best be studied through the historical analysis of concrete cases of particular African countries.

Nevertheless, certain features of history and class structure appear common to the African countries. They are useful for achieving some theoretical understanding of ethnicity. Central to these is their common colonial history, and the origin of ethnicity in the colonial ideology. [We have seen how ethnic consciousness in Africa was the offspring of colonial racism whose objective basis was the alienation of the African for easy foreign exploitation. It was in the colonial enclaves that the colonised African made contact with the colonial environment, the coloniser, and the Africans from different communal groups. The dynamics of this quadrupartite contact gave rise to ethnicity in colonial and post-colonial African countries.]

In the colonial contact situation the African migrant could not relate meaningfully to or conquer his physical and biological environments. The discrepancy between the resources used in the enclaves' dominant activities with the Africans' needs and traditional consumption habits rendered him unable to adapt to the new environment, and impotent to manipulate it. At the same time he was the victim of a complex international, national

21

and local division of labour which thoroughly alienated him from the products of his work. He received barely subsistence wages for his labour and artificially low prices for his farm products. Under such conditions labour ceased to be a liberating force and turned instead into an oppressive instrument. Frustration and disorientation of the colonised African were reinforced by his humiliating relationship with the coloniser.

The latter dominated the commanding heights of the economy through his ownership of the means of production, distribution and exchange, controlled the foreign production relations which unjustly exploited the labour of the vast majority of Africans, dictated the work roles, and expropriated the surplus from production. The exploited African soon experienced the coloniser's racial prejudice and discrimination in the fields of jobs, remunerations, housing, sports, and even churches and burial grounds.[43] Having been uprooted from the pre-colonial setting which had valid meaning for him, in which history had effectively and organically related him to his local environment and culture had produced salutary patterns of interactions with others, the African migrant found the door to the coloniser's glorified world securely barred to him. The resultant anomie and alienation affected his socio-economic and political activities. Even in interactions with his fellow Africans he experienced tension, anxiety, and insecurity. Disoriented, subjugated, and humiliated by the coloniser he directed his aggressive impulses against other colonised "natives" with whom he competed on the basis of equality. Ethnic group membership was useful for this competition.[44]

The colonialists also encouraged the emergent competitive groupings to run along linguistic and communal lines. For example, they chose administrative units which coincided with the communal homelands of the various linguistic groups and which, with the introduction of elective politics, became political constituencies. The resultant competition among the administrative units and political constituencies was enhanced by the uneven development inherent in imperialism. Colonial socioeconomic projects were located in areas of gainful exploitation. They were not guided by the desire for intersectoral and inter-

---

43. S. O. Osoba, "Intellectual Aridity in Nigeria," in *Theory and Practice*, Vol. I, No. 1 (1974), p. 51.
44. J. Rex, "The Plural Society in Sociological Theory," *British Journal of Sociology*, Vol. X, No. 1 (1959), pp. 116–117.

regional balance in socioeconomic achievement. Ultimately certain linguistic and communal homelands became better "developed" socioeconomically than others. This imbalance deepened antipathies between ethnic groups. In Nigeria, for example, the South achieved a higher level than the North. Similarly, the Baganda advanced farther than the other Uganda linguistic groups, the Chagga and Haya were ahead of the other Tanzanian groups, and the Kikuyu and Ashanti made a more rapid "progress" than the other Kenyan and Ghanaian communal groups respectively.

In order to cut the costs of maintaining law and order necessary for colonial exploitation, the colonialists were forced to depend to a greater or lesser extent on the pre-colonial African institutions, authority, and personnel. Even the French who were not enarmoured by the doctrine of indirect rule could not ignore the utility of these local forces; they tried to subordinate and westernise them. In some cases this policy actually meant the organisation of people into new communal units. Its net effect was to create and perpetuate a traditional symbolic focus for the new urban population, thereby strengthening the ethnocentric component of ethnicity. Under such conditions it was not easy to make a complete break with the communal homelands.

A similar effect was produced by the colonialists' categorisation of African peoples into tribes, their emphasis on what was different among them to the utter neglect of what was common to them, and the pervasive colonial bureaucratic requirement that official forms should contain information about the "tribal" origins of the local population. The continual reminder by official forms and documents of his communal homelands constantly reinforced ethnocentric sentiments and the parochial loyalty of the colonised. He feared that since he was regarded as a member of an ethnic group by others he would likely be discriminated against by them and would be lost in the struggle for socioeconomic rewards if he did not identify with this ethnic group.

An urbanisation process, which is rooted in the organic relationship between the population and the local physical environment, ultimately arises from increased specialisation of functions in the traditional pattern of economic activities and leads inevitably to the urban migrant's total break with the rural and communal homeland, essentially because of his economic irrelevance there. But the colonial urban process was divorced from pre-colonial activities. The colonialists paid subsistence wages to urban migrants, thereby ensuring that the communal home-lands remained a reservoir of cheap labour, and, what is more, that the urban migrant carried on some economic activities there to supplement his meagre wages. Therefore, the new urban dwellers remained closely linked emotionally, culturally, socially, and even economically to their communal homelands. This link continually reinforced the parochial components of ethnicity.

Finally, ethnicity served the colonialists as a mechanism to divide the colonised and, therefore, maintain domination over them. As a political line, the colonisers used ethnicity to curb African nationalism and maintain their power. For example, in 1920 when the National Congress of British West Africa was organised, and demanded reforms in the British West African colonies, Sir Hugh Clifford the then governor of Nigeria immed-iately sought to divide the nationalists by arguing that "The peoples of West Africa do not belong to the same stock and are not of common descent."[45] He contended that any suggestions of a possible future West African nation were "mischievous, because . . . it is the consistent policy of the Government of Nigeria to maintain and support the local tribal institutions and the indigenous forms of Government . . . which are to be regarded as the natural expressions of [African] political genius."[46] Thus to the colonial governor, not only was the idea of a West African nation anathema, that of a Nigerian nation was inconceivable. True patriotism and nationalism were attributes that must be associated with the "natural and self-contained" "tribal" home-lands.

Again the colonialists tried to check the march to independence by sponsoring reactionary political parties. Often the ethnic base was adopted, with the colonialist manipulating the prevalent fears of ethnic domination, exploiting regional imbalances or preying on interethnic hostility and tension. For example, in colonial Zaire the pioneering nationalist activity of the Abako party whose leadership was dominated by the Bakongo led the Belgian colonial rulers to look for a "moderate" political organ-isation among the Bangala known to be hostile to the Bakongo. In Kasai, the radical articulation of nationalist views by Albert Kalonji and Joseph Ngalula of the Baluba linguistic group led the

45. Quoted in J. S. Coleman, *Nigeria: Background to Nationalism* (Berkeley and Los Angeles: University of California Press, 1958), p. 193.
46. Quoted in *ibid.*, pp. 193–194.

Belgian colonial administration to find renewed sympathy for the grievances of the Lulua who had always "complained" of oppression by the Baluba.[47] In colonial Guinea (Conakry) the colonial administration first sponsored the Socialist Party headed by Yacine Diallo from the Fouta Djallon and later by Barry Diawadou from the plateau region, both supported by the Foula of the Fouta Djallon, to oppose the radical political party led by Ahmed Sekou Toure.[48]

In the French Cameroons, the Cameroons Peoples Union (UPC) was a political party dedicated to the revolutionary overthrow of French rule and the unification of the English and French speaking Cameroonians. At birth it found support among workers in the growing urban centres of the Trust Territory, as well as among the Bassa, Douala, Bamileke, Boulou and Ewondo linguistic groups. When in 1958-1959, the Bamileke rebelled against the mounting socioeconomic oppression of colonialism in their region, the UPC, which had not inspired the dissatisfaction and consequent insurrection, championed their cause. Thereupon the imperialist regime and its local agents fanned the anti-Bamileke feeling in the country and used this as one of the instruments with which to isolate and destroy the party.[49]

In these various ways, ethnicity in Africa emerged and persisted either as a mechanism for adaptation to the imperialist system or as an instrument for ensuring a facile and more effective domination and exploitation of the colonised. In both cases it served the reactionary purpose of the system: the degradation of the African in order to better and more easily exploit him. At best, ethnicity diverted attention away from the foreign oppression and exploitation inherent in the imported relations of production, thereby consolidating the system. At worst, it constituted an instrument for channelling aggressive impulses arising from the frustrations of the colonial situation against fellow Africans.

Even in the post-colonial period ethnicity has continued to serve the interests of imperialism. During the early period of independence in Zaire, the progressive anti-imperialist move-

---

47. Crawford Young, *Politics in the Congo* (Princeton, New Jersey: Princeton University Press, 1965), pp. 269–270.
48. L. Gray Cowan, "Guinea," in Gwendolen M. Carter, ed., *African One-Party States* (Ithaca, New York: Cornell University Press, 1962), pp. 159–162.
49. David E. Gardiner, *Cameroon* (London: Oxford University Press, 1963), pp. 90–92.

ment, led by Patrice Lumumba, was destroyed by reactionary foreign and local neocolonialist forces who relied essentially on ethnic sentiments. Lumumba's major political rivals were Joseph Kasavubu and Moise Tshombe. Close to the Bakongo's ethnic religionalists, the Kimbanguists, Kasavubu based his political power and career on a passionate appeal to Bakongo patriotism. Tshombe was related to the royal family of the Lunda ethnic group which was powerful in Katanga. Never part of the pre-independence nationalist movement, he stuck close to the Belgian colonialists. His attempt to sever Katanga from Zaire was actively supported not only by Belgian financial circles, and settlers in Katanga but also by the Lunda linguistic group. It contributed immensely to the death of Lumumba and the elimination of his movement.[50]

Finally, the recent history of Angola is illuminating. In its struggle against imperialism in general and Portuguese colonialism in particular, the Popular Movement for the Liberation of Angola (MPLA) encountered major opposition in the National Front for the Liberation of Angola (FNLA) and the Union for the Total Independence of Angola (UNITA), which counted first and foremost on ethnic support, and then on imperialist reaction and South African invasion. The origin of the FNLA lies in the protest in 1955 of the largely protestant Bakongo of northern Angola against the Portuguese imposition of a catholic chief on them. Ever since then it had been confined essentially to the Bakongo and derived its major support from its appeal to their ethnic sensibilities. Similarly, UNITA and its foreign backers confined their major activities to the Ovimbundu ethnic group of the central highland region, and preyed on their ethnic sentiments.[51]

As may have already become evident, ethnicity also objectively served the interests of the African petty bourgeoisie and the comprador bourgeoisie reared by colonialism. The former comprised essentially those in the professions, teaching, petty trading, the middle and upper echelons of the African section of the Civil Service, the middle and upper ranks of the army, and the petty contractors and independent artisans. The latter was made up of those in the import-export business, wholesale trade, produce

---

50. Colin Legum, *Congo Disaster* (Harmondsworth, England: Penguin, 1961) pp. 98–101.
51. Armando Entralgo, "Angola is Independent," and "Binguem Impedira A Chuva," in *Tricontinental*, Vol. X, (1975), pp. 35–51.

merchants and large-scale cash crop farmers. In their search for the crumbs from colonial production, contending regional factions of these parasitic classes emphasised the exclusion of their counterpart from the other regions. And when they got into positions of political power they used the government to exclude them. A careful examination of the election manifestoes of the nationalist movements and parties led by these classes shows an overwhelming emphasis on relations of distribution rather than those of production and on the superstructure of society such as the principles of social and political interaction rather than the infrastructure, the relations of production. Unable historically to increase production because of their parasitic role in the production process, these classes depend on this device of exclusion to increase their benefits from the society. First, foreigners are excluded, then members of different linguistic groups, cultural groups, provinces, districts, clans, towns, villages, and extended families are excluded in that order as the "cake" being divided diminishes in size.

In the atmosphere of extreme socioeconomic and political scarcity that prevailed in the colonial societies and are still prevailing in the post-colonial societies, few members of these privileged classes are confident enough of their own ability to survive and prosper to advocate a merit system of hiring, promotion, trade and business. Most prefer the security of at least being able to rely on exploiting ethnic preferences whenever and wherever this is possible. Each gives preferences to members of his group whenever he can as a means of ensuring that they will return the gesture sometime when he may need it. The whole system is rationalised by these classes in terms of ethnic diversity and the need to accord to each group a say and a share in national life.

Members of these classes benefited most from the salary conditions, opportunities for contract work and business, in the professions and various other fields of economic endeavour. They saw their path to a fuller life blocked by the racism of the colonial order and thereafter by competion from their own kind. Against racism they opposed nationalism. They travelled round the country to mobilise mass support against this ideology having been dismissed by the colonial authorities as representing no one but themselves. Against competition from other members of their classes, they employed the myth of ethnic identity along lines previously fabricated by the colonialists. And mobilised mass support along these lines. Like the colonialists they had no objective interest in encouraging class identity. This would have exposed the exploitation inherent in the colonial production process and the parasitic character of the petty bourgeoisie and comprador bourgeoisie in that process.

Interest of these local privileged classes in ethnicity was reinforced by some objective conditions of the colonial economy. The economy lacked integration and balance and was, therefore, fragmented. The metropole's imposition of an international division of labour on the colony and its usurpation of a superior role in this specialisation of function caused the local economy to be import-export oriented well before the home capitalist market had become regional and national. This pattern of economic transactions hampered the economic integration of the various parts of the colony. Instead, the various parts of the colonial economy were integrated with those of the metropole and the other advanced capitalist societies. Raw materials from one part of the colony were not used in the factories of another but in Europe. Similarly, manufactured goods sold in one part did not come from another but from Europe.

Thus the colonial economy was organised around regional enclaves isolated from each other. Consequently, the petty bourgeoisie and comprador bourgeoisie were fragmented along regional ethnic lines and they tended to regard the regional enclaves as exclusive reservoirs of benefits for those of them from the region-ethnic homeland. The participation of those from other regions in the petty bourgeois fortunes of a regional enclave was fiercely resisted by the local faction. Resistance was waged in the name of ethnicity, the protection of the socioeconomic interests of the ethnic group.

In their pursuit of gainful economic activities the colonialists were impelled first and foremost by the profit motive of exploiting cheap labour and raw materials and seldom by any desire for balanced socioeconomic development of the various regions and ethnic homelands of the colony. Therefore, those regions, or sections of them, which were neither significant centers of colonial economic production nor situated along the major centres of the colonial system of communication and administration suffered socioeconomically. For example, the Haya and Chagga enjoyed early socioeconomic advantages in Tanzania because of the cultivation of coffee in their homelands. Similarly, the Baganda of Uganda capitalised on cofee production, the Ashanti of Ghana on cocoa production, and the Bemba of Zambia on copper mining.

These disparities deepened the antipathies among the various regional factions of the petty bourgeoisie and comprador bourgeoisie and thereby contributed to ethnicity. For example, as Colin Leys has pointed out, in Kenya before colonial rule there was no enmity between the Luo and Kikuyu. But by the end of 1960 a strong feeling had developed. The pre-colonial enemies of the Kikuyu were the Masai although inter-marriage among the two groups existed. Ethnic consciousness among the Kikuyu developed during the colonial period, not as is popularly believed primarily as a result of their loss of land to the white settlers since the Masai and the Giriama lost equal or more land, but essentially because of forced Kikuyu participation in wage labour and trade which led to the growth of petty bourgeois fortunes among them. Semi-proletarianised within colonial capitalist mode of production, the Kikuyu entered the colonial enclaves earlier than the other groups and its petty bourgeois members took advantage of new opportunities in the new economy out of proportion to their share of the total population. Members of other groups in competition for these opportunities began to resent this Kikuyu advantage. Hence, inter-ethnic relations in Kenya has been characterised by the hostility of all the other groups to the Kikuyu.[52]

Finally, in some colonies the interest of the privileged local classes in ethnicity was conditioned by certain peculiarities of the colonial order. Of particular reference here are those countries where, for historical reasons, whites, Asians and Africans coexist. As a result of deliberate racist policies these various communities were officially stratified, with the Africans at the bottom followed by the Asians, with the whites at the very top. This system of stratification also coincided with different roles in the production process officially assigned to the various groups. For example, in East Africa, official policy ensured that the whites went into large-scale capitalist farming, manufacturing, the largest-scale trading, and shipping, the Asians went into medium-sized and petty trading while the Africans were predominantly peasant procedures and wage earners.

The African met the Asian mainly as a producer and consumer. The Asian was the trader, middleman, and the creditor. The white was the employer of the African. Similarly, in white minority regimes where such stratification also existed, the African met the white as an employee in the service of an employer. Unlike the

52. Colin Leys, *Underdevelopment in Kenya* (London: Hieneman, 1975).

situation in other countries, relations among various communal groups tended to coincide with antagonistic production relations.[53] It is no longer a question of various factions of the same class contending for dominance but of different and opposed classes locked in the class struggle. The role of ethnicity in the latter case is slightly different from its role in the former case. It serves to mask the exploitation of a class composed of an ethnic group by another class made up of another ethnic group. In the former, ethnicity functions to obscure the class differences within a communal group as well as to mobilise mass support for the contending factions of the same privileged classes.

Thus ethnicity in Africa has a class character. Its understanding cannot be achieved in isolation from the general class struggles in the society. No meaningful solution of the ethnic problems of Africa, including ethnic balancing, can succeed without a fundamental change in the nature of the national leaderships in Africa. Above all, the struggle against ethnic chauvinism cannot be successfully waged under the leadership of that segment of the population which benefits most substantially and concretely from the prevailing interethnic situation. As a result of their success in ethnic politics, the present leaders now occupy political and economic positions of power and privilege in the inherited colonial structures which gave rise to and continues to reinforce those politics. Therefore, they have an objective interest in maintaining the ethnic pattern of activities and the imperialist structures, both of which are inimical to interethnic harmony.

Sociopsychological Factors

Most leftist theoretical discussions tend to end at this point of the class character of ethnicity. Such analyses are incomplete. In order to fully comprehend the ethnic phenomenon, particularly the aspect involving struggle among various factions of the same petty bourgeois class, it is necessary to understand why the underprivileged classes have tended to rally behind the struggles of these factions. Why has their mobilisation not taken on a class

53. Rodolfo Stavenhagen, "Classes, Colonialism, and Acculturation" in J. Kahl, ed., *Comparative Perspectives on Stratification: Mexico, Great Britain, Japan* (Boston: Little, Brown and Co., 1968), pp. 31–45; Issa Shivyi, *Tanzania: The Class Struggle Continues* (Dar es Salaam, Tanzania: Mimeo), pp. 35–38.

form against these privileged classes? Why are the economic and political leaders able to manipulate and divide the workers and peasants by playing on their ethnic sentiments? In light of the tendency of the ethnic boundaries to shift, how did these sentiments arise in the first place? These are questions whose answers will greatly enrich the understanding and, therefore, solution of the ethnic problems of Africa.

Ethnicity services some interests of the underprivileged classes of the colonial urban areas, albeit to a lesser extent than it does the interests of the privileged classes. Max Gluckman[54] and Immanuel Wallerstein[55] have observed the major role which communal voluntary associations play in the lives of the African urban dweller by offering socioeconomic security. They ameliorated the pervasive insecurity of the individual in the colonial urban setting. D. S. Dustin and H. P. Davis have demonstrated that the individual is more confident and secure in a group than when alone.[56] When, as in the colonies, the society is not occupationally highly differentiated, the level of class consciousness is low, and the incidence of destructive competition for scarce valuable resources is high, the individual tends to ally with those who share certain communal characteristics in common: members of the same nuclear family, extended family, clan, culture, language, religion and race. Only in such alliances is he confident of mutual trust, useful communication and mutual aid. This is reflected in the tendency of ethnically-conscious town dwellers of different communal groups to live apart wherever the housing policy permits it,[57] and their marriages to be confined to members of the same communal group.[58]

The communal unit chosen for alignment at any time and place

---

54. Max Gluckman, *op. cit.,* p. 259.
55. I. Wallerstein, "Voluntary Associations", in James Coleman and Carl Rosberg, eds., *op. cit.,* pp. 318–339.
56. D. S. Dustin and H. P. Davis, "Evaluative Bias in Group and Individual Competition," *Journal of Social Psychology,* Vol. LXXX, No. 1 (1970), pp. 103–108.
57. P. C. Gutkind, "Urban Conditions in Africa," *The Town Planning Review,* Vol. XXXII, No. 1, (April 1961), p. 11.
58. J. C. Mitchell, "Aspects of African Marriages in the Copperbelt of Northern Rhodesia," *Human Relations in Africa,* Vol. XXII, No 1 (1957); A. Izzett, "Family Life Among the Yorubas in Lagos, Nigeria," in A. Southall, ed., *Social Change in Modern Africa* (London: Oxford University Press, 1961) pp. 31–37; Peter Morris, *Family and Social Change in an African City* (London: Routledge and Kegan Paul, 1961).

varies with the nature of the units in competition. Within the extended family, the nuclear family alignment prevails, in the clan the extended family, and in the urban area the linguistic group. Therefore, as the level of social relations widens from the extended family to the city, the unit of group affiliation shifts from the nuclear family to the linguistic group. It is the latter which is usually referred to as the ethnic group. However, at each higher level there is a mixture of alignments including units at lower levels. For example, the relevant focus of alliances in the city includes the nuclear family, extended family, clan, district and the linguistic or ethnic group. Each competes with its counterparts: clan with clans, and ethnic groups with ethnic groups.[59] For national politics, ethnic group affiliation is the most relevant and significant form of alignment. It is also usually dominant in the urban areas.

The most significant all-inclusive alliance which the individual enters into in order to ameliorate his insecurity and increase his capacity for socioeconomic competition is the ethnic group-wide voluntary association. In most cases, however, these alignments are not formal in nature; the individual does not necessarily join any voluntary association. It is a question of mutual identification on the part of the relevant individuals. The resultant sense of identity, feeling of solidarity and increased power for socioeconomic competition provide the needed security. It provides a buffer for new entrants into the cities and for those who find themselves in difficulty there by ensuring mutual aid and leadership, providing common welfare, security, and credit, and offering a basis for links with the rural areas.[60] Heightened socioeconomic frustration is a crucial element in the motivational complex leading to ethnicity.[61]

A feeling of both belonging and rejection becomes the basis for distinguishing individuals in the city and at the national level. Under these circumstances, each member of X ethnic group fears that he is regarded as an X by any member of Y or Z ethnic group and would, therefore, be discriminated against by them in the

59. This tendency for communal groups to be the basis for alignments even at the very local level had been observed by Audery Smock in "The NCNC and ethnic Unions in Biafra," *Journal of Modern African Studies*, Vol. VII, No. 1 (1969), pp. 21–34.
60. Audery I. Richards, *op. cit.*, p. 30.
61. Joseph S. Himes, "A Theory of Racial Conflict," *Social Forces*, Vol. L, No. 3 (September 1971), p. 54.

struggle for the scarce socioeconomic resources. He believes that he can expect preferences from any member of X in a position to help him, and perceives it to be in his interest to promote the activities of all Xs in competition with Ys and Zs. If any X or Z does not favour his own kind he gets no preference from his kind in return, and no one of the other groups would give him preference over their own people. As a result, anyone who finds himself outside the system of ethnic preferences is lost.

As this happens, members of an ethnic group tend to look more and more towards their group for support. The consequent intra-group cohesion acts to further separate it from the other ethnic groups. Members begin to develop common experiences in relation to others and, therefore, a common history, tradition and interest. Under these circumstances, further conflicts of interest increase their social distance in economic and security considerations as well as in ideology. If ethnic group lines coincide with regional geographical boundaires, the resultant territorial cohesion acts to convert ethnic group boundaries into cultural, economic and, just before secession, military barriers.

These factors are reinforced by a political process such as the Western parliamentary system where candidates for political office are chosen from constituencies defined along spatial lines rather than lines of specialisation of production functions. Michael Parenti has observed that in such systems ethnically salient parliamentary candidates tend to emerge and persist because of the political gains likely to accrue from appeals to ethnic sentiments, and their presence acts to ensure the persistence of ethnicity by continually fanning the embers of ethnic identification.

As ethnic consciousness thus increases in scope and intensity, the socioeconomic and political atmosphere becomes charged with tension. Under these circumstances, the ethnic factor assumes a self-fulfilling and self-sustaining dynamic of its own. Ethnic hostility, loyalty and identification are passed on to successive generations through the process of socialisation. The family, press, private and public conversation and other agencies of socialisation are infected by ethnicity. Therefore, even when the original basis of ethnicity, socioeconomic competition among classes and individuals, is eliminated, there remains the problem posed by the internalised dimension. Under such conditions the persistence and sometimes growth of ethnicity is assured. An adequate solution to the ethnic problem must, therefore, in addition to tackling the question of external and local class interests, come to grips with individual insecurity and the internalised dimension of his ethnic sentiments. It must, however, be preceded by a detailed examination of how ethnicity has emerged, persisted and grown in a concrete case such as Nigeria.

Chapter 2

THE CRADLE OF ETHNICITY

The Colonial Urban Setting as the Cradle of Ethnicity

In Nigeria, the colonial urban setting constitute the cradle of contemporary ethnicity. As will become evident later, it was there that what we refer to today as ethnic groups first acquired a common consciousness. In other words, contemporary Nigerian ethnicity is not the result of some barbarous mystique peculiar to the African. Nor is it basically the consequence of the pre-colonial pattern of conflict among the various pre-colonial polities. In fact, in the various Nigerian languages there is no equivalent concept for tribalism. Given the pervasive presence of the word in our present political vocabulary it certainly would have been represented in the pre-colonial linguistic dictionaries if its origin lies in the pre-colonial order. The fact is that tribalism or ethnicity in Nigeria is a creature of the colonial and post-colonial order.

For example, it was only after colonisation that the term Yorubaland began to be used to refer to the domains of all rulers who claim descent from the mythical Oduduwa, instead of the kingdom of Oyo to which it was previously limited.[1] Historical records indicate that before the British came, these various kingdoms fought disastrous interestate wars among themselves. On one occasion the Ibadan people were opposed by an alliance of the Egba, Ijebu, Ekiti, Ijesha and Ilorin peoples over the control of trade in the area. Similarly, the Igbo were organised into separate and autonomous political societies coterminous with the village. International wars among these polities sometimes occurred. Nri and Aro civilisations spread to practically all corners of Igbo land, indicating contact between the Nri and Aro Igbo with the rest of Igbo societies. However, only the Aros made contact with most of the various other Igbo-speaking people on a permanent and an extensive basis. But this was characterised by a cooperative symbiotic relationship between the host and migrant

---

1. P. C. Lloyd, *Africa in Social Change* (Harmondsworth, England: Penguin, 1967), pp. 288–303.

communities. Many times the various Igbo pre-colonial polities did not make any contact whatsoever before colonisation, and were even in certain cases oblivious of the existence of one another. In fact, the Igbo speaking people were self-consciously divided into the Olu and the Igbo peoples. Even today the Olu are very reluctant, except sometimes in the urban centres, to refer to themselves as Igbo. Therefore, among certain neighbouring peoples, there was a definite distinction between Olu and Igbo, while in what is today known as Igboland there was no history of common pre-colonial consciousness and identity. Certainly there were no wars fought together by the Igbo as a collectivity. Such wars usually marked the boundaries of mutual identification and group identity. Only a rudimentary common consciousness based on a myth of common descent existed among some of the pre-colonial linguistic groups. For example, the Yoruba traced descent from Oduduwa, and the Edo from the younger son of Ogiso. The Hausa-Fulani have the myth of Bayajidda.

This colonial and urban origin of ethnicity becomes clear when it is realised that the phenomenon cannot exist unless individuals from different communal groups are in contact. It is a social and not a biological phenomenon. Such contact is a prerequisite for the emergence of ethnicity. This point is widely recognised, but most explicity stated by the proponents of the race-cycle.[2] It is also reflected in the views held by Frederick Barth[3], Gunnar Haaland[4],

---

2. The race-cycle framework was initially formulated by Robert E. Park in his *Race and Culture* (Glencoe: Free Press, 1950). Since then others have written about it: Ernest Barth and Donald Noel, "Conceptual Frameworks for the Analysis of Race Relations: An Evaluation," *Social Forces*, Vol. L, No. 3 (1964) pp. 333–348; Emory Bogardus, "Race Relations Cycle," *American Journal of Sociology*, Vol. XXXV No. 1 (January 1930), pp. 612–617; W. O. Brown, "Culture Contact and Race Conflict," in E. B. Butler, ed., *Race and Culture Contact* (New York: McGraw Hill, 1943), pp. 34–47; E. F. Frazier, *Race and Culture Contacts in the Modern World* (New York: Alfred A. Knopf, 1957); C. E. Glick, "Social Roles and Types in Race Relations," in Andrew W. Lind, ed., *Race Relations in World Perspective* (Honolulu: University of Hawaii Press, 1955), pp. 243–262; E. N. Palmer, "Culture Contacts and Population Growth," in Joseph J. Spengler and Otis Dudley Duncan, eds., *Population Theory and Policy* (Glencoe: Free Press, 1956), pp. 410–415; A. Grenfell, *White Settlers and Native Peoples* (Melbourne: Georgian House, 1950). For summaries of several of these cycles, see Brewton Berry, *Race and Ethnic Relations* (Boston: Houghton Mifflin, 1958), Chapter 6.
3. Fredrick Barth, "Competition and Symbiosis in North East Baluchistan," *Folk*, Vol. VI No. 1 (1964), pp. 1–15.
4. Gunnar Haaland, "Economic Determinants in Ethnic Processes," in Fredrick

and Henning Siverts[5] that the origin and persistence of ethnic
boundaries, the incorporation of ethnic populations, and the
organisation of interethnic relations are generally related to factors affecting the competition for environmental resources.[6] They
change with changes in the spheres of such competition. G. W.
Skinner has also observed with respect to Indonesia that ethnicity
is essentially associated with urban centres and villages near ethnically heterogenous cities where contact among members of various
ethnic groups is significant.[7] Robert Grey's preliminary study of
Ethiopia, which shows that increased education positively affects
national identification in the rural but not the urban areas, provides empiral evidence.[8]

It is essentially in these urban areas that an extensive and significant contact takes place between members of the different pre-
colonial polities and diverse linguistic and cultural formations.
Rural-rural migration also provides intercommunal contact but,
for various reasons, it is not significant for the emergence of ethnicity in the country. First, horizontal mobility within the rural areas
is hampered by the land tenure system which, especially in the
South, emphasises ancestral heritage. As an official economic
corollary of the colonial administrative policy of indirect rule but
also as a result of the hostility of the areas to white settlement, the
British supported the maintenance of the traditional land tenure
system. With the exception of small palm oil plantations in
Calabar and a rubber plantation in Benin province, no agricultural units were owned or controlled by European farmers.

Although the land tenure system varied from one area of
Nigeria to another, it was usually communal in character and
vested in the family, village or town. On receiving the allocation of
rights of occupation and usufruct from the traditional authorities of the communities the peasant farmers were free to use their
land in the way they desired. They were limited by only one stipula-

Barth, ed., *Ethnic Groups and Boundaries* (Boston: Little, Brown and Co.,
1969), pp. 52–81.

5. Henning Siverts, "Ethnic Stability and Boundary Dynamics in Southern
Mexico," in Fredrick Barth, *Ethnic Groups and Boundaries, op. cit.*, pp. 105–
130.

6. Leo A. Depres, "Introduction", in Leo A. Depres, ed., *Ethnicity and
Resource Competition in Plural Societies* (The Hague: Mouton, 1975), p. 3.

7. G. W. Skinner, "The Nature of Loyalties in Indonesia," in I. Wallerstain,
Social Change: The Colonial Situation (New York: Wiley, 1966), pp. 265–277.

8. Robert Grey, "Determinants of National Identification in Ethiopia: A
Research Note," *The African Review*, Vol. III, No. 1 (1973), pp. 72–81.

tion which enjoins them not to alienate the land through sale, or other means, from the community.[9] Consequently, it was difficult for Nigerians to secure land in rural areas other than their own. With increased colonial influence there was gradually a general shift toward individual land ownership and the assignment of a market value to land which was formerly free. Sales of land and rent from land payable in cash are now common in suburbs of urban areas and, to a lesser extent, in rural areas, particularly where cash crops are grown.[10]

Nevertheless, a large number of Nigerians migrate to food farms, cocoa and rubber estates, and timber concessions in the rural areas to work. Long distance migrants from Sokoto usually spend the months of the dry season working for cash in the cocoa belt in Yorubaland, then return home in time for the next farming season. Igbira food farmers and Isoko oil palm exploiters who are also found in the cocoa belt are usually self-employed and tend to spend several years in the area. Some wage-earning migrants also farm for subsistence as well as cash. Examples include Igbo migrants in the cocoa and rubber estates, the Igbira in parts of Ekiti, Owo and Afemai divisions, and Isoko migrants whose main work consists of harvesting palm fruits. The non-indigenous food farmers in Asaba Division, the lower Benue valley, the cross river districts, and the fishermen of the creeks and lagoons of southern Nigeria form another group of rural-rural migrants. In Asaba there are Igbo migrants from the impoverished and overcrowded areas around Awka. They produce yams and cassava for the Onitsha food market. Cassava is the main crop around Okonyong in the lower Cross River valley where Igbo and Ibibio migrants generally cultivate larger acreage than the local people. Along the creeks of Okitipupa and Eket in the Western and Southeastern states respectively, there are several migrant fishermen from other coastal areas of Nigeria, Ghana, and the Republic of Benin.[11]

9. T. O. Elias, *Nigerian Land Law and Custom* (London: Routledge and Kegan Paul, 1953); P. C. Lloyd, *Yoruba Land Law* (London: Oxford University Press, 1962); C. K. Meek, *Land Tenure and Land Administration in Nigeria and the Cameroons* (London: Colonial Research Studies No. 22, HMSO 1957).

10. T. C. Mbagwu, "Oil Palm Economy in Ngwaland (Eastern Nigeria)," Ph.D. thesis, University of Ibadan, 1970.

11. R. K. Udo, "Rural-rural Migration in Nigeria," in *Nigeria Magazine*, (December 1969/February 1970), pp. 616–624; R. K. Udo, "Food Deficit Areas of Nigeria,"in *Geographical Review*, Vol. LXI, No. 3 (1971), pp. 415–430.

However, the number of such rural migrants relative to their host communities is quite small. Therefore contact among members of the various communal groups is insignificant. When, as in areas such as Okonyong near Calabar and Umudioga near Ahoada, the migrant population is numerically significant, ethnicity tends to emerge and persist. For example, in Umudioga during the late 1950s, when the migrant tenant farmers who out-numbered the local inhabitants began to demand the right to have a say in the expenditure of local rates they paid, the host community, fearing their domination from political control, became hostile. Thereafter, ingroup-outgroup exclusiveness emerged in their relations.[12] This supports the conclusion that significant contact between members of different communal groups is a prerequisite for the emergence of ethnicity.

The significant level of contact for the emergence of contemporary ethnicity took place in the colonial urban areas. Such intercommunal contact is reflected in the linguistic group composition of some Nigerian urban centres (Table 2.1). In comparison, migrants to the rural areas hardly constituted 1 per cent of the total population. Significant and relevant intercommunal contacts at the village level were confined to those villages near the periphery of the linguistic group and those close to the urban areas.[13] Otherwise, salient intercommunal experiences of the rural population were obtained indirectly from the stories of the urban dwellers who returned occasionally to their villages to visit,[14] and from letters written by the urban dweller to his family, relatives or friends back home.

The Origin of the Colonial Contact Situation

It is important in explaining ethnicity that the contact situation of the diverse communal groups is clearly understood. It is in such situations that ethnocentrism leads to ethnicity. The critical question for analysis at this point becomes: why is it that often when these groups are in a contact situation, ethnicity develops? In other words, what characteristics of the contact situation turn

---

12. R. K. Udo, "Rural-rural Migration in Nigeria," op. cit., p. 622.
13. G. W. Skinner, "The Nature of Loyalties in Rural Indonesia," in J. Wallerstein, ed., Social Change: The Colonial Situation (New York: Wiley, 1969), p. 271.
14. Ibid., 272.

TABLE 2.1 *Linguistic group composition of selected colonial urban centres, 1952*

	Ibadan	Lagos	Benin	Sapele	Onitsha	Enugu	Port-Harcourt	Calabar	Kano	Zaria	Kaduna	Jos	Minna
Indigenous group	Yoruba	Yoruba	Edo	Mixed	Ibo	Ibo	Mixed	Efik	Hausa	Hausa	Mixed	Birom	Gwari
Percentage of population, i.e. non-indigenous	5.4	26.7	18.0	77.2	14.0	13.3	22.6	65.8	22.5	23.5	51.6	99.1	98.1

Sources: Nigeria, *Population Census of the Western Region of Nigeria 1952* (Lagos: Govt. Statistician, 1953); Nigeria, *Population Census of Eastern Nigeria, 1952* (Lagos: Govt. Statistician, 1953); Nigeria, *Population Census of the Northern Region of Nigeria, 1952* (Lagos; Govt. Statistician, 1953).

ethnocentrism of the communal group into ethnicity? These questions cannot be fully answered without closely examining the factors which define the Nigerian urban situation. Often analysts identify the origin of ethnic conflict in group interaction, but they fail to investigate fully the causes and nature of such contact.

Several factors explain the Nigerian urban setting and its relationship to ethnicity. These include its colonial origin, the pattern of migration to it, the colonial heritage of the country, particularly its status as a dependent and peripheral appendage of the advanced capitalist societies, its participation and inferior role in an imposed international division of labour, the resultant scarcity of socioeconomic goods and services, socioeconomic competition of the type underlined by J. S. Furnivall,[15] inegalitarianism in socioeconomic life, social atomisation of the population, the pervasive socioeconomic insecurity of the individual, and the low level of class consciousness of the population. Analyses that exclude these factors mystify rather than clarify the ethnic problem.

In any normal society, no matter how primitive or civilised, an organic link unites the pattern of interhuman relations and symbols with the technology and physical environment. The crucial point here is that the link is organic. It is a natural inescapable and inseparable tissue which joins technology and the local physical environment with the activities of the vast majority of the population as they make their living. It is a central element in the creativity of a people. Without it they would lack the necessary confidence to harness their resources creatively and originally to their needs and interests.

In Nigeria, colonialism disrupted this organic interdependence in the various pre-colonial political antities which it agglomerated into one political unit. The colonialists decided what crops were needed in the European industries and if they were already produced in Nigeria they encouraged increased production. If not, and the conditions were favourable, they introduced them from outside. For example, the development of the soap industry in Britain required vegetable oil such as palm oil, palm kernel oil, groundnut oil and oil from copra. Since palm oil was considered one of the best of such oils its production in Southern Nigeria was

---

15. J. S. Furnivall, *Colonial Policy and Practice* (Cambridge: Cambridge University Press, 1943).

accelerated. Similarly, increased output of groundnut, the source of groundnut oil, was promoted. The requisite oil was exported for use in the Sunlight, Lux, Lifebouy, and Vim soap factories in Britain and other soap factories in Canada, U.S.A., Switzerland, Germany and Belgium.

In order to meet the demands of British factories for raw materials and to raise the financial capacity of the local population to buy British goods, the colonialists in the Ibadan area first introduced rubber production. It failed. The Malayan rubber boom of 1913 destroyed the fledgling rubber economy. Cotton cultivation was also encouraged. In 1903 cotton seeds and ginning machines were introduced and the Ibadan Council was persuaded to grant a lease on approximately four square miles of land to the British Cotton Growers' Association for fifty years. Cash loans were also made to cotton farmers by the Bank of West Africa. But cotton never became an important export crop. It was not until the extensive cultivation of cocoa introduced into the area in 1910 that the colonialists' efforts succeeded.[16]

Other governmental encouragements for export crops included the establishment of the Lagos Botanical Station in 1887 to explore the possibility of introducing cocoa into Western Nigeria. In 1902 the British Cotton Growers Association was formed to encourage cotton production for sale in Lancashire. Samples of soil and vegetation were shipped to imperial institutes for analysis designed to show what crops should be introduced into the country. During the inter-war years, the task of stimulating production rested with the government departments of Agriculture, Forestry and Veterinary Services. Despite the retrenchment of the staff of other government departments in the 1930s, the technical personnel of those departments trebled. Their programme encompassed not only the further development of existing export crops, but also the fostering of new products such as sugar, rice and gumarabic.

There was no attempt to design industries and activities relevant to the needs and taste patterns of the local population. Rather efforts were directed at changing the local needs and consumption habits to conform to those which the industries catered for, those of the advanced capitalist countries. As a result, whatever technical

16. Akin Mabogunje, *Urbanization in Nigeria* (London: University of London Press, 1968), pp. 194–195.

skills were brought to colonial Nigeria were transferred in isolation from the original technology of the pre-colonial societies. Foreign technology did not act or seek to act to modify the local one but completely ignored it. Thus, although this importation of know-how led to a substantial increase in the pre-colonial level of technology in Nigeria, it did so in a way which made it difficult for technical innovations to stem from the local population and to be geared to the conquest of the immediate local environment. It was divorced from the needs, interests, and resources of the colonised people.

Under the circumstances, the pre-colonial social relations and symbols could not support it. The colonialists had to establish a new set of social relations and symbols linked to the imported technology. But such a link could not be organically related to the vast majority of the population. Therefore, in order to make the colonial system work, the commanding heights of the Nigerian economy were dominated by foreign ownership of the means of production, distribution, and exchange, foreign production relations which unjustly exploited the labour of the vast majority of Nigerians, foreign work roles, and a skewed distribution of the surplus from production in the direction of Britain and the other advanced capitalist societies. As a British official aptly put it, the overall purpose of colonial enterprise was "one of exploitation and development for the people of Britain."[17] This system of domination and exploitation was buttressed by British sociopolitical norms and institutions.

The need to cut costs and concentrate their limited foreign manpower forced the colonialists to confine their activities to colonial enclaves the most significant of which were the colonial urban centres. They were the peripheral nerve centres of imperialism. They formed the relay centres from where monopoly capital penetrated all geographical areas of the country and all aspects of socioeconomic and political life. Simultaneously, they provided the necessary link between activities within the colony and their centres of organisation, manipulation, and control in the metropolitan country. The limited structural changes which took place at this time occurred in these enclaves or areas close to them.

17. H. S. Scott, "The Development of the Education of the African in Relation to Western Contact," in *The Year Book of Education, 1938* (London: Evans Bros., 1938), p. 737.

Three interrelated activities dominated socioeconomic and political changes in these new centres, British private enterprises, the British colonial government, and the Christian missionaries. They stimulated the growth of the colonial urban enclaves. In the operation of these activities the private firms were the most instrumental in structurally transforming the country. The colonial economy was dominated by the firms' investment capital, employment facilities, and general influence.

During the early colonial period, private trading firms were the most significant of these enterprises. In the 1930s, aggregate expatriate profits on the export-import trade were three times as high as those earned in the mines.[18] Their business consisted of export of agricultural products which they purchased from Nigerian middlemen, and the import of various consumer goods for sale directly to consumers or indirectly through petty traders. For example, Akin Mabogunje reports that by 1918 many European firms which were already established in Lagos had opened up branches in Ibadan. These firms included the African and Eastern Trade Corporation, Miller Brothers, G. B. Ollivant and Co., Patterson Zachonis, G. Gottschalk and Co., W. B. MacIver and Co., the Société Commerciale et Industrièlle de l'Afrique Occidental, John Holt and Co. (Liverpool) Ltd., Lagos Stores Ltd., John Walkden and Co., the Anglo-Colonial Trading Corporation, Ayer and Wintle, and H. B. Russel and Co.[19] These trading firms, especially the United Africa Company (UAC), accounted for the largest share of the estimated ₦73,580,000 which was invested by private European interests in Nigeria from 1870 to 1936.[20] In comparison, the British Government invested ₦69,442,000 in loans and grants-in-aid during the same period.[21] The firms organised their operations in the new urban enclaves because of the heavy consumer demand from the high income groups which lived there, and the concentration of capitalist and administrative infrastructure in the enclaves.

The colonial government emphasised the expansion of these enclaves. Although in 1900, governmental expenditure amounted to only ₦1,470,000 or 40 per cent of export value, in 1929 it

18. J. Mars, "Extraterritorial Enterprises," in Margery Perham, ed., *Mining, Commerce and Finance in Nigeria* (London: Faber and Faber, 1948), p. 58.
19. Akin Mabogunje, *op. cit.*, pp. 194–195.
20. S. H. Frankl, *Capital Investment in Africa* (London: Oxford University Press, 1938), p. 158.
21. *Ibid.* p. 158.

was ₦12.6 million.[22] This expansion kept pace with the growth in the value of exports. In anticipation of the high returns from new trading outlets, and because of the demands of increased political control of the hinterland, the colonial government built the railway system from 1898 to 1932. For example, when the railway reached Kano in 1911 the exports of groundnuts jumped from 1,179 to 19,288 tons.[23] It also engaged in considerable road construction throughout the country, and harbor construction at Lagos and Port Harcourt to promote import and export trade.

The building of railways and roads became a significant feature of colonial activity during the interwar period 1914–1939. Rail lines were built from Lagos to Ibadan and through to Kano, from Jos to the main line, from Enugu to Port Harcourt and eventually to Maiduguri. In 1926 the southeastern section was linked to the northern. Meanwhile, district commissioners constructed every type of road, from the modern metaled highway to the dusty laterite track to facilitate both administrative communication and the movement of goods and services. Telegraph and postal services were added to these activities and infrastructure. By 1913 deep water berths had been opened in Lagos; thirteen years later some were opened in Apapa. One common feature characterised this web of communications. Their respective paths all ran from the enclaves of colonial production, distribution and exchange to the ships that would carry the colony's produce to the advanced capitalist countries.

Governmental policies which equated development with the expansion of these enclaves encouraged and subsidised investments in them, provided them with infrastructural facilities at subsidised rates, extended low-interest loans to their activities, imposed tariffs to protect their industries, and made some (albeit inadequate) response to labor's demand for better wages and living conditions. The Government directed research projects toward satisfying the enclaves industrial and agricultural needs. The West African Cocoa Research Institute, the West African Institute for Oil Palm Research, West African Stored Products Research Unit, the Expanded School of Agriculture at Samaru, and the faculties of Agriculture in the country were created for this purpose. In addition the Government operated

22. *Ibid.*, p. 317; G. K. Helleiner, *op. cit.*, p. 13.
23. Margery Perham, ed., *The Native Economies of Nigeria* (London: Faber and Faber, 1946), p. 9.

the coal mine at Enugu, ran a stone quarry at Aro near Abeokuta and a furniture and sawmill plant at Ijora near Lagos.

As a result of these activities the colonial government needed centers for administration and for the effective political control of the country. The specific requirements of the new railways for fueling and other facilities reinforced the need for such centres. In 1917 a Township Ordinance came into force for the creation, control, and administration of these towns and municipalities. Three categories of townships were created: first, second and third classes. Lagos was the only first class township in the country. There were 18 second class townships in 1919. They were principally large centres of trade. Twelve were located in the South and six in the North. As Akin Mabogunje has observed they

"were centres either along the railway line or on the coast, so that they represented places where European traders had set up stores. They were not particularly distinguished by the size of their population nor their traditional importance as is evidenced by the absence of many of the larger Yoruba towns."[24]

Also, in 1919 third class townships numbered fifty, thirty-eight in the South and twelve in the North. These were officially described as "government stations," underlining once more the association of the colonial urban centres with colonial order and rule.

Prior to British intrusion, urban areas existed in Nigeria. A few Yoruba towns had populations of between 20,000 and 70,000. They were Ibadan, Abeokuta, Oshogbo, Ogbomosho, Ife and Oyo. Although the degree of urbanisation in Yorubaland was unique in tropical Africa, urban centers also existed in northern Nigeria. They included Kano, Zazzau (Zaria), Sokoto, Katsina, Kakawa and Yerwa. Such cities were quite different from the new colonial ones. Basically they arose as a result of growth in production above the needs and wants of the local population as dictated by their habitual pattern of consumption. The resultant surplus enabled a veritable division of labour in which individuals specialised in trade, crafts, and administration in addition to agriculture. The urban centres provided the necessary infrastructure to the practitioners of the specialised activities. These specialised urban professional groups were organically related to the food producers, providing them with the necessary implements for

24. Akin Mabogunje, *op. cit.*, pp. 112–113.

improved agricultural production in exchange for food and other farm produce. In contrast, the colonial cities were not similarly organically related to the growth of food production or to the emergence of locally relevant specialisation of functions. This abnormal and distorted pattern of colonial urbanisation failed to uproot the urbanite from his rural base; he was in the city, but not of it. He worked there but diverted his savings to his village. Also those pre-colonial cities not located on the rail line, major roads, or other centres of colonial activities disintegrated.[25]

Ogbomosho which in 1911 was the second largest city in Nigeria stagnated for more than 30 years because the railway was routed through Oshogbo. Abeokuta, a famous Yoruba city was eclipsed by Lagos and Ibadan in part because of its location midway between these two larger colonial centers. Kaduna rather than Zaria or Kano became the northern governmental headquarters out of Lord Lugard's personal wish, as well as because of its central location in the region. The famous northern centers of Sokoto, Katsina and Yerwa have deteriorated in importance because of their unfavourable location in the colonial scheme of things.

Wage employment, small scale business, hospitals, water supply, electricity, and education, although severely limited, were concentrated in the new towns. Township status guided the distribution of social services; they were provided to the first, second and third class towns in that order. For example, in 1917 there were European hospitals at Calabar, Kaduna, Kano, Lagos, Lokoja, Onitsha and Warri. These were either first or second class townships. By 1924 such hospitals had been built in Jos, and Port Harcourt. In addition, there were hospitals for Africans at Calabar, Ikot Ekpene, Ilorin, Kaduna, Kano, Lagos, Lokoja, Minna, Onitsha, Port Harcourt, Warri, Zaria. A minority of these were third-class townships. By 1929 the list of places with such hospitals had grown to include more third-class towns such as Aba, Abakaliki, Ado-Ekiti, Agbor, Bauchi, Benin, Degema, Ibi, Ijebu-Ode, Maiduguri, Ogoja, Okigwi, Owerri and Sokoto.

Similarly, water supply and electricity were allocated on the basis of township status. By 1914 only Lagos had water supply. However, by 1932 twelve centres had efficient water supply. Out

25. Akin Mabogunje, "The Economic Implications of the Pattern of Urbanisation in Nigeria," in *Nigerian Journal of Economic and Social Studies*, Vol. VII, No. 1 (March 1965), pp. 16–17.

of these, nine were either first or second class townships. Eight other centres, mostly third class townships, had smaller water schemes. By 1950, water had been supplied on a large scale to nineteen towns. In terms of the 1917 categories, one of these cities was in the first class category, twelve in the second class, three in the third class, and four were unclassified. In the same manner electricity was gradually extended from Lagos in 1896 to Enugu, Port Harcourt and Kaduna in 1929 and so on until 1950 when twenty towns had electricity supply. Although by the latter date the township categories no longer operated, no less than twelve of these centres were either first or second class townships.[26]

In Southern Nigeria this urban centered pattern of colonial activities was reinforced by the work of the Christian missions which monopolised colonial education.[27] Until 1898 all education was under the direct control of the missionaries. As late as 1942 they controlled 99 per cent of the schools, and more than 97 per cent of the students were enrolled in Mission schools.[28] Schools were concentrated in the urban areas where the colonial population and employment opportunities were concentrated. Nigeria's first secondary school was founded in Lagos in 1859.[29] In 1895 the Hope Waddel Training Institute was set up on Calabar by the Church of Scotland Mission. These two advanced coastal towns took the lead in colonial education. By 1900 there were eight secondary schools in Nigeria as follows: five in Lagos, one in Calabar, one in Oyo and one in Ogbomosho.[30]

In 1921 about 40 per cent of "educated" Southern Nigerians lived in thirteen urban centres with a population of less than 2 per cent of the total Southern population.[31] In 1953 about 34 per cent of those with four or more years of education in Onitsha province

26. Sources: *Nigeria, Handbook of Commerce and Industry* (Lagos: Govt. Printer, 1952), pp. 87–88; *Nigeria, Handbook of Commerce and Industry* (Lagos: Govt. printer, 1954), p. 45; Akin Mabogunje, *Urbanization in Nigeria, op. cit.*, p. 115 Tables 7 and 8.

27. In northern Nigeria pre-colonial forms of education in the Koran continued to dominate education in the new order.

28. Nigeria, *Ten Year Educational Plan* (Lagos: Nigerian sessional paper No. 6/1944), p. 11.

29. David Abernethy, *The Political Dilemma of Popular Education: An African Case* (Stanford: Stanford University Press, 1969), pp. 34, 36.

30. *Ibid.*, p. 36.

31. Nigeria, *Annual Report, Department of Education 1953* (Lagos: Govt. printer, 1954), pp. 5–6.

lived in Enugu and Onitsha, 60 per cent in Rivers province lived in Port Harcourt, 61 per cent in Ibadan province lived in Ibadan, and 89 per cent of those in Kano province who had completed six or more years of Western education lived in Kano.[32] Colonial schools were further concentrated in these urban areas. For example, Lagos was not only the capital of the country, but also the headquarters of most of the European enterprises. In 1921, 43 per cent of Europeans in the country lived in Lagos.[33] Thirty years later, in 1951, 60 per cent of Europeans in the South lived in the city.[34] In the former year Lagos alone had 20 per cent of the schools in Nigeria.[35]

Thus the activities of the foreign private firms, local colonial administration, and the Christian missionaries stimulated the growth of the colonial urban areas. The process of urbanisation which accompanied the growth of colonial activities during the period prior to 1929 was slowed down by the economic depression of the 1930s. In fact, the growth of the Nigerian economy was effectively halted until after the Second World War. Post-war growth in colonial activities gave rise to an unprecedented structural transformation of the country. Urban centres of 20,000 or more inhabitants grew from 0.8 million in 1921 to 1.4 million in 1931.[36] By 1952 the figure had reached 3.2 million representing 10.6 per cent of the total population in comparison with 7 per cent in 1931.[37] As late as 1931 there were no urban centres of more than 20,000 in Eastern Nigeria. But by 1952 there were four cities of more than 50,000.[38]

All evidence from the immediate post-war period, 1945–1954, points to a rapid acceleration in the rate of migration from the rural to the urban areas. After 1945 colonial activities became dominant over all others, particularly in the cocoa and ground-nut areas. By 1948 about 43 per cent of the adult male population

32. *Ibid.*, p. 5.
33. J. S. Coleman, *op. cit.*, p. 144.
34. *Ibid.*, p. 144.
35. *Ibid.*, pp. 144–145.
36. Sources: *Ibid.*, p. 74; Nigeria, Department of Statistics, *Census of Nigeria, 1952–1953* (Lagos: Govt. Printer, 1955); Nigeria, Dept. of Statistics *Census of Nigeria 1931* (Lagos: Govt. Printer, 1932). Note that because of the stagnation and deurbanization of the periods of the depression and the Second World War, the figures of urbanization in the post-war period are more significant than they seem.
37. *Ibid.*
38. J. S. Coleman, *op. cit.*, p. 75.

TABLE 2.2   *Population over time of some Nigerian urban centres*

Urban centre	1911	1931	1953
Lagos	73,766	126,108	267,407
Sapele	2,107	4,143	33,638
Enugu	—	12,959	62,764
Port Harcourt	—	15,201	71,634
Kano	unknown	97,031	130,173
Kaduna	—	10,628	38,527

Sources: P. Amoury Talbot, *The Peoples of Southern Nigeria, Vol. IV: Linguistics and Statistics* (London: Oxford University Press, 1926); C. K. Meek, *The Northern Tribes of Nigeria* (London: Oxford University Press, 1925); Nigeria, *Census of Nigeria, 1931* (Lagos: Govt. Printer, 1932); Nigeria, *The Population Census of the Western Region of Nigeria, 1952* (Lagos: Govt. Statistician, 1953); Nigeria, *The Population Census of the Eastern Region of Nigeria, 1953* (Lagos: Govt. Statistician, 1954); Nigeria, *The Population Census of the Northern Region of Nigeria 1952* (Lagos: Govt. Statistician, 1953).

were actively involved in the new order.[39] As a result, growth in cash crop production accelerated (Table 2.3). Also there was an increased drift to wage employment. Whereas in 1938 the number of persons in wage employment was approximately 150,000, by 1948 the number had risen to 260,000 and by 1951 to 300,000.[40]

TABLE 2.3 *Growth of Nigerian cash crops during the colonial period (in thousands of tons)*

Year	Palm products	Groundnuts	Cocoa	Cotton
1919–1921	272	45	20	4
1934	402	245	78	6
1939	426	147	114	4
1944	439	156	70	4
1949	546	378	104	10
1953	604	327	105	18

Sources: Margery Perham, ed., *Mining Commerce and Finance in Nigeria* (London: Faber and Faber, 1948), p. 9; B. T. Bauer, *West African Trade* (London: Oxford University Press, 1950), p. 195; J. S. Coleman, *Nigeria, Background to Nationalism* (Barkeley and Los Angeles, Calif: University of California Press, 1958), p. 67; International Bank for Reconstruction and Development, *Economic Development of Nigeria* (Baltimore: IBRD, 1955, pp. 18–19.

39. See K. M. Buchanan and J. C. Pugh, *Land and People of Nigeria* (London: University of London Press, 1955); International Bank for Reconstruction and Development (IBRD), *Economic Development of Nigeria* (Baltimore: IBRD, 1955), p. 616.
40. Margery Perham, ed., *op. cit.*, pp. 18, 97; J. S. Coleman, *op. cit.*, pp. 68–70.

This drift weakened the equilibrium of the villages which began to lose their power, function, and traditional industries, in addition to their manpower. Migration from the rural to the urban areas was thus further accelerated. Kano recorded a 26.8 per cent increase in population between 1911 and 1921. By 1952 the 1921 figure had trebled. Between 1952 and 1962 the population again doubled.[41] However, in Lagos the most rapid increase in population occurred from 1901 to 1910. Growth was retarded during 1910–1921 by the First World War, an influenza epidemic which broke out soon after the war, and the immediate post-war slump in trade. This trend continued until the Second World War because of more deaths from a bubonic plague and the general world economic depression. But by 1950 the population had grown to almost twice the size in 1931.[42]

Differential Migration to the Colonial Contact Situation

Migration to the colonial urban areas was caused by the needs and pressures of the new order. Foreign personnel was inadequate to man the various colonial enterprises. Local labour was required. Several devices were used to procure this labour. Some analysts contend that Nigerians voluntarily migrated to areas of colonial activities because the latter offered them greater and better social and economic rewards than village life. The same analytical perspective is reflected by G. K. Helleiner who, although he recognises the British use of forced labour for building the railways, and for work in the mines, argues that, in general, the colonialists merely dangled "sufficiently attractive prizes before the producers' noses to persuade them to convert potential into actual surpluses by increasing their output.[43] While this may have been true for such products as palm oil, palm kernels and groundnuts which were consumed locally, it certainly was different for cocoa which was introduced from outside the

---

41. John Paden, "Communal Competition, Conflict and Violence in Kano," in Robert Melson and Howard Wolpe, eds., *Nigeria: Modernization and the Politics of Communalism* (East Lansing, Michigan: State University Press, 1971), pp. 116–117.
42. Akin Mabogunje, *op. cit., Urbanization in Nigeria*, p. 257.
43. G. K. Helleiner, *Peasant Agriculture, Government and Economic Growth in Nigeria* (Homewood, Illinois: Irwin Inc., 1966), p. 12.

country. In any case as Samir Amin has aptly pointed out, the transformation of a natural subsistence economy into a commodity economy is never a spontaneous consequence of the introduction of new manufactured goods causing the subsistence farmers to produce agricultural products for export in order to satisfy new wants.[44]

Pierre-Philippe Rey and Claude Meillassou have shown that strictly economic mechanisms do not suffice because of the resistance of the traditional social structures to the spread of commodity exchange.[45] For example, the persistence of the right of all villagers to use the village land makes the simple mechanism of competition that played a determining role in the transition from feudalism to capitalism in Europe ineffective. Therefore, the colonial authority must stimulate the "monetarisation of the primitive economy." In the process, violence, a method of primitive accumulation, is inevitable. Specific distortions of the traditional society are forced through which compel people to go in search of money, and so cause them to become commodity producers or to sell their labour power. Also, competition from imported products causes the ruin of local craftsmen, forcing them to seek new means of livelihood in the new colonial enclaves.

This approach to rural-urban migration characteristic of pro-colonialist economic analysis assumes that export crop production by foreign capital is beneficial to the colony. Therefore, labour moves in the direction of its highest remuneration. The theoretical alternative of capital, which is more mobile than labour, moving to areas of cheap labour for the production of local pre-colonial goods and services is not entertained. Why was capital invested exclusively in certain areas of export crop production and manufacturing for import substitution goods and not in agriculture for local consumption in other areas? Why does labour have to move to areas where foreign capital has decided to install itself and not the other way around?[46]

As Samir Amin has correctly pointed out this approach begins with two mistaken assumptions. First, it sees the distribution of the factors of production as given rather than as the result of a

---

44. Samir Amin, *Unequal Development* (New York: Monthly Review, 1976), p. 204.
45. Summarized in *ibid.*, pp. 203–205.
46. Samir Amin, "Introduction," in Samir Amin, ed. *Modern Migrations in Western Africa* (London: Oxford University Press, 1974), pp. 85–87.

strategy of development. Second, it supposes that the migrant is an individual whose decision to move is the function of the gap between his real income in the city and the rural areas, and the probability that he will be employed in the city.[47] It fails to see that the migrants do not move indifferently from all the poor rural regions and are not recruited from all the individuals who constitute their populations. In fact, Akin Mabogunje has observed that in Nigeria such migration is principally from regions with a higher income, stronger growth rate, and population density towards regions with lower income, and sparser population, except for the cocoa region of Western Nigeria.[48] The colonialist view-point pays little attention to the society of origin of the migrant. It is merely assumed to be an aggregate of individuals who have a choice of moving or staying. Consequently, why certain individuals migrate is never probed and all discussion of the modes of production and organisation of society is eliminated. By taking its point of departure from the observations of motivations, such a viewpoint is prevented from the beginning from seeing the essential facts such as the processes, rules, and needs of the system which cannot be discovered from the motivations but which lie behind individual motivations because they determine the alternative choices avilable to the individual. Motivations are really nothing but rationalisations of behaviour within the system.[49]

Oshomha Imoagene has shown that during the initial period of migration the urban dweller retains his rural system of traditional values and links, coming only to earn money. He necessarily regards the town as an extension of his village community, leaves his family back in the village and reduces rural-urban migration to a mechanical process of backward and forward movement between the town and his village. While in the city he keeps up all the channels of communication with the home people through regular and frequent visits, letters, messages and gifts, thereby keeping himself within the rural network of social relations. At the end of his career in the town, particularly if it is a short career,

47. *Ibid.*, pp. 88–90.
48. Akin Mabogunje, "Migration Policy and Regional Development in Nigeria," *Nigerian Journal of Social and Economic Studies*, Vol. XII, No. 3 (July 1970), p. 256.
49. Samir Amin, *Modern Migration in Western Africa, op. cit.*, pp. 90–91; Rott. Sabor, "Urban Migrations in Tanzania," (University of Dar es Salaam Tanzania 1972) (unpublished Mineo) p. 12.

the forced migrant quickly resumes his village life as if he had never left it. For him there is meaning in this existence which does not exist in the town.

Therefore, the labour migration which tends to characterise the initial phase of colonial urban development involves hardly any learning, nor is it motivated by the glamour of urban life. Since the colonial towns grew out of the need to establish centres for trade and administration rather than the desire for a direct connection with the lives of the indigenous population, they were not conducive to the integration of the migrant into colonial life. Physically, the emergent city is inadequately equipped to provide the migrants with the social amenities which they need in order to adjust to a new set of values. Culturally, there is a vacuum which results from the neglect of traditional norms and values with nothing yet to take its place. Under these conditions the migrant is not attracted to the city. He is forced to go there. Only later does he acquire a second system of values, those of the town which then become in themselves a motive for migration, in particular to bigger and better cities such as the capital.[50]

Even as recently as 1977 Ray Ofoegbu has observed that the Igbo in the towns are still a product of both the village and the urban worlds. While they live and work in the latter, they do not regard it as their home. They view their stay there as temporary and believe that their roots and future lie together with their village communities. "Their emotional and sentimental attachments are not with the urban communities but with their home towns. Hence, they are willing to endure any hardships, deprivations and sufferings in the towns without protesting because they feel their stay is temporary and essentially instrumental."[51] In his survey of Igbo urbanites' attitudes on the subject, he found that the home village still holds the ultimate attraction for 51 per cent to 64 per cent to invest their earnings, and for between 60 per cent and 79 per cent to retire to with their earnings and savings.[52]

A comparative costs and benefits analysis condu·cted at the microeconomic level of the migrant only gives the appearance of

50. Oshomha Imoagene, "Some Sociological Aspects of Modern Migration in Western Africa," in Samir Amin; ed., *op. cit.*, p. 343.
51. Mazi Ray Ofoegbu, "Urban Politics Among the Igbo of Nigeria," Ph.D thesis, University of Nigeria, 1977, p. 16.
52. *Ibid.*, p. 34.

objective rationality to a choice by the migrant which in reality does not exist because in the given system he has no other alternatives. It is forgotten that the migrant had to find money within the framework of a system that gave him no other alternative for getting this money. Therefore, migration is hardly voluntary. The migrants, usually from among the poorest or the least powerful socially, go to earn money for their taxes. And who migrates can not be explained without analysing the mode of production in the region considered and its deformation as a result of its integration into colonial capitalism.

In fact, in 1898 Sir George C. Denton, the Lieutenant Governor for Lagos complained bitterly about the reluctance of Nigerians to serve in the colonial service: "To obtain carriers to go out of the colony is most difficult. Recently, to quote an instance, as much as two shillings a day was offered with head money of 5s, and yet very few carriers were prevailed upon to go to Gold Coast . . . The fact is that the Lagosian does not like foreign service."[53] He variously explained this reluctance as arising from the Nigerian's dislike for working away from his home, or because he is not fond of work: "the native of the Protectorate, with very few exceptions, is not fond of work, and it is very difficult to get out of him anything like the worth of the money paid."[54]

The colonialist view-point ignores the compulsion inherent in the enforcement of British currency as the only means of economic exchange, and the introduction of fixed recurrent taxes whose equivalent was hitherto unknown in the country except in the northern emirates. British money was introduced into the country around 1900. Without the new money it was difficult to buy and sell goods and services in the new order. Nigerians were thus forced to engage in colonial activities. Local resistance to it is reflected by the fact that as late as 1919 Lord Lugard complained about the persistence of barter as a means of exchange in some parts of the country: "trading by barter is still carried on in some parts of Nigeria in spite of all efforts of the Government to put a stop to it."[55] In fact, in Eastern Nigeria the pre-colonial currency

53. Quoted in Wogu Ananaba, *The Trade Union Movement in Nigeria* (London: Ethiope, 1969) p. 6.
54. Quoted in *ibid.*
55. Quoted in Alan McPhee, *The Economic Revolution in Britisv West Africa* (Aberdeen, Scotland: Routledge and Sons, 1926), p. 233; and reproduced in James S. Coleman, *Nigeria: Background to Nationalism* (Berkeley and Los Angeles, Calif.: University of California Press, 1958), pp. 56–47.

was not completely abandoned until 1950 when it was compulsorily out-lawed.

Similarly, the introduction of taxation increased indigenous participation in the colonial economy. After transforming the tax system in the northern emirates to conform to British norms, Lord Lugard extended a similar framework to Southern Nigeria where such taxation was alien. His motive was, in part, to stimulate the use of British currency. In order to raise money for these taxes, Nigerians had to engage in colonial activities. Resistance flared up in the Iseyin uprising of 1916, the Abeokuta revolt of 1918, riots and demonstrations in Sapele and Warri in 1927, and the Aba riots of 1929. Such reactions attended the decision to impose a land and house tax in Lagos in 1895, and to levy a water rate on its inhabitants in 1908.[56]

The reactionary local colonial administration also created artificial scarcity in order to compel Nigerians into colonial activities. It paid such low wages that more than one worker was needed to feed the extended family. In addition it maintained huge surpluses every year whenever possible, even during the 1930–1935 economic depression. For example, between 1947 and 1954 the publicly-owned Nigerian Marketing Boards amassed enormous surplusses: ₦92,086,600 from cocoa, ₦70,029,600 from palm oil, ₦61,070,600 from groundnuts, and ₦16,642,600 from cotton.[57] By 1954 about ₦240 million in trading profits had been mobilised by the four boards during this seven-year span. Over the same period the two principal sources of government tax revenue each earned less than this amount. Import duties realised ₦187 million and export duties earned ₦113.4 million.[58]

These accumulations were meant to be distributed to farmers during the lean years or used for socioeconomic services. Only palm oil producers received subsidies and price supports during the lean years of this period. In 1953 they received about ₦13.8 million in subsidies; and in 1954 benefited from price support. In spite of these measures, however, the Oil Palm Produce Marketing Board still maintained large resources. Even after palm oil export prices began to fall in the latter half of the 1950s it continued to maintain surpluses. In 1964 the real export prices

56. *Ibid.*, p. 178.
57. Sources: *Annual Reports of the Nigerian Marketing Boards*, G. K. Helleiner, *op. cit.*, p. 160.
58. *Ibid.*, p. 162.

for palm oil and palm kernels were below their levels during the Depression of the 1930s.[59] More money was even withheld from growers through export duties and, from 1958, regional sales taxes on produce sold by the boards. In this way, during the period 1947 to 1954, over 42 per cent of the producer income earned from cotton, 40 per cent from groundnuts, 39 per cent from cocoa, 29 per cent from palm kernels, and 17 per cent from palm oil were withheld from the producer.[60]

Forced labour was also used for colonial activities. In the building of the railways and bridges, and in the mines, indentured and free labour was forcibly recruited by the colonialists. Paul Iyorpuu Unongo graphically recalls the consequent suffering of the Tiv.

"The callous assaults started with the mass conscriptions, the forced labour, and physical forceful uprootment of male members of families who were carted away in wagons, to work in mines in unknown far away places without any financial compensations. Perhaps as Tiv, you may recall these atrocities, which were perpetrated by British Administrators beginning in the late twenties and continuing through to the early forties under two familiar names: ADOGON (reference to the railway construction and the work on the Makurdi bridge over River Benue) and KUZA (reference to tin-mining on the Jos plateau)."[61]

Thus, four British colonial policies – forced labour, alien currency, taxation, and artificial scarcity – forced many members of the local population to migrate to areas of new colonial activity for longer or shorter periods to work or trade. Increasingly fewer Nigerians could subsist by performing their pre-colonial activities. In a general way, this migration led to a significant alteration of the Nigerian colonial economy. Between 1900 and 1929 its export sector greatly expanded. Export value increased more than seven times, and export volume more than five times, amounting to annual growth rates of seven per cent and five and half per cent respectively.

New cash crops, groundnuts, cocoa, rubber and cotton were introduced. In 1900 palm products constituted from 80 per cent

59. *Ibid.*, p. 32, pp. 162–163.
60. *Ibid.* p. 163.
61. Paul Iyorpuu Unongo, "Where do We Go From Here," an unpublished open letter to the Tiv people, 1969, quoted in J. I. Tseayo, *Conflict and Incorporation in Nigeria* (Zaria: Gaskya, 1975), pp. 150–151.

to 90 per cent of the total export. But by 1929 although its volume had trebled it accounted for only 47 per cent of the total export; groundnut products accounted for 15 per cent and cocoa for 30 per cent of total exports.[62] Tin deposits on the Bauchi plateau were exploited by British mining concerns, while coal resources at Enugu were discovered and exploited. An extensive railway system linking the northern with the eastern and western parts of the country was built to service these and other forms of exploitation. Export production grew at a faster rate than the traditional economic activities.

Nevertheless, the overall structures of the economy altered very little during this period. Precolonial economic activities for domestic use rather than export predominated. In 1929 they accounted for 85 per cent of the value of goods and services produced in the country. Very little Western technology was introduced into this sector. Even the activities connected with the new export sector altered the indigenous way of life only very slightly. During the interwar years, total government exployment of the local population amounted to only 50,000.[63] However, export production grew faster than the pre-colonial activities. Export volume doubled between 1900 and 1912 and doubled again between 1924 and 1929. On the other hand, over the entire period from 1900 to 1929, traditional output increased by at most only 10 per cent.[64] Governmental emphasis was certainly placed on the growth of the new colonial activities.

The impact of the colonial economic order on the country was crucial regarding the differential in the number and communal background of migrants to the urban areas of Nigeria. This economic order created three types of areas. First, there were areas for large-scale export production and/or administration in which private capitalist appropriation of land and the availability of labour were characteristic features. Such areas included, but were not limited to, the new urban centres. Second, other areas served essentially as reserves which supplied wage labour and which had been fully penetrated by colonial capitalism. Third, there were other areas which were only marginally penetrated by peripheral capitalism. Migratory flow took place from the second towards the first areas with the third areas supplying

62. *Ibid.*, pp. 5–7.
63. *Ibid.*, p. 15.
64. *Ibid.*, p. 7.

no migrants even though their real incomes were quite low.

Several factors accounted for the possibility of a communal homeland developing into a labour reserve supplying migrants to the areas of colonial activity. Among these is the nature of the pre-colonial socioeconomic conditions. When the members of a communal group were unable to pay their taxes and fulfill their other financial obligations in the new colonial order by continuing their precolonial economic activity, their rate of migration was high. They had to seek new fortunes in the colonial order in order to ensure bare existence. Otherwise, their rate of migration was low. Therefore, among and within communal groups the pre-colonial level of production, which is the outcome of the prevailing mode of production, the level of growth of the productive forces, and the relations of production, was crucial for migration.

Thus for example Igbo primitive communalist mode of production under patriachal domination was accompanied by a low level of production, underdevelopment of the productive forces, and the increasing pauperisation of the younger sons. And since production was based on the cultivation of land, low production, and pauperisation were worst in areas of poor soil. Here the rate of migration was highest. Igboland is one of the most densely populated areas of the world. In some places the density is more than 1,000 persons to the square mile.[65] Moreover, the soil is comparatively poor because it is highly leached and acidic. Hence, a large number of Igbo-speaking people have migrated to colonial life. For example, in 1952 about 99,000 Igbo residents lived in the eleven main urban areas of the North, West, Midwest and Lagos. They constituted 8 per cent of the total urban population of these areas of 1.2 million, and 51 per cent of the non-indigenous population. In Lagos, Benin, Kano and Kaduna they constituted over 30 per cent of the non-indigenous residents.[66] Therefore, unlike the more materially-developed Hausa and Yoruba linguistic peoples, the Igbo were more impelled to move. The younger sons who were the poorest because of the disadvantages imposed on them by the land tenure system constituted the bulk of the migrants. Similarly, the secular and sacred slaves, Oru and Osu respectively, also migrated in large numbers. They constituted the most exploited and down-

65. R. K. Udo, "The Migrant Tenant Farmer of Eastern Nigeria," *Africa*, Vol. XXXIV, No. 4 (1964), pp. 326–327.
66. Mazi Ray Ofoegbu, *op. cit.*, p. 13.

trodden of Igbo societies, and were without social, economic or political rights. In fact, colonial activity, although itself generally degrading and dehumanising, offered them an opportunity to escape the inhuman conditions under which they lived.

There were sections of the Igbo such as the Abakaliki and Anam peoples who fiercely resisted migration. They are blessed with fertile lands and, therefore, high productivity of agriculture. Consequently, they were able to maintain a high level of subsistence existence similar to that obtained during the pre-colonial times. At the same time, they were able to generate agricultural surpluses which provided them with the necessary funds for paying taxes and buying some of the colonial goods and services which they wanted. Under these circumstances, there was no serious pressure to migrate. Ikenna Nzimiro has successfully related the higher rate of migration of certain sections of the Igbo to (a) land hunger, particularly around Onitsha, Awka, Okigwi, and Orlu (b) a dearth of fertile land as in Nnewi and (c) rising costs of farming as in Oguta.[67]

Another major determinant of the differential migration from the labour reserves to the urban areas was the timing of contact of the homelands of the various communal groups with colonialism. The coastal peoples, such as the Yoruba and the Efik of Calabar who first made contact with colonialism, gained an earlier start than others in acquiring socioeconomic resources within the new order. Initially, colonialism was essentially oriented to import-export trade. At its outset, the dominant international mode of transportation was by ocean-going ships. Therefore, the initial points of contact between the metropole and the colony were the latter's seaports. Here, the colonialists entered into trade and other relations with the inhabitants of the coastal strip and established outposts from where they ventured into the hinterland.

Thus, the coastal peoples entered into colonial activities well before those further inland. They were the first to receive education, get a job in the Civil Service and the firms, act as middlemen between the peasant producer and the foreign marketing firms, enter into petty trading, and serve as interpreters for the Christian missionaries. For example, by 1900, of the eight secondary

67. Ikenna Nzimiro, "A Study of Mobility Among the Ibos of Southern Nigeria," in *International Journal of Comparative Sociology*, Vol. VI, No. 1 (March, 1965), p. 53–54.

schools in the country, seven were situated in Yoruba-speaking towns and one in Calabar.[68]

The manner in which contact with colonialism was made also affected migration by members of communal groups. There were two patterns of such contact. Among such groups as the Igbo and Ibibio, where the pre-colonial productive forces were underdeveloped and the mode of production and division of labour were rather rudimentary, socioeconomic integration was weak. Similarly, the central authority was weak. Colonial penetration occurred essentially through economic activities. The colonial devices for obtaining cheap labour could not be successfully resisted by the central authority. The local economy and the political order were powerless to regulate the flow of labour to colonial enterprises.

The capitalist mode of production tends to disintegrate the pre-capitalist modes when interaction is unrestricted and limited to the economic level. This disintegration enables cheap labour to be released for capitalist production. At the same time the weakness of the central authority makes it easy for the members of the local society to cast off their ties in the pre-colonial production process for new ones in the colonial setting. The Igbo citizen could more easily defy his pre-colonial authority in pursuit of the new economic activities than his Yoruba and Hausa counterparts. The Yoruba Oba wielded much greater influence over his subjects than the Igbo chief. And the Hausa subject usually held his Emir in awe, often prostrating before his presence. This explains, in part, the greater tendency of the Igbo in comparison to the Yoruba and of the Yoruba in comparison to Hausa to migrate to colonial activities, particularly far away from their homelands.

On the other hand, in the Hausa Emirates the pre-colonial level of production and the growth of the productive forces had advanced sufficiently to generate a veritable complex division of labour and consequent powerful central authority. The disintegration of the pre-capitalist by the capitalist mode of production could, therefore, be resisted, particularly when the capitalist mode was exogenous and governed by a restrictive division of labour imposed from outside. The colonialists' attempt to penetrate the emirates met with fierce resistance organised under

68. David Abernethy, *The Political Dilemma of Popular Education* (Stanford: Stanford University Press, 1969), pp. 34–37.

the central authority. Therefore, colonialism operated through an agreement with the Emirs which left them with enough power to regulate the migration of their populations to centres of colonial activity. The colonialists could only make contact with the members of the emirates through the rulers.

This situation was reinforced by the vast expanses of the emirates, the consequent inability of the colonialists to provide enough personnel for their administration, and the absence of other avenues for revenues for the colonial coffers than the inhabitants of the emirates. The compromise deal which allowed the emir continued domination over his people with as little interference from the colonialists as possible in exchange for the maintenance of law and order in the emirate and the collection of taxes for the colonial authorities gave rise to the system of Indirect Rule. For religious reasons related to the security of their system of domination the Hausa rulers discouraged the migration of their subjects. Much of the emir's authority over his subjects came from his religious role in society. Exposure of the latter to Christian influences of the colonial order might weaken this authority. Hence, the Hausa have lagged behind their Igbo and Yoruba compatriots who were not under similar restraints in migrating the colonial activities.

The pattern of location of colonial socioeconmic projects also affected the differential migration of communal groups. Those communal homelands or sections of them which were neither significant centres of colonial economic production nor situated along the major routes of the new system of communications produced very few migrants. Akin Mabogunje has shown that, with the exception of Lagos, the vast bulk of migration to the colonial urban areas came from the provinces immediately around them.[69] With the reluctance of the migrants to venture far away from home it could not be otherwise.

Lagos in Yorubaland had a disproportionate share of colonial activities. Apart from its early contact with colonialism it was one of the earliest port towns and, therefore, an important commercial centre for the import-export trade. It was also a terminal of that section of the Nigerian railway system which served the

69. Akin Mabogunje, Regional Mobility and Resource Development in West Africa (Montreal: McGill University, Center for Developing Area Studies, n.d.).

important cash crop areas of cocoa in Western Nigeria, and cotton and groundnuts in Northern Nigeria. At the same time it was not only the administrative capital of the country but also the headquarters of most of the European enterprises.[70] This socioeconomic importance of Lagos in the colonial order together with the significance of cocoa produced in Yorubaland accounts, in part, for the high rate of migration of the Yoruba-speaking peoples.

Capitalism in general, and the peripheral capitalism purveyed by colonialism in particular, contain an inherent tendency to marginalise people, areas, and economic sectors not directly involved in the expanded reproduction of private capital through profit maximisation. In Nigeria, foreign private companies organised colonial economic activities first and foremost in areas of the gainful exploitation of local resources. And since the gainful colonial economic activities were only marginally related to the traditional economic activities the question of geographical balance in the location of colonial socioeconomic projects could not arise. Therefore, those communal homelands where these colonial projects were located experienced an earlier and higher rate of migration than other areas. This lack of concern for an all-round balance in economic growth characteristic of colonialism is the historical origin and basis of contemporary imbalance in the achievement of petty bourgeois and comprador bourgeois fortunes among the various communal homelands of the country.

The Locational Feature of the Contact Situation

It is not enough for an explanation of the origin of ethnicity in Nigeria to understand that the colonial urban area was its cradle and that various factors contributed to differential migration to it by the various communities. Not all the urban centres were the birth places of ethnic identification; certainly they were not equally so. If it is accepted that contemporary ethnicity in Nigeria refers to the phenomenon associated with contact among various linguistic groups in the colonial and post-colonial situations, it is also necessary to determine those urban areas where

70. James Coleman, *Nigeria: Background to Nationalism* (Berkeley and Los Angeles: University of California Press, 1958), p. 144.

such contact was significant and, therefore, salient, in order to distinguish them from others where contact was almost exclusively among members of the same linguistic groups. It is the former areas that actually constitute the cradle of ethnicity and, therefore, must occupy the attention of any effort to understand and, eventually solve the ethnic problem of the country.

Much of the available literature on migration in West Africa indicates that the pattern of migration in Nigeria is different from that in the rest of West Africa. As in the other countries, the source of Nigeria's migration is still almost entirely certain rural zones with the inter-urban migration being, for the most part, a relay point in the rural-urban chain. However, the country does not experience that emptying of the labour force of the interior at the coast so characteristic of the other countries of West Africa with the exception of Ghana. The provinces with the highest non-indigenous populations in colonial Nigeria proportionately were not those of the coast, except Lagos, but plateau 20 per cent, Niger 18 per cent, Kabba 10 per cent, Benue, Rivers and Ilorin 9 per cent each, and Zaria, Bornu, Adamawa and Calabar 7 per cent each.[71] In fact, regarding the rural-urban component of this migration, a significant proportion takes place from the South close to the coast to the North. In the years before and after 1950, about 35,000 persons left the South to the North each year to find employment in the administration, commercial firms and industries.[72] According to Peter Kilby, around 1960, the majority of the workers in the factories of the North were southerners, mostly Igbo-speaking.[73]

The major factor accounting for this unique character of migration in Nigeria is the consistent and self-sufficient unity of the three geographical regions of the country, the North, West and East. There is no doubt that the existence of the overall large and dense population groups of the Yoruba, Igbo and Hausa-speaking peoples occupying these various regions has prevented any one region from becoming a mere source of labour for the other as is generally the case elsewhere in West Africa in the relation between the coast and the interior. Hence, migratory movements in Nigeria comprise the migration of skilled labour from the

71. Akin Mabogunje, *Regional Mobility and Resource Development in West Africa*, *op. cit.*, pp. 5–8.
72. Samir Amin, ed., *op. cit.*, p. 81.
73. Peter Kilby, *Industrialization in an Open Economy* (Cambridge, England: Cambridge University Press, 1966), p. 205.

South to the North; migration of rural farm workers to the Middle Belt, the cocoa belt of the West, the Niger Delta, and the region of Calabar; migration from various parts of the North to the Bornu and Adamawa areas of the region; flows associated with urbanisation in each region; and interregional and intraregional flows of seasonal labour.

In the light of the consistency and self-sufficiency of the regions, three core areas of urbanisation and high increase of population may be identified. The first region, is the Southwest in which is located the port city, federal capital and industrial complex of metropolitan Lagos, the commercial and transport hub of Nigeria, and the important commercial and administrative centre of Ibadan. The second region is the North in which is located a central and densely populated region containing the cities of Kano, Zaria, Kaduna and Jos which together make up the administrative, commercial, manufacturing and transport nodes of Northern Nigeria, as well as the surrounding rural areas which are intensely farmed for cash crops. The third is in the Southeast and consists of a network of urban centres closely knit together by road, rail and river communications, dominated by the cities of Port Harcourt, Onitsha, Aba and Enugu, and again primarily industrial, commercial and administrative in character.[74]

These towns were the major recipients of the colonial rural-urban migrants. This is reflected in their phenomenal growth. Between 1952 and 1963 the Lagos metropole grew at 11.5 per cent a year, Kano 7.6 per cent a year, Kaduna 10.6 per cent a year, Zaria 5.5 per cent a year, Jos 7.6 per cent a year, Port Harcourt 10.5 per cent a year, Aba 7.6 per cent a year, Enugu 7.4 per cent a year and Onitsha 7.0 per cent a year. Other centres of urban growth were the provincial capitals, and towns located in the eastern parts of the cocoa belt in the West. During the period 1952–1963, the rate of growth of the population of these cities per annum were as follows: Ibadan 3.0 per cent, Maiduguri 4.8 per cent, Ilorin 4.0 per cent, Katsina 5.0 per cent, Sokoto 5.9 per cent, Benin 5.8 per cent and Calabar 4.5 per cent.[75] At the top of the emergent hierarchy of urban areas was metropolitan Lagos whose population expanded at about four times the national rate of growth. Following it are the core areas of the North and Southeast whose urban populations ex-

---

74. Leslie Green, "Migration, Urbanization, and National Development in Nigeria," in Samir Amin, ed., *op. cit.*, p. 287.
75. *Ibid.*, p. 288.

panded at about three times the national rate. And finally came the provincial capitals and locally important towns whose rate of growth of population was about twice the national rate.[76]

Of particular importance for the emergence of ethnicity is the fact that these rates of urbanisation have, in some cases, been sustained by migration from different linguistic groups. Between 1952 and 1963 an estimated 644,000 migrants poured into the Lagos metropole at a yearly rate of nearly 59,000. Out of these migrants 79 per cent are estimated to have come from Yorubaland, particularly the colony province and the southern divisions of Abeokuta and Ijebu provinces. About 16 per cent came from the Southeast, of which a significant majority were Igbo, but including Efik, Ibibio and Ijaw-speaking peoples. Only 4 per cent came from the Midwest, especially the Benin and Urhobo divisions. A mere 1 per cent came from the North, especially the zone of Kano-Zaria-Kaduna.[77]

In the North during the period 1952–1963, a total of 124,989 migrants came from the South. Out of these, 54 per cent went to the central core area of Kano, Zaria and Jos divisions, and Kaduna capital territory. A further 41 per cent migrated to a belt surrounding this core area and peripheral to it, and 5 per cent went to the fringe areas to the north, east and west of this belt. Of these immigrants, 110,742 or 88.6 per cent came from the East and was composed overwhelmingly of Igbo-speaking peoples. A little over 50 per cent of these Easterners went into the commercial, industrial and mining areas in the Kano, Zaria, Kaduna and Jos areas. The rest moved to the rural areas lying mainly between this core area and Southern Nigeria. On the other hand, 167,689 migrants came from the North itself to the three main cities of Kano, Zaria and Kaduna. Of these nearly 60 per cent originated from this central core area of the North.[78]

Thus, over 19 per cent of the migrants to Kaduna, 13 per cent in Kano and 10 per cent in Zaria came from the East. By contrast during the same period virtually all the 262,000 migrants to the urban areas of Port Harcourt, Onitsha and Aba originated from the local area, notably Igboland.[79]

Two major conclusions of relevance for the emergence of ethni-

76. *Ibid.*
77. *Ibid.*, p. 289.
78. *Ibid.*, p. 290.
79. *Ibid.*, p. 291.

city are inescapable from the above figures. First, it is not all the colonial urban areas that were important as cradles of ethnicity. Certainly in those in the East and many parts of the West where virtually the whole population came from one linguistic group, the indigenous one, no significant relevant contact was possible. Therefore, ethnicity could not be formented there. The cradles of ethnicity were instead constituted by the Lagos metropolitan area in the South, and Kano, Zaria, Jos and Kaduna in the North. It was in these urban towns that significant contact between different linguistic groups was possible, the prerequisite for the emergence of ethnicity. Although in these towns members of the indigenous population accounted for the majority of the population, figures of between 10 per cent and 19 per cent for migrants from different linguistic groups were high enough to be significant.

It is noteworthy that the major cases of interethnic tension and violence in the history of the country have either occurred in these towns or originated from them. In 1932, ethnic tension in Jos was so high that a riot nearly occurred there. In 1945 the smouldering ethnic hostility in the city erupted into violence causing death and damage to property. In Lagos in 1948 an interethnic cold war raged between the Yoruba and Igbo residents causing a great deal of insecurity to life and property. The Kano riots of 1953 also had an essentially ethnic character. It was also in Kano, Zaria and Kaduna that the May and September-October, 1966 ethnic massacres began and raged with vengeful intensity before spreading to other towns.[80] The relatively insignificant participation of the rural population in these cases is a clear indication of the urban nature of contemporary ethnicity.

Second, distinction must be made between the linguistic groups in contact in the North and those in contact in the South. An understanding of the emergence of ethnicity in Nigeria must come to grips with the relations between the Igbo, Yoruba and Hausa linguistic groups. But it is obvious from the pattern of migration that, in the North, only the relations between the Igbo and Hausa groups were relevant. There, the bulk of the migrants from the South were Igbo-speaking. The greatest possibility for contact among linguistic groups existed between the Hausa majority and the Igbo who predominated among the Southern minority of migrants. It is not surprising, therefore, that practically all erup-

80. A more detailed discussion of these cases of ethnic tension and violence appears in Chapter 7.

tions of interethnic hostility and violence in the northern cities have involved attacks by the Hausa on the Igbo with only the marginal involvement of the other language groups. However, in Jos significant relevant contact existed between the Hausa migrants from areas to the North, and linguistic groups such as the Birom and Tiv more immediately located near to the city. Hence the near riot of Jos in 1932 involved Birom hostility against the Hausa. And in 1960 and 1964 the Tiv rose against the Hausa all over Tiv land. In the Lagos metropolitan area on the other hand, the significant relevant interaction was between the Igbo again and the Yoruba-speaking peoples. The latter indigenous group constituted the majority while the former formed a significant minority, being dominant among the less numerous non-indigenous immigrant language groups. Relations between the Yoruba and Hausa-speaking peoples were, therefore, not relevant for the emergence of ethnicity in the country. In this way the pervasive involvement of the Igbo-speaking peoples in ethnic conflicts of Nigeria may be understood.

Chapter 3

RESOURCE COMPETITION AND THE EMERGENCE OF CONTEMPORARY ETHNICITY

The Impact of Socioeconomic Competition

Contact alone does not fully account for the emergence of ethnicity. In fact, Ethel Lindgreen has observed a case of culture contact and ethnocentrism without ethnicity, involving the Reindeer Tungus and the Cossacks of Northwest Manchuria.[1] Kenneth Dike has even observed a case of intercommunal assimilation between the Igbo and Ijaw in the Niger Delta area during the precolonial times.[2] R. K. Udo has similarly shown that, in the cocoa belt of Nigeria, the demand for labour is so serious that the migrant laborer is quite popular.[3] In the Asa area of Ngwaland where the local inhabitants grow and grate cassava to such an extent that they neglect to harvest their palm trees, the migrant palm tree cutters live in harmony with them.[4] The same is true along the creeks of Okitipupa and Eket where migrant fishermen depend on the host population for fishing traps, raffia nets used for catching shrimps, crayfish, and lobsters, and raw materials for making canoes.[5]

Two other major classes of variables are also significant for the emergence of ethnicity. These are the cultural and socio-structural characteristics of the primary groups prior to contact, and the

---

1. Ethel, J. Lindgreen, "An Example of Culture Contact Without Conflict: Reindeer Tungus and Cossacks of Northwest Manchuria," *American Anthropologist*, Vol. XL, No. 4 (October–December 1938), pp. 605–621.

2. K. O. Dike, *Trade and Politics in the Niger Delta, 1830–1885* (London: Oxford University Press, 1956).

3. R. K. Udo, "Rural-rural Migration in Nigeria," *Nigeria Magazine*, (December 1969/February 1970), p. 621.

4. *Ibid.*, p. 622.

5. *Ibid.*, pp. 619–620.

nature and context of the initial contact.[6] Since, however, the characteristics of the groups which they bring to the contact situation are more or less "givens" and, therefore, relatively constant, the context of initial contact which is more prone to change, especially over time, is of greater explanatory significance. Therefore, neither contact nor ethnocentrism arising from biocultural and political particularisms suffices to generate ethnicity.[7] The influence of the precontact variables is mediated by the structure of initial contact.[8]

The most critical factor in this structure is the degree of socioeconomic competition involved. In the case of the Reindeer Tungus and the Cossacks of Northwest Manchuria, for example, both groups remained racially and culturally dissimilar and characterised by a general ethnocentric preference for the in-group. But there was no socioeconomic competition among them. Their two economies were complementary. Each admitted that the other was superior in certain specific aspects of life. And they shared a wide range of values and interests.[9]

In his study of the Puyallup Indians of North America, M. W. Smith observes that the complementarity of economic interests between them and the early white migrants to their territory led to a quick and peaceful social interaction and economic transaction. But when other whites came to acquire Indian land and exploit timber they entered into destructive competition with the Puyallup for these scarce resources. Relations between the two groups became strained and ethnic exclusiveness emerged.[10] Similarly,

6. Ernest Barth and Donald Noel identify three classes of variables. In addition to the two mentioned here they include the characteristic of the migration of the communal group. While this may be significant in the United States, it is of little importance in Africa where the ethnic problem is not related to immigration from foreign countries and the motives for migration are similar across communal groups. Cf. Ernest Barth and Donald Noel, "Conceptual Framework for the Analysis of Race Relations: An Evaluation," *Social Forces*, Vol. L, No. 3 (1964), pp. 333–348.

7. The insufficiency of ethnocentrism is well discussed in Donald Noel, "A Theory of the Origin of Ethnic Stratification," *Social Problems*, Vol. XVI, No. 3 (Fall 1968), pp. 157–172.

8. *Ibid.*; Ernest Barth and Donald Noel, *op. cit.*, p. 337; Pierre Van den Berghe, *Race and Ethnicity* (New York: Basic Books, 1970); R. A. Schermerhorn, *Comparative Ethnic Relations* (New York: Random House, 1970); Philip Mason, *Race Relations* (London: Oxford University Press, 1970); A. B. Riddleberger and A. B. Motz, "Prejudice and Perception," *American Journal of Sociology*, Vol. LXII, No. 2 (March 1967), pp. 498–503.

9. Ethel Lingreen, *op. cit.*, pp. 617–619.

10. M. W. Smith, "The Puyallup of Washington," in Ralph Linton, ed.,

the intense competition for land between the Kikiyu and the white settlers who occupied their land created serious tension which has not yet been satisfactorily resolved.[11] More convincing still is Carey McWilliam's study of Japanese-Americans, which shows that even when no racial and cultural differences exist, intense socioeconomic competition may produce ethnic-like identities and antagonism.[12] Also the study of North Americans in Guatemala by H N. Seelye and M. B. Brewer shows that the nature and degree of contact among members of different communal groups are determined more by socioeconomic than attitudinal factors.[13]

With regard to Nigeria, when in 1943 some Awka rural-rural migrant farmers in Nkwelle claimed that the land they were occupying had been purchased outright from Nkwelle families, the prevailing good relations between the two communities rapidly deteriorated and rigid ingroup-outgroup identities emerged.[14] A similar situation in the Owo division gave rise to a new regulation whereby migrants can only take short land leases of rarely more than two years, after which they may be renewed.[15] Soil impoverishment through overcultivation of land, and the destruction of rubber trees through "slaughter tapping" by migrant share-tappers are some of the other malpractices which generate conflict with the host population and thereby cause ethnic exclusiveness.[16]

Abner Cohen has noted that in the kolanut trade between the Hausa and Yoruba, conflict first arose in 1934 when some Yorubas tried to enter the trade in competition with the Hausa. As a result, during the course of the 1930s and 1940s, scores of highly-knit Hausa communities sprang up in Ibadan, Shagamu, Abeokuta, Agege, Ife, Ijebu and other Yoruba areas which enabled the Hausa to control the kolanut trade and even dictate prices to the Yoruba kolanut farmers. This incipient ethnicity was later reinforced by the struggle over who should pay the "lada," a commission paid for trade in kolanuts, the Yoruba farmers or the Hausa buyers.

Acculturation in Seven American Indian Tribes (New York: Appleton-Century, 1940), pp. 3–36.

11. Louis Leakey, *Mau Mau and Kikuyu* (London: Metheun, 1952).

12. Carey McWilliams, *Prejudice: Japanese-Americans* (Boston: Little, Brown, 1943), pp. 51–103.

13. H. N. Seelye and M. B. Brewer, "Ethnocentrism and Acculturation of North Americans in Guatemala, "*Journal of Social Psychology* Vol. LXXX, No. 2 (1970), p. 145.

14. R. K. Udo, *op. cit.*, p. 622.

15. *Ibid.*

16. *Ibid.*

The farmers who hitherto had paid it, wanted the buyers to take over payment.[17]

Also, in his study of the Ibadan cattle market, Cohen notes that until the early 1930s both the cattle landlords and butchers were Hausa. But later, the Yoruba began to displace them as butchers. Ever since then, the cleavage in the market between the buyer and seller became perceived as one between the Yoruba and Hausa. The Yoruba began to refer to the exploitation and greed of the Hausa; the latter began to talk of the machinations and treachery of the former. When the cattle landlords appealed for support from their counterparts in the other markets they did so, not in the name of the profession, but as Hausa. Similarly, butchers began to confront the landlords as an ethnic group and to rely on the support of various other Yoruba groupings in these confrontations. This emergent ethnicity based on the rationalisation and mystification of class relations (relations of production) and the class struggle was later reinforced by the resentment of the butcher over their payment of the cattle trade commission to the cattle landlords, and the unsuccessful attempts by the Yoruba to displace the Hausa as cattle landlords or even as cattle dealers.[18]

Colonial urban life was marked by socioeconomic competition because it offered very little socioeconomic security. There was no guarantee of employment, no provision for the care of the old, compensation for sickness or accident was low, and the few existing pension schemes were quite meagre. The effects were as J. H. Boeke has observed with respect to tropical colonies,

"materialism, individualism, and a concentration on economic ends far more complete and absolute than in homogenous Western lands; and a total absorption in the exchange and market; a capitalist structure with the business concern a subject far more typical of capitalism than one can imagine in the so-called capitalist countries which have grown up slowly out of the past and are still bound to it by a hundred roots."[19]

J. S. Furnivall recognises this fact when he observed that in colonial situations "the working of economic forces makes for tension

---

17. Abner Cohen, "Politics of the Kola Trade," in Robert Melsen and Howard Wolpe, *op. cit.*, pp. 306–307.

18. Abner Cohen, "The Social Origin of Credit in a West African Cattle Market," in Robert Melsen and Howard Wolpe, *op. cit.*, pp. 93–112.

19. J. H. Boeke, *The Structure of Netherlands Indian Economy* (New York: Day Publishers, 1942), p. 452.

between groups with competing interests; between town and country, industry and agriculture, capital and labour."[20]

Given the capitalistic structures and values of colonial Nigeria and its dependent relations with British and in general Western capitalism, competition was the most dominant feature of the urban setting. In the face of an extreme scarcity of socioeconomic rewards and an intolerable degree of inequality, it could hardly be otherwise. For example, according to Governor Bourdillon, "a low percentage expenditure on social services is inevitable in a poor country like Nigeria in which essential expenditure on administration and security, and on the service of the public debt must absorb an unduly large percentage of the available revenue."[21] Since the very limited opportunities for jobs, trade, business, and social amenities existed in the few urban centres, it was essentially there that a significant degree of destructive socioeconomic competition occurred.

In the rural areas contact among members of different communal groups is made essentially on the basis of either complementarity of economic interests or superordination and subordination. The hosts employ the migrant labourers; there is mutual understanding of the formers' domination and the latters' subservience. In addition, the most important needs such as jobs, food and housing are secured. It is in the urban areas, where intercommunal contact by individuals is made on the basis of equality and basic necessities are limited, that competition which breeds ethnicity can ensue. Marvin Harris has shown that the critical difference in ethnic relations between the deep south U.S.A. and Brazil lies in the fact that, in the former, a white yeomanry is in direct competition with ex-slaves whereas in the latter, the Portuguese owners of plantation worked by the ex-slaves were not in any such competition because they were in a dominant position.[22] Also such thinking underlies South Africa's reprehensible policy of apartheid which prevents equal competition between blacks and whites in all spheres of national life. Under the circumstances intercommunal competition in the rural areas is limited to interactions among migrants from different communal groups. But

---

20. J. S. Furnivall, *Colonial Policy and Practice* (Cambridge, England: Cambridge University Press, 1942), p. 452.
21. Nigeria, *Ten Year Educational Plan, op. cit.*, p. 11.
22. Marvin Harris, *Patterns of Race in the Americas* (New York: Walker, 1964), p. 00.

their very presence in the host locality means that they are at least guaranteed employment. Therefore, unlike in the urban areas the scope of socioeconomic scarcity is relatively narrower.

As a determinant of ethnicity competition alone is not enough. Charles Wagley and Marvin Harris suggest that it is important to know the objective of competition. The more vital or valuable the resources over which there is competition, the more intense is the resultant insecurity which gives rise to ethnicity.[23] Aaron Antonovsky contends that a discriminatory system of social relations requires both shared goals and scarcity of rewards.[24] With the increasing dominance of colonial activities, rewards accruing from the colonial enclaves became increasingly important, not only for enjoying a better livelihood, but, in many cases, for maintaining even the precolonial standard of living. For example, in the absence of any meaningful old age security benefit colonial education was widely regarded as an investment for the future. Educated children were expected to look after their aging parents. The scarcity of much highly-valued resources encouraged destructive competition.

Also the inequitable allocation of resources in society gives rise to intense competition. It is reinforced by an attitude to social relations which accepts such inequality as inevitable. The resultant struggle of individuals and groups not to be consigned to the bottom of the ladder of inequality has anti-social effects. Competition rather than cooperation predominates in human interaction and hostility is the dominant feature of such competition. A high degree of inequality characterised the Nigerian colonial situation. The private ownership of the means of production, distribution and exchange gives rise to exploitative relationships which encourage inequality in social relations.

The net effect of this intense socioeconomic competition arising from scarcity and inequality in colonial Nigeria was the insecurity of the individual regarding its outcome. First, there was the insecurity and anomie resulting from the search for the very limited job opportunities and social services. Second, these were reinforced by the low wages and deplorable social services provided for those who succeeded in securing jobs or businesses in the colonial enclaves. Raymond Wolfe has shown that anomie and

23. Charles Wagely and Marvin Harris, *Minorities in the New World* (New York: Columbia University Press, 1958), pp. 263–264.
24. Aaron Antonovsky, "The Social Meaning of Discrimination", *Phylon*, Vol. XXI, No. 2 (Spring 1960), pp. 81–95.

insecurity are directly related to threats of economic hardship.[25] J. S. Furnivall has observed that capitalism in tropical colonies creates conditions of social atomisation. Thus communal group affiliation and identity in the colonial urban setting can be understood as a mechanism to overcome the pervasive insecurity and anomie of colonial society. J. Rex recognizes this fact in his criticism of J. S. Furnivall for ignoring the extent to which the colonial market system itself produces new group affiliations. He argues that although it draws people together into a single social system it also divides them into new dynamically related groupings.[26] The emergence and persistence of significant ethnic organisation and interethnic boundaries is always an indication that there is differential access to resources, and that ethnic identity has payoffs with respect to access to the resources, as well as their utilisation.[27] Ethnicity arises from the desire of individuals to organise themselves in ways to enhance their competitive efficiency in a situation where they perceive each other as competitors for resources and positions.

Scarcity in the Colonial Urban Setting

Resource competition implies that the disputed resources are scarce and that their accessibility is limited. Of course, all economic goods and services are limited, in an objective sense. However, subjectively they may not be. A population may acquire a subjective notion of abundance. It is this latter notion that determines the behaviour of its members, at least in the short run. Also, scarcity can be manipulated. As a result of certain mechanisms of production and distribution of products in a particular society, one and the same resource may be abundant for some members of society, scarce for others, and inaccessible for the rest. Ideally, therefore, scarcity refers to resources that are limited both objectively and subjectively.[28]

25. Raymond Wolfe, "Effects of Economic Threat on Anomie and Perceived Locus of Control," *Journal of Social Psychology*, Vol. LXXXVI (1972), pp. 233–240.
26. J. Rex, "The Plural Society in Sociological Theory," *British Journal of Sociology*, Voo. X, No. 2 (1959), pp. 116–117.
27. Regina E. Holloman, "Ethnic Boundary Maintenance, Readaptation and Societal Evolution in the San Blas Islands of Panama," in Leo A. Despres, ed., *Ethnicity and Resource Competition in Plural Societies* (The Hague: Mouton, 1975), pp. 30–31.
28. H. Hoetink, "Resource Competition, Monopoly and Socioracial Diversity," in *ibid.*, p. 10.

Colonialism ushered in a period of significant scarcity in Nigeria. It did so essentially through the importation of the capitalist mode of production from outside. Prior to it, various precapitalist modes of production prevailed, each with its characteristic social formation. However, they all shared certain features in common including a low level of production, underdeveloped productive forces, and a meagre surplus from production. Objectively, therefore, they suffered from a high degree of scarcity. In absolute terms the quantity and quality of food was low, medical services were primitive, and very little leisure time was available because the poverty of the means of production and transportation caused much time to be devoted to production and transportation.

Nevertheless, at the subjective level this scarcity was not immense and, therefore, not socially disruptive. Although the productive forces were underdeveloped, there was no unemployment. Each member of the society was gainfully employed in accordance with the prevailing norms and the local physical and biological environments. More importantly, relative deprivation was not a component of the perceptual map of the population. Within the norms of the societies, each individual accepted his station in life and, therefore, his share of the surplus from production. There was no discrepancy between the expected and actual patterns of benefits. Above all, there was no divergence between the pattern of consumption and the need of the vast majority of the population; the pattern of production was oriented to the needs and consumption habits of the vast majority of the population. The importation of the capitalist mode of production through colonialism disrupted this organic link between the pattern of use of resources and the needs and consumption habits of the population. It thereby created scarcity at both the objective and subjective levels.

This colonial pattern of economic activities hampered balanced growth among the different sectors of the economy and segments of the population, the expansion of income-earning opportunities in agriculture, and an increase in the capacity of the industrial sector to provide, in part, its own needs for intermediate and capital goods, and to process the nation's products to a more valuable stage before exportation. Similarly, it frustrated the growth of the productive forces by confining the country to imitative rather than innovative technology, prevented the capitalist mode of production from expanding in accordance with its own internal dynamics by tying it to an international division of labour dominated by external forces, limited the size of the dominant market, hampered the geometric growth of economic activities by promoting the export of profits to foreign countries, and limited local economic expansion by creating a propensity to import consumer goods.[29]

Regarding the production process, only a few Nigerian cash crop farmers and those few Europeans and Africans in the mining industry participated in this import-export economy. A small proportion of the population acted as middlemen and participated in the construction, transportation, and service sectors. In relation to consumption, only the wealthiest and most prestigeous segment of the population took part. This segment included European and other expatriates, Nigerian large-scale cash crop farmers, a sprinkling of local businessmen including middlemen, largescale traders, and contractors, leaders of marketing cooperatives, professionals, university teachers, and senior civil servants. Since they enjoyed a disproportionate share of the economic surplus of the country they were financially able to participate. On the other hand, the limited incomes of the middle-income civil servants and semi-skilled labour force constrained their participation. Consisting of the unskilled labour force, the urban unemployed, and the mass of sibsistence farmers, the vast majority of the population could only marginally afford these consumer goods.

Colonial education in Nigeria was a very scarce commodity. Particularly in the south of the country, it was designed to prepare Nigerians for meaningful participation in colonial activities. Its character was, therefore, molded by the motives and dynamics of colonial enterprise. According to a British educator, "the conception [of colonialism] was one of exploitation and development for the people of Great Britain – it was to this purpose that such education as was given was directed."[30] Initially, educated Nigerians were needed essentially as clerks and artisans in the Civil Service and commercial firms and as subordinates in the army and police force. Later a small beginning was made in training

---

29. For a good, detailed analysis of how the colonial economy hampers domestic growth refer to Sami Amin, *Accumulation on a World Scale*, Vols. I and II, (New York: Monthly Review, 1974).

30. H. S. Scott, "The Development of the Education of the African in Relation to Western Contact" in *The Yearbook of Education, 1938* (London: Evans Bros., 1938), p. 737.

them for higher positions in the technical services. A fitful effort was also made to train native administration officials and chiefs' sons. In addition to the goal of preparing Nigerians for employment in the colonial administration of mines and private firms, the Christain missionaries, who largely imparted the education, also sought converts to Christianity and their respective denominations.

This origin of colonial education in the socioeconomic and political activities had important consequences for the official and local attitude to education in the country. The centrality of the metropolitan profit motive in colonialism ensured that educational expenditure would be tailored to the profits accruing from colonial activity. During the years before the Second World War, the colonial government devoted most of its expenditure to administration, defense, and the preservation of law and order so crucial for profitable activities by metropolitan enterprises.

Also the colonial government's consistent treatment of education as a low priority item was even politically motivated. Lord Lugard contended that, in the face of limited potentialities for the growth of job opportunities, an increase in the number of educated Nigerians would lead to political instability in the future.[31] In fact, in 1938 a public Board of Education observed that "this country is in the invidious position of providing fewer opportunities in regard to elementary education than any other British possession in Africa."[32]

As late as the early 1950s. Nigeria still had a lower percentage of

TABLE 3.1   *Central government expenditure per item as percentage of total expenditure*

	1930	1933	1938	1947	1961
Administration	18.3	18.4	14.1	13.5	16.6
Defense	8.0	8.1	6.1	3.5	8.3
Justice and Police	9.2	8.0	8.0	11.9	9.4
Education	6.4	6.2	5.3	12.2	6.1

Sources: G. K. Helleiner, *Peasant Agriculture, Government and Economic Growth in Nigeria* (Homewood, Illinois: Irwin Inc., 1966); *Nigeria Handbook, 1936* (Lagos: Govt. Printer, 1937) p. 164; IBRD, *The Economic Development of Nigeria* (Baltimore, John Hopkins University Press, 1955), pp. 626–633.

31. Nigeria, *Annual Report, Department of Education, 1938* (Lagos: Government Printer, 1938), pp. 8–10.
32. *Ibid.*, p. 8.

children of school age in school than any other African territory.[33] For example the percentage of children of school age actually in school were: Northern Rhodesia 46 per cent, Gold Coast 45 per cent, Belgian Congo 42 per cent, Kenya 32 per cent, Uganda 28 per cent, and Nigeria 19 per cent.[34] Education was a marketable commodity. The government bought as much as was profitable and the rest was sold to the local population.

Second, to the colonised Nigerians, education was a very valuable commodity. Entrance to good colonial employment, particularly in the South, required some level of colonial education. Employment in a good office provided at one and the same time relatively high income, high security, high social status, and a good opportunity to escape from what, in the new colonial environment, had become tiresome, tedious, and non-lucrative traditional agricultural work. Therefore, those who had savings spent them on the education of their children and wards because they saw that only the educated salaried people enjoyed any form of socioeconomic security. Communities occasionally got together to educate some of their sons and daughters. But, although education was a highly valued resource, it was a very scarce one.

The British colonialists believed that the payment of school fees was not only a good way of financing education, but also a useful device for building character. Prior to 1955, parents in the South paid ₦4 to ₦6 a year to send a child to primary school. The cost of tuition and boarding in the predominantly boarding

TABLE 3.2   *Number of schools and pupils in colonial Nigeria*

Year	Primary school	Secondary school	Primary pupils	Secondary pupils
1906	127	1	11,872	20
1912	184	10	36,670	67
1926	3,953	18	143,459	518
1937	4,072	27	238,879	4,350
1947	6,094	46	609,353	9,908
1957	15,553	194	2,528,801	31,851

Source: J. S. Coleman, *Nigeria: Background to Nationalism* (Berkeley, California: University of California Press, 1965), p. 134, Table 14.

33. J. S. Coleman, *Nigeria, Background to Nationalism* (Berkeley and Los Angeles, California: University of California Press, 1958), p. 125.
34. *Ibid.*

secondary schools averaged ₦30 a year per student.[35] Only the few financially able families, those on scholarship, and those whose families made heavy sacrifices could pay such fees. The costs of books, school uniforms, and incidental expenses added to the burden. The resultant impact on the ability of the population to acquire education is evident in the comparative dropout rates of the primary school pupils in the various regions in 1965. The percentages of those initially enrolled who did not complete the sixth year in 1965 were as follows: Western Region 55 per cent, Midwestern Region 58 per cent and Eastern Region 74 per cent. Only in the Eastern Region did pupils pay fees. That the ₦10 enrollment fees paid from primary class four in the Eastern Region deterred many prospective pupils, is reflected in the dropout figure from primary class three to four. In the Eastern Region it was 33 per cent but only 8 per cent in the Western and 8 per cent in the Midwest Regions.[36]

In addition, the colonial government's scholarship programme left much to be desired. It started in 1938 as a result of pressure from Nigerian nationalists and was only expanded in 1948. By 1944, only 40 government scholars were studying abroad. But in 1950 alone, 111 overseas scholarships were awarded and the total number of scholars abroad was 207.[37] Similarly, government support for post-secondary education did not begin until 1930 when the Yaba Higher College, Lagos was opened. In 1948 the University College, Ibadan superseded the Lagos institution as the premier post-secondary institution in the country. Later in the 1950s three colleges of Arts, Science and Technology were established.

The colonialists rationalised their unwillingness to establish free and universal primary education on grounds of scarcity. First, they argued, the cost would be prohibitive. Second, they contended that, in the face of limited potentialities for the growth of job opportunities, the growth in the number of educated Nigerians would be socially destabilising. Nigerian nationalists were more optimistic. Propelled by a strong nationalistic fervour

35. Nigeria, *Annual Report, Department of Education 1938. op. cit.*, pp. 11–16.
36. These comparative figures have been calculated from Education and World Affairs, Nigeria Project Task Force, Committee on Education and Human Resource Development, *Nigerian Human Resource Development and Utilization* (New York: Education and World Affairs, December 1967).
37. *Report of the Commission on Higher Education in West Africa* Cmnd, 6655 (London: HMSO, 1945).

but largely unguided by an adequate socioeconomic theory or analysis of the colonial social structures, they could not comprehend the effects of colonialism on socioeconomic scarcity in the country. Therefore, prior to independence, nationalist-led governments embarked on programmes of universal free primary education. But they were soon brought face to face with the harsh realities of economic scarcity in a colonial situation.

The first to embark on the project was the Western Regional government. It was the wealthiest regional government at that time and, therefore, in the best financial position to mount it. Nevertheless, in order to help pay for the cost of the programme it announced an education and health levy in 1952. As a result of this, tax riots ensued in Oyo in which several people were killed; the tax also contributed to the failure of the ruling Action Group in the 1954 federal election in the West. Following the introduction of the programme in the West, the much poorer Eastern Region came under intense political pressure to follow suit. But with a per capita income of ₦50, it had financial difficulties doing so. As soon as the project took off the ground in 1956, it began to face financial problems. The expected revenues of ₦10 million from which it was to be mounted was not realised; only ₦4.8 million was collected. By mid-1957 the Eastern Region had spent about ₦4 million more than the ₦5.8 million it had allocated for the whole year. The trend in expenditure showed that by 1958, the education bill would be ₦13.2 million and ₦29.6 million in 1964. Since these amounts would constitute about 50 per cent of the region's expenditure in 1958 and virtually all of it in 1964, the government drastically diluted the programme.[38]

On 8 January 1958 the Eastern Region reintroduced fees at certain levels. Pupils in Standard Five had to pay ₦12 per year and those in Standard Six, ₦16. In addition, pupils in Infant One and Infant Two had to pay an enrollment fee of ₦1 and ₦2 each respectively. These new measures caused violence in Owerri where crowds of women surged through the town in protest. They burned school buildings and looted the homes of politicians or threatened them with destruction. Protest demonstrations spread

38. Nigeria, Eastern Region, Ministry of Education, *Dike Report*: *Official Document No. 19 of 1962* (Enugu: Government Printer, 1962), p. 12; Eastern Region, *Annual Report, 1956* (Enugu: Government Printer, 1957), p. 33., Eastern Region, *Annual Report, 1957* (Enugu: Government Printer, 1958), p. 32.

to other parts of Owerri and Onitsha provinces. In reaction, the colonial government declared a state of emergency in nine divisions of the Eastern Region and sent in 500 federal police to repress the aggrieved populace. However, by 17 February 1958, the programme was further modified to reduce some school fees and eliminate others. Similarly, efforts in 1962 and 1963 to stabilise the region's recurrent expenditure on primary education by raising the Assumed Local Contribution, created a great furor particularly in the rural areas. Consequently, in 1964 the scheme was abandoned.[39]

Unemployment was also a reflection of scarcity. Four basic factors accounted for unemployment in colonial Nigeria. All of them stem from the intrinsic character of colonialism. First, the total divorce of the dominant economic activities of the colony from the precolonial pattern of economic life, needs, and consumption habits ensured that the precolonial skills could not be employed in the new economic scheme of things. Since the vast majority of the working population relied exclusively on such skills, massive unemployment was inevitable in the society.

Second, and related to the first, in spite of this massive unemployable labour force, the colonial administration embarked on extensive propaganda which portrayed colonial activities as being more rewarding than their precolonial counterparts. Consequently, people entered the colonial economy at a rate faster than the economy could provide them with employment. Those without education were the first to be adversely affected and had to take recourse in petty trading and in such jobs as domestic servants. Later, however, even those with higher education became increasingly affected.

Third, colonial economic activity was first and foremost oriented to, and motivated by, the desire of foreign enterprise to amass profits to be repatriated to the metropole. Employment to Nigerians was carefully tailored to this profit motive. Just sufficient employment was given as was deemed suitable to maintain the enormous profits reaped by the foreign enterprises. Even employment in colonial governmental administration was similarly indirectly affected because the colonial government existed essentially to provide a stable and peaceful environment for the exploitation of the country by foreign capital. Since the foreign

39. David Abernethy, *The Dilemma of Popular Education* (Stanford, California: Stanford University Press, 1969), pp. 181, 223.

enterprises spent some of their earnings on the wages and salari\
of their employees, the more of them they employed, the less their
profits. Therefore, they tended to increase their profits, in part,
by limiting the number they employed.

It is not surprising, therefore, that these enterprises carted
away huge profits from the territory. In fact, their annual profits
exceeded annual expenditures on education. Part of the profits
(in the form of royalties) of one of the mining firms alone over a
ten-year period was nearly equivalent to one-sixth of the country's
total budget for that period.[40] There was very little, if any, governmental restrictions on the capacity of these enterprises to amass
wealth. In fact, by encouraging the concentration of economic
power in the hands of a small group of European firms, the
government contributed to this capacity.[41] The 1946 colonial
development plan, the first of its kind in the territory, together
with its colonial successors, had nothing to say about the creation
of employment as an objective. The first Nigerian plan to do so
was the 1962–1968 Plan.

Fourth, the interest of foreign firms in using equipment and
services from their home countries also contributed to unemployment. The technology that was used by both the foreign enterprises and their local subsidiaries, were very much influenced
by the choice of production techniques that were used in the rich
countries. Such techniques were developed in an economic
environment in which labour was relatively costly and capital
relatively abundant. Therefore, they tended to be more capital-
intensive and labour-saving than was warranted by the resource
condition of Nigeria in which there was very little capital and a
desperate need for large-scale employment.

Thus, the Nigerian colonial economy could not satisfy the needs
of the Nigerian population for employment. By 1960, there was
only a very small wage-earning labour force. That year the
National Manpower Board estimated total wage employment to
be between 0.8 and 1 million or between 12.8 per cent and 16
per cent of the total possible labour force.[42] Even when manu-

40. J. S. Coleman, op. cit., p. 89.
41. Ibid., pp. 80–81.
42. K. C. Doctor and Hans Gallis, "Size and Characteristics of Wage Employment in Africa: Some Empirical Estimates" in International Labour Review,
   Vol. XV, No. 6, (December 1964), pp. 544–568; Nigeria, Ministry of
   Labour, Report on Employment and Earnings Enquiry (Lagos: Government
   Printer, 1961), p. 6.

facturing was initiated after the Second World War, the employment situation was not significantly affected. Between 1950 and 1962 manufacturing expanded rapidly. The same situation obtained for the production of electricity. The discovery and exploitation of petroleum began in 1958. Consequently, the overall pattern of the previous sixty years was altered, especially by the insertion of a rich mineral enclave. Nevertheless, employment rose only marginally and, in the petroleum industry, direct employment effects were minimal.

This low level of employment contributed to a generally low standard of living of the population which, in turn, reflected the high degree of scarcity in the colony. Also, the wages and salaries of Nigerians were not large enough to meet personal and family obligations. The wage rates were low and did not keep pace with changes in the cost of living. For example, the wage rate in 1912 showed no improvement on that of 1899. This general situation "led to materialism, venality and almost pathological obsession regarding money."[43] The consequent alienation occasionally found vent in violent crowd actions such as those which followed the introduction of new currencies in Eastern Nigeria, taxes in Southern Nigeria, and school fees and levies in Eastern and Western Nigeria. It was accentuated by the anonimity and atomisation which were characteristic of the colonial urban setting. In such urban centres as Lagos, Port Harcourt, and Sapele, with tenuous links to the countryside, the problem of alienation could be quite acute. Ethnic group identity provided solace.

During the colonial times, but especially before 1951, opportunities for Nigerians to participate politically in the formulation of national policies were severely limited. Hence, the struggle for the scarce political offices contributed to the emergence of contemporary ethnic sentiments. The 1862 Legislative Council had been confined to the Lagos Colony. It had consisted of a small body of persons nominated by the colonialists to "advise and assist the Governor",[44] and also to scrutinise the estimates of the expenditure in the colony.[45]

In 1914 following the amalgamation of the northern and southern provinces a larger but still advisory legislative body was estab-

43. Quoted in J. S. Coleman, *op. cit.*, Alan Burns, *History of Nigeria* (London: Allen and Unwin, 1955), p. 145.
44. Alan Burns, *History of Nigeria* (London: Allen and Unwin, 1955), p. 145.
45. *Ibid.*, p. 237.

lished. Its activities covered the whole country. It was composed of the Governor, members of his Executive Council, certain other colonial officials who represented the Chambers of Commerce, Shipping, Banking and Mining interests. Of the 36 members, only 6 were Africans. They were nominated to represent the coastal districts and the hinterland areas. Two of them were Emirs from the North; the Alafin of Oyo represented the West; and one member each was elected from Lagos, Calabar, and Benin-Warri. Again the function of the Council was merely advisory.

In 1920, dissatisfaction among Nigerians over this scarcity of political resources was expressed through the National Congress of British West Africa which called for a Legislative Council in which at least half of the members would be elected and not more than half nominated. The Congress also demanded the setting up of a House of Assembly for the whole of West Africa. In it, the members of the legislative councils of Nigeria, the Gold Coast, and Sierra Leone would, together with six elected financial representatives, would "have the powers of imposing all taxes and discussing freely and without reserve the items of the annual estimates."[46] In Nigeria, the colonial authorities dismissed the Congress as representing the opinion of only a few educated Africans and not that of the vast majority.

Nevertheless, following the 1922 Constitution a new Legislative Council was formed consisting of 46 members. Colonial officials, including the Governor, accounted for 27 of the total. Only 19 were not government functionaries. Of the officials, 23 held their seats *exofficio* and three were nominated. Among the ordinary members, 15 could be nominated and 4 elected from Lagos and Calabar. Those elected served for five years and were eligible for reelection. Also, those nominated were appointed by the Governor for five years in the first instance and could be renominated. In 1922, the number of non-officials who were nominated was 13 among whom were 7 Europeans and 6 Africans. The Council legislated for the Colony and the Southern Provinces while the Governor continued to legislate for the Northern Provinces.[47]

Throughout the period 1922–1946 the Legislative Council

46. M. Wight, *The Gold Coast Legislative Council* (London: Allen and Unwin, 1947), pp. 26–27.
47. Nigeria, *Nigerian (Lesgislative Council), Order-In-Council, 1922* (Lagos: Government Printer, 1922).

hardly changed. With regard to the colonial officials, there was a slight increase in the number of the *exofficio* members from 23 to 24. As far as the ordinary members were concerned there were no changes involving the elected members nor until 1938 with the nominated members. However, during that year a member was nominated to represent the Oil Rivers Division instead of the African Traders. In 1941 the maximum number of ordinary members nominated by the colonialists was fixed at 17 instead of 15. After 1943, three ordinary members were appointed to the Executive Council, one European and two Africans. At first these three officials were members of the Legislative Council. But, after 1944, the Africans were limited to the Executive Council and only the European participated in the activities of both councils. The percentage of the legislative councils composed of Africans was as follows:

1906–1914	=	18 per cent
1914–1921	=	17 per cent
1922–1945	=	22 per cent
1946–1950	=	64 per cent

The situation changed in 1946 when, following the Richard's Constitution of that year, a new Legislative Council was established for the whole country. This council consisted of 45 members. Of these, 28 were Nigerians, 4 of which were elected, 24 appointed. In addition, for the first time, Regional Assemblies were created in the North, West and East. There the majority were nominees of the native authorities with a minority of colonial officials. A Regional House of Chiefs was also created in the North. All afforded Nigerians opportunities to participate in some political decision-making at the regional level and to select their representatives to the Legislative Council in Lagos. Nigerian nationalists vigorously protested various aspects of that constitution as grossly inadequate for satisfying the popular demand for effective participation in political decision-making for the nation. It was not until the Macpherson Constitution of 1951, that these demands began to be met. An 18-man Council of Ministers was formed at the federal level. Out of these, 12 were Nigerians and 6 colonial officials. In addition, there was a Federal House of Representatives of 136 Nigerians and three regional legislatures dominated by Nigerians, most of whom were elected. There were also two Houses of Chiefs.

On another level, the number of people who took part in the

choice of their political leaders and representatives has also grown haltingly. The franchise was first given to the people of Lagos and Calabar after 1922 to elect 3 and 1 members to the Legislative Council respectively. But voters had to satisfy a salary requirement of a gross annual income of ₦200. In addition, only those who were not receiving salaries from public revenue were eligible. In Lagos, only 3,000 out of a possible 40,000 adult male Africans qualified. In Calabar only 1,000 out of 10,000 were eligible.[48] Following the Richards Constitution of 1946, the franchise was extended beyond Lagos and Calabar.[49] However, it was not until 1958 that universal adult suffrage was adopted for the whole country, except in Northern Nigeria where, on religious grounds, women were denied the vote.

Therefore, scarcity was pervasive of the colonial order. It was evident in the economic, social, and political spheres of life. It affected employment, education, political participation and the provision of social services to the population. Under these circumstances, the competition for the limited resources and opportunities could only be intense and destructive. Individuals had to rely on various useful devices to gain access to the scarce goods and services. One of these was alignment with other members of the individual's communal groups, including the most inclusive of them, the ethnic group. Under conditions of low-class consciousness and the manipulation of communal sentiments by the privileged classes as well as the colonialists, such an alignment was inevitable.

Inequality in the Colonial Urban Setting

Colonialism introduced capitalist relations of production into Nigeria. These relations are characterised primarily by exploitation. Capitalism cannot survive without exploitation.[50] The expanded reproduction of private capital so central to the survival of the system necessitates the appropriation of the surplus from production by the owners of capital, the capitalists, from the producers of the surplus product, the workers. Also, capitalism

48. Joan Wheare, *The Nigerian Legislative Council* (London: Faber and Faber, 1950), pp. 38–39, 55–56.
49. Nigeria, *(Lesiglative Council), Order-In-Council, 1946, No. 1370* (Lagos: Government Printer), Part VI, Chapter 56.
50. R. Milliband, *The State in Capitalist Society* (London: Quartet Books, 1973), p. 24.

transforms social services, and even labour-power, into commodities which are bought and sold in the market place. In these market transactions the owners of capital make large profits. This inherent exploitative tendency of capitalist relations of production lie at the heart of inequality in capitalist societies. It is, therefore, illusory to believe that inequality will be eliminated under capitalism.

Thus situations of exploitation in colonial Nigeria best reflect inequality during the period. Taxation was a major instrument of colonial exploitation. It further reduced the already very low receipt of the working population from the surplus product, while most of the benefits from their use accrued to the owners of capital who dominated the use of the public enterprises, infrastructural projects, and public administration financed by these taxes. It is not surprising, therefore, that the imposition of taxes in colonial Nigeria frequently led to violent incidents. The earliest of these occurred in Lagos in 1895 following the colonial government's proposals for a house and land tax in the city. In reaction, over 5,000 Lagosians protested, and the new tax measure was never enforced.[51] Again in late 1907, the Land Acquisition Ordinance came into force empowering the government to expropriate land on Lagos Island for official residences. The irate inhabitants sent a petition to the Secretary of State for the Colonies in which they made it clear that "the people look at their own poor little huts alongside the palatial buildings of the European and wonder how long and how far this thing will go."[52]

In 1908 the government again levied a water rate on the inhabitants of the capital city. Over 400 young people demonstrated against the measure smashing the windows of buildings belonging to expatriate firms. Lagos chiefs and land owners presented a long petition to the Governor opposing the new rate and complaining that, although Nigerians paid high taxes, they received hardly any social benefits which they argued were confined to Europeans. In a letter to a newspaper, one Lagos resident wrote: "What we daily feel, and every action of the present Administration justifies and deepens, is that we are exploited for the benefit of those who came among us."[53]

51. J. S. Coleman, *op. cit.*, p. 187.
52. *African Mail*, Lagos, 31 January 1908, p. 1, quoted in *ibid.* pp. 178–179.
53. *African Mail*, Lagos, 26 December 1909, quoted in J. S. Coleman, *op. cit.*, p. 179.

Another Lagos protest occurred in 1912 when the Colonial Office set up the West African Lands Commission to determine the feasibility of extending the Northern Nigerian system of land tenure to Southern Nigeria. Under that system all rights over land were under the control, and subject to, the disposition of the Governor. In response the Anti-Slavery and Aborigines Protection Society was formed to protect indigenous land. This society sent a protest delegation to London in 1913. In addition, mass demonstrations which sometimes attracted 6,000 people protested the measure.[54]

Direct taxes on individual income and wealth contributed nearly as much to governmental revenue during the colonial period as did customs and excise duties which received the greatest emphasis. Before 1916 only the North knew any taxation. That year, a new tax was introduced into Yorubaland and the Benin area consisting of a head tax calculated at $2\frac{1}{2}$ per cent of the income of the average farmer, plus various special rates for those in certain trades and professions, and certain types of property owners.[55] By 1928, direct taxation had been extended throughout the West and introduced into the East.

Since the Second World War there have been considerable increases in local tax rates and personal income taxes in all parts of the country. In the North, for example, tax rates increased from a range of 70k to ₦1.52 in 1947 to a range of ₦1.66 to ₦5.10 in 1961.[56] Jagali or cattle tax rates also increased during this period. Such increases represented real increases because the price level in the North rose by only 27 per cent between 1948 and 1962.[57] A similar growth in taxes also took place in the East and West. In 1956 the local authorities in the East were restricted to levying a maximum tax per head of 50k but this was later raised to ₦1.50 per head in 1962.[58] By this time, however, most local councils in the area were collecting rates of ₦2.00 per head and one was collecting ₦3.00 per head.[59] In 1962, when the West

54. J. S. Coleman, *op. cit.*, pp. 180–182.

55. For a good discussion of the introduction of taxation into the West see G. K. Helleiner, *Peasant Agriculture, Government, and Economic Growth in Nigeria* (Homewood, Illinois: Irwin, 1966), pp. 219–221; G. O. Arewa, *Taxation in Western Nigeria* (London: Oxford University Press, 1962), pp. 10–27.

56. G. K. Helleiner, *op. cit.*, fl. 220.

57. *Ibid.*, p. 221.

58. *Ibid.*

59. *Ibid.*

ran into serious financial difficulties the Western Regional Government added an additional development levy.[60]

Among the upheavals arising from the hardships imposed by these taxes was the Egba uprising (Adubi war) of 1918. Yorubaland had retained a substantial measure of autonomy until 1914 when the treaty governing its relations with Britain came to an end. In 1918, accumulated grievances over British authority, especially the imposition of direct taxes, led to an uprising in Egbaland. A spontaneous expression of popular anger and discontent erupted. It was brutally and violently repressed by the colonialists.[61] Nevertheless, violent protest against taxes occurred in Calabar on 1 April 1925. Under the Market Ordinance, tolls were imposed on the two markets in the town. The Ibibio and Efik women refused to pay. They drove off laborers building a fence around the Marina market. In addition, they disrupted activities at the Bush market, closed all factories on the river front, and assaulted Europeans and the police. It required a strong contingent of police weilding rifle butts to disperse them.[62] In 1927, following a tax assessment survey in the South, violence erupted in Warri province. During the disturbances, which lasted from August to the end of the year, over 200 police patrolled the area. The protest was eventually suppressed with the loss of four lives.[63]

Initially, the exercise in the East was carried out with less trouble than was expected, but in Ogoja and Onitsha provinces some trouble broke out. The Ezza and Ezzi of Abakaliki division refused to pay and crowds of women broke up many of the meetings called to discuss taxation. The police finally succeeded in repressing the uprising. Similarly, in Onitsha province demonstrations against these taxes were suppressed by the police.[64]

In 1929, the most intensive, extensive, and violent anti-tax

60. *Ibid*.
61. Raymond Leslie Buell, *The Native Problem in Africa* (New York: MacMillan, Vol. 1 1928), pp. 710 ff; Ajayi Ajifase, *History of Abeokuta* (Suffolk, England; Richard Clay, 1924), pp. 198–204.
62. Nigeria, *Legislative Council Sessional Paper, Paragraph 28, Report of a Commission of Inquiry Appointed to Inquire Into the Disturbances in Calabar and Owerri Provinces, December 1929* (Lagos': Government Printer, 1930), p. 11.
63. Nigeria, *Annual Report, Southern Provinces, 1927* (Lagos: Government Printer, 1927), pp. 75–77.
64. Nigeria, *Annual Report Southern Provinces, 1929* (Lagos: Government Printer, 1929), p. 33.

protests occurred in the East. Young men who had no real earning power were taxed equally with their more well-off neighbours. Assessment was based not only on the man's wealth but also on items which traditionally belonged to women. Again, taxation reduced the men's ability to provide the women with traditional welfare services. The effects of taxation were reinforced by the deteriorating economic situation of the women. Many of them were deeply involved in trading. In some cases they acted as intermediaries providing European firms with palm oil and palm kernels. They also traded in imported items such as cloth, tobacco, cigarettes and spirits. In 1929, traders suffered a loss of between 8 to 12 per cent in earning capacity as a result of the Great Depression.[65]

In 1928 the government had introduced a new scale of duties which adversely affected the goods sold by the traders. Import duties on tobacco rose from 16k to 20k per pound, that on cigarettes rose from 16k to 20k per hundred, and that on spirits from ₦2.50 to ₦2.76 per gallon.[66] As a result market women suffered a substantial loss in profits. Also, in 1929, the produce houses changed their method of purchase from buying by measure to buying by weight. This change, together with the lower prices of products, convinced the women that they were being cheated. By instituting a programme of inspection of produce the government further reinforced this conviction.

Thus, when in October 1929 Captain John Cook sought to obtain information on the number of men, women, children and livestock in Oloko Native Court Area of Bende Division in Owerri Province, the women began a protest movement which spread from Oloko to various parts of Owerri, Rivers and Calabar provinces. On 12 December of that year women destroyed the Ayaba Native Court, and on 19 and 20 December they forced warrant chiefs at Umuahia to surrender their chieftaincy caps. However, it was the disturbances at Aba on 11 December of that same year that gave the name of this town to these riots. Over 10,000 angry women beseiged the government offices and looted the Barclays Bank, the Post Office, the Survey Office, and the African Merchants Store, the major agencies of exploitation. They were finally repelled by a large contingent of troops firing shots into the air.[67]

---

65. *Legislative Council Sessional Paper Paragraph 28, op. cit.*, pp. 101–103.
66. *Ibid.*, p. 103.
67. *Ibid.* Appendix V and pp. 44–47.

From Aba the violence spread. On 12 December rioting at Imo River led to the looting of several factories. Native courts at Azumini, Obohia, and Asa were destroyed. At Omuma Native Court, the offices were attacked and prisoners released from jail. Similarly, the women of Obowa in Okigwi division released men from the town's jail. On 13 December 1929, Owerri province was declared a "proclaimed area" under the Peace Preservation Ordinance. However, on 17 December serious rioting occurred in Okigwi town, and on 18 December women burnt the Omuma Native Court, and the Umuaturu Native Court and Rest House.

In Calabar province, demonstrations in Abak district practically ended with the clashes which took place on 14 December in which three people died, and at Utu-Etim-Ekpo on 15 December in which 18 women were killed and 19 injured. On 16 December women wrecked the dispensary and Native Court in Opobo and looted the postal agency. Police opened fire on them killing 32 and wounding 25. But it was not until 20 December that Calabar province was completely pacified.

In spite of the colonial government's repression of these riots, disturbances re-occurred in many areas of the East in 1930. Areas affected were Afikpo division of Ogoja province, Umuachieze in Onitsha province, Aloyi in Bende division and Isoba in Ahoada division. As late as October, 1930, there was a serious situation at Mgbidi near Oguta arising from dissatisfaction over governmental regulation of the priority of palm oil. Before it ended, one man had been killed and several others wounded by the police.[68]

The riots and protests led the government to reassess its tax policies. In April 1931, there was a general reduction of taxes, amounting in some cases to 50 per cent. The government also adopted a more lenient attitude toward payment. In December 1932, 19 per cent of the tax due for the year was still outstanding. One year later, 44 per cent of the tax was not collected. And a further tax reduction was granted in Owerri province.[69]

In addition, the occurrence of labour actions and strikes attests to the degree of deprivation imposed on the workers by the prevailing exploitative conditions. Not only were strikes illegal for a long time, but the brutal and punitive reaction of the colonialists was clearly predictable. For example, "the brutal shooting by the

68. Harry A. Gailey, *The Road to Aba* (London: University of London Press, 1971), pp. 118–129.
69. *Ibid.*, pp. 137, 141,

police on 21 June 1947, of defenceless UAC employees in Burutu, who went on strike in furtherance of a wage demand did not deter the workers of Enugu colliery from going on strike in 1949."[70] In one of the addresses of welcome presented to a trade union leader, Nduka Eze, during his tour of the country, a group of workers complained that "for so many years the United Africa Company Limited has applied instrument of transforming the total African employees here in the Plateau Region into perpetual slaves, without the least regard for our comfort, without provision for us when we are old or incapacitated."[71]

In August 1950, employees of the UAC went on strike over matters concerning conditions of employment and the payment of a cost-of-living allowance. Violence erupted, resulting in damage to property and assaults on strike breakers. The strike was called off when the company acceded to most of the workers' requests. However, disagreement re-emerged over the effective date of implementation of the remedies to the grievances. Another strike followed on 14 December 1950, which, in comparison with the massive response of the earlier one, was a failure. Similarly, the strike called by the Nigerian Labour Congress on the same day and involving 29,860 mercantile workers and a loss of 39,663 man-days ended in failure.[72]

By far the bloodiest of these strikes was that of the Enugu coal miners. It occurred at the Enugu Colliery on 18 November 1949, the climax of a period of unrest and dissatisfaction among the miners. Claims by miners for a wage increase, the payment of daily allowances for certain categories of miners, and for their arrears which the colliery management was withholding led to the strike. The workers first staged an unprecedented go-slow strike. Fearful that the strikers may capture the mine's explosives the colonial government rushed in a strong contingent of armed police to guard them. This action was in turn perceived by the strikers as part of an attempt by the government to remove the explosives and, therefore, effectively close the mines. In order to prevent this they surrounded the police guards. Thereupon the latter opened fire killing 21 and wounding 51 miners.[73]

---

70. Wogu Ananaba, *The Trade Union Movement in Nigeria* (Benin, Nigeria: Ethiope, 1969), p. 72.
71. Quoted in *ibid.*, p. 76.
72. *Ibid.*, pp. 122–123.
73. *Ibid.*, pp. 98–119; Nigeria, *Report of the Commission of Inquiry into the*

In other ways, exploitation and, therefore, inequality were expressed in colonial Nigeria. Economic power was concentrated in the hands of a few expatriate firms, notably the United Africa Company (UAC). By the late 1930s the UAC controlled more than 40 per cent of import and export trade. As late as 1949, this company handled 34 per cent of all commercial merchandise imports and purchased 43 per cent of all Nigerian non-mineral exports.[74] In association with a few other foreign firms, the UAC formed the Association of West African Merchants (AWAM) which controlled import agreements and allocated export quotas. In 1949, AWAM handled about 66 per cent of Nigeria's exports and nearly 70 per cent of its imports.[75] In addition, extensive European ownership and control of shipping and banking facilities prevailed. Until 1933, two British banks, Barclays Bank and the Bank of British West Africa, exercised a virtual monopoly of the banking business in the country. This near totality of economic power exercised by a small group of European firms was supported by governmental power. The Government dealt mostly with these few large firms in the allocation of trading licences, administration of trade control, and formulation of tax policies.

A few Nigerians acted as middlemen in the import and export trade. They numbered about 100,000 during the interwar period.[76] With cash advances from the European firms they purchased produce from farms and in turn were credited by the firms. Their excessive profits depended on their skill in taking advantage of price changes as well as the illiteracy of the primary producer. Thus, they amassed capital often in an exploitative manner and used it in other entrepreneurial activities.[77] This system of marketing and related activities gave rise to a wide socioeconomic gulf between the producers and their middlemen exploiters. Such a

Footnote 73 continued

    Disorders in the Eastern Provinces of Nigeria, November 1949 (Lagos: Government Printer, 1950).

74. P. T. Bauer, "Concentration in Tropical Trade" in *Economica*, Vol. XX, No. 4 (November 1953), pp. 302–321.

75. P. T. Bauer, *West African Trade* (Cambridge England: Cambridge University Press, 1954); pp. 66–67.

76. Gilber Burck, "The World of Unilever," in *Fortune* (January/February 1948), p. 136.

77. K. D. S. Baldwin, *The Marketing of Cocoa in Western Nigeria* (London: Oxford University Press, 1954), esp. pp. 7–10, 34 ff.; *Report of the Commission on the Marketing of West African Cocoa* Cmnd. 5845 (London: HMSO, 1938).

pattern of inequality has persisted in spite of the statutory market-ing arrangements of 1939 which tended to thwart the activities of this increasingly affluent group. The firms became licensed buying agents, and the middlemen became accredited to them. Prices and profits for both became largely determined by the marketing board. Although this arrangement drastically curtailed the op-portunity of the middlemen to exploit the farmer, enough ex-ploitation was still possible to maintain the socioeconomic distance between the two groups.

Inequality existed even among the farmers themselves. For example, in the early 1950s a survey of the cocoa growing areas of Western Nigeria found a great degree of inequality among the cocoa farmers. About 55 per cent of them held only 19 per cent of the cocoa land. At the other end of the spectrum, 1.5 per cent of the farmers held 12 per cent of the land, and 10 per cent of them held 41 per cent of the cocoa land. Inequality in the distri-bution of food farm land was even greater than that of cocoa. Therefore, the inclusion of all the other land to the cocoa land area worsened rather than improved the situation. In fact, a little over 2 per cent of the families held 20.5 per cent of all the land; 9 per cent held 38 per cent; 37 per cent held less than 10 per cent; and 55 per cent held only 19.5 per cent of the land.[78]

Evidence of inequality in colonial Nigeria exists in the tax system. Taxes on incomes above ₦1,000 were more regressive in Southern Nigeria than in England.[79] In general, personal direct taxes are the most equitable of tax arrangements. In Nigerian practice, however, they have been grossly inequitable. Tax evasion was not difficult and not considered unethical. Therefore, it was widespread. Those who escaped with the highest share of their legal tax burden were the traders, shopkeepers, lorry-owners, middlemen of the import and export trade and land-lords. Comparatively they were the wealthy members of the society who travelled a lot and had widespread interests. On the other hand, the stationary village farmer found it difficult to escape the taxes levied by the colonial authorities. Under the circumstance, the socioeconomic inequality among individuals was exacerbated.

78. R. Galletti, K. D. S. Baldwin, and I. O. Dina, *Nigerian Cocoa Farmers; An Economic Survey of Yoruba Cocoa Farming Families* (London: Oxford Univer-sity Press, 1956), pp. 149–152.

79. G. O. Arewa, *Taxation in Western Nigeria* (London: Oxford University Press, 1962), p. 104.

In addition, the acceptance of inequality as an inevitable aspect of colonial life was reflected in the racially discriminatory character of income distribution and political participation. For example, the salaries of 3,000 odd European employers exceeded the total wages paid to the 100,000 odd Africans employed by the firms. There were separate salary scales for Europeans and Africans. The African scale ranged from ₦72 to ₦800 a year. Most Africans received an annual salary of ₦100 or less. By contrast a European official usually started at ₦900 a year and in seventeen years could reach ₦2,000 a year. This gap between the European and Nigerian was further widened by the more favorable service conditions of the former.[80]

Racial inequality was further reflected in the decision-making processes of the public service. As late as 1938, provincial committees were created to advise on the rates of pay for employees but it was not until 1941 that an African was named to one of them. Despite the comparatively large number of Nigerian lawyers, the country's judiciary remained predominantly European until the 1940s. By 1939, there were only 23 educated Africans in the Senior Service of the Government. Most of them were either repatriated Brazilians or non-Nigerian Africans.[81] Blacks had their own Civil Service sector. Here, by 1936, only 3 per cent of the positions had been classified as "Senior", that is, carrying a salary above ₦200 a year.[82]

This colonial system of inequality generated a feeling of deprivation and insecurity among Nigerians. In comparison to the Europeans, they sought to be elevated to the Senior Service and other financially rewarding jobs and enterprises. Among the Africans themselves, the higher up the ladder of inequality one was, the greater was one's financial and political power. Under these circumstances, scheming for a better position in colonial life became a significant aspect of the individual's socioeconomic behaviour. Nigerians sought ways and means of preventing one another from ascending this ladder to their own detriment while ensuring their own success in the ascent. The consequence was ethnic group alignment which was increasingly useful as a device for this competition.

80. *Ibid.*, p. 155.
81. *Ibid.*, pp. 153–154.
82. *Nigeria Handbook 1936* (Lagos: Government Printer, 1936), pp. 225, 357–359.

The Gestation of Ethnic Identity

Thus, the contemporary ethnic phenomenon of Nigeria is not the result of the mere agglomeration of disparate linguistic and cultural groups. In fact, as will become clear later on in this study, the social boundaries of the various language groups drastically changed from its precolonial character to its colonial form. People who did not share a common ethnic identity during the former period began to do so during the latter. The new ethnic boundaries are associated with the insecurity arising from the scarcity and inequality of colonial order. This is illustrated by the effect of the Depression and the Second World War on ethnicity in the country. The relevant ethnic identification became salient and significant between 1928 and 1948. The years of the Depression and the Second World War constituted the gestation period of ethnic identity and therefore the birth period of contemporary ethnic politics in Nigeria.

As the British colonialists developed roads, railways, postal communications, and other media of communication, individuals from one linguistic group could more easily migrate to another. Initially, the socioeconomic competition between the migrants and their hosts was not sharp. Consequently, the latter did not feel threatened by the activities of the former and very little hostility existed between the groups. Therefore, as J. A. Sofola observed, interactions between them were so positive that intergroup marriage was fairly common.[83] However, when migrants became many and socioeconomic competition with the hosts became more distinct, relations were strained. In reaction, both migrants and hosts organized themselves along communal lines in order to safeguard their interests in the struggle for the scarce and unequally distributed resources.

During the 1920s, kinship and communal unions sprang up in the main urban centers of Nigeria. They were known by various names such as Naze Family Meeting, Ngwa Clan Union, Owerri Divisional Union, Calabar Improvement League, Igbirra Progressive Union, and Urhobo Renascent Convention. They were established in several urban centers in the South and North as

---

83. J. A. Sofola, "Some Aspects of Pre-Crisis Inter-Ethnic Relations in Nigeria: The Yoruba Repatriate's Social Relations in the Former Eastern Region," in *The Nigerian Journal of Economic and Social Studies*, Vol. 12, No. 7, March 1970), pp. 115–131.

well as in Fernanda Po and the Gold Coast. In 1918, the Egba Society was formed in Lagos to promote the interests of Egbaland. Throughout the interwar period similar associations were formed first in Lagos and then in other urban centres in Yorubaland and elsewhere. These groups included the Union of Ijebu Youngmen formed in 1923, the Yoruba Union established in 1924, the Egbado Union, the Ekiti National Union, the Ife Union, the Ijaiye National Society, the Offa Descandant's Union, the Ogbomosho Progressive Union, the Owo Progressive Union, and the Oyo Progressive Union. In the late 1930s these associations formed federations. In 1942 the Yoruba Language Society was formed. This development of Yoruba associations paralleled a similar development among the Igbo.[84]

Since the migrants were too poorly educated to compete against the British for socioeconomic resources they turned their competitive energies against fellow Nigerians. The resultant struggle produced frustrations. The unsuccessful competitors found it easy and convenient to blame their plight on advantages possessed by members of other groups. Once the members of a particular group gained access to the best jobs and other resources they used their positions to find jobs for others or at least pass on news of job opportunities to them. The repercussions were felt in unequal levels of unemployment and income, as well as in different degrees of social status among the communal groups. Attempts by each group to escape the negative consequences of this phenomenon led to the further strengthening of communal associations.

Most of the communal unions may have been formed prior to 1928. But it was during the period 1928–1948 that their most significant developments took place. This was the period of the Great Depression and the Second World War, a period of great scarcity, inequality, and socioeconomic insecurity. An expansion of the governmental sector of the economy was halted by the Depression. The government depended largely on revenues from external trade. But customs revenues fell from ₦6.8 million in 1929 to ₦4.2 million in 1931.[85] However, direct tax revenues constituting about 40 per cent of total public revenue did not fall so dramatically. While the sources of income were, in fact, diminishing, the taxpayers continued to bear the same burden of taxation, thereby

84. J. S. Coleman, *op. cit.*, p. 343.
85. G. K. Helleiner, *op. cit.*, pp. 17–20.

suffering severe exploitation and socioeconomic hardships.[86]

Nigerian exports dropped in value from ₦35.6 million in 1928 to ₦17.6 million in 1931. During the same period the purchasing power of the exports fell by 38 per cent from ₦26.4 million to ₦16.0 million.[87] Apart from a brief surge in the late 1930s the levels of real value of exports during the predepression years were not regained. In fact, the growth of the Nigerian colonial economy was effectively halted until after the Second World War. Over the period 1929–1945, the volume of exports increased by only about the same proportion as the population and the output of traditional goods and services. Therefore in 1945 the per capita GDP was about the same as in 1929.[88] However, since the terms of trade of the colony had deteriorated sharply during the same period per capita income was actually greater in the former than in the latter year.

The unit values of the major Nigerian export crops fell by 53 per cent in the case of cotton and 78 per cent for rubber, with the others in between. Most severely hit in terms of total export value were the least important crops, rubber and cotton, whose value fell by 90 per cent and 88 per cent respectively. Palm oil came next with 77 per cent decline. Least affected were groundnut exports whose value fell by only 39 per cent but which continued to expand in volume throughout the period. The growth in the volume of cocoa exports was also not seriously affected by the Depression.[89]

After some attempts at deficit spending in 1931, the government cut back its expenditures. By 1932 gross expenditures of the Central Government had fallen to ₦10 million from ₦78 million in 1928.[90] Various public schemes had to be postponed, causing much hardship in urban areas such as Lagos. During the interwar years, urban activities did not keep pace with the growing number of school dropouts migrating from the rural to the urban areas. As a result of the Depression, there was severe retrenchment in both the government and private enterprises. Job openings in urban centres were drastically reduced.

---

86. *Administrative and Financial Procedures Under the New Constitution: Financial Relations Between the Government of Nigeria and the Native Administration* (Lagos: Government Printer, 1947), p. 170.

87. G. K. Helleiner, *op. cit.*, p. 18.

88. *Ibid.*, p. 19.

89. *Ibid.*

90. *Ibid.*, pp. 19–20.

Following the outbreak of the Second World War, wartime controls were applied. Agricultural producers, middlemen, importers, traders, and wage earners were confronted with wage ceilings and price controls. All felt the impact of scarcity. These measures most adversely affected the emergent Nigerians who wished to enter import and export trade. One of the wartime measures was the government's assumption of complete control over exports and imports. It issued licenses only to established non-African firms and the firms concluded an agreement among themselves which created a rather effectual oligarchy in the import trade.

Following the outbreak of the Second World War in 1939, the British government sought to protect British consumer prices, control the direction of the trade in raw materials, and increase the degree of general control over colonial economies. The major underlying purpose of these efforts was to forestall the collapse of the cocoa producing areas consequent to the cutting off of important overseas markets. As the expatriate buying enterprises also cut back on their purchases from the farmers, the British Ministry of Food agreed to buy the entire cocoa crop during the 1939 to 1940 period at prices then prevailing in Africa. The government of the United Kingdom agreed to return ultimately any profits thus made to the producers. It also assumed the risk of acquiring undisposable stocks of cocoa. Similar arrangements were made for palm produce and groundnuts; the Ministry of Food undertook to purchase the entire oilseed surplus.

In the absence of a market, export prices were set by agreement between the colonial government and the British Ministry of Food. Prices to be paid by the traders to the peasant producers were regulated in such a way as to allow the buying foreign firms a reasonable profit. During the period 1939 to 1940, a modest loss of ₦417,000 was suffered by the British government. At the end of that period a Marketing Board proper (the West African Control Board) took over from the Ministry of Food the purchasing and disposal of cocoa. It was financed by the British government under the jurisdiction of the Colonial Office. With the fall of the British Far Eastern Territories in 1942, control over the sale of palm produce and groundnut was added to the control over the sale of cocoa in order to ensure adequate supplies to Britain. The Board was renamed the West African Produce Control Board (WAPCB).[91]

91. G. K. Helleiner, *op. cit.*, pp. 153–154.

However, the manner of sale of palm produce and groundnut remained different from that of cocoa until 1947. These products were supplied to the Ministry of Foods by WAPCB. The farmer received whatever income the Ministry of Food had decided to pay. The latter always made sure that it was the major beneficiary of the interaction. This arrangement was made possible by the Ministry's total monopsony. There was no question of surpluses or deficits being run by the Board. With respect to palm produce and groundnuts, the Board operated in such a way as to break even while serving as an agent between the producers and the Ministry of Food. In this way, Nigerian groundnut and palm produce farmers were being taxed to aid the war effort.

Regarding cocoa, provisions were made for the Board to make profits and losses. In fact, the Board made profits for all but one of the seven years from 1940 to 1946.[92] About ₦18 million was realised in profits. Over half of this amount was realised in 1946 after the removal of wartime price ceiling in the United States. These profits were invested in British securities.[93] The harsh producer price policy of the earlier years of the war was rationalised by the need to protect the British taxpayer, the undesirability of making cocoa too attractive when other war needs were more pressing, the danger of inflation, and the fact that profits earned were ultimately to be returned to the producers.[94] Cocoa producers were thus placed in a position of offering forced loans to the British government, to be repayed subsequently in much depreciated currency and without interest. Only from February 1947 did the question of the WAPCB maintaining surpluses and deficits on oilseed accounts arise. The result was a rapid accumulation of surpluses, as in cocoa, which were again invested in British securities. In the meantime, cash crop farmers suffered under the burden of socioeconomic scarcity artificially created by this policy.

In spite of the depression and the war, however, there was some economic recovery in the late 1930s. The spread of the war to North Africa, the Middle East, and India enhanced the strategic value of Nigeria as a station for troops and supplies enroute to

92. *Statement on Future Marketing of West African Cocoa* Cmnd 6950 (London: HMSO, 1946); P. T. Bauer, *West African Trade, op. cit.*, pp. 396–397.
93. *Ibid.*
94. *Report on Cocoa Control in West Africa 1939–1943 and Statement on Future Policy*, Cmnd. 6544 (London: HMSO, 1944), p. 8.

these areas. Consequently, airports, military camps, new roads and related infrastructure were constructed. These activities took place in key urban centers, particularly Lagos, Ibadan, Kaduna, Kano, Maiduguri, Jos, and Enugu. One of the effects was an acceleration of urbanisation. In 1939, the total number of wage and salary earners in Nigeria was about 183,000. By 1946 this number had increased to 300,000.[95] This trend toward urbanisation was most marked in centres of military and industrial activity. For example, the population of Enugu increased by 400 per cent between 1939 and 1946.[96]

However, even though the value of Nigerian exports during the period rose from ₦20.6 million to ₦49.2 million, and that of imports increased from ₦13.6 million to ₦39.6 million, socio-economic scarcity prevailed.[97] Between 1939 and 1942, the cost of living rose by 50 per cent in the urban centres. This rise caused considerable unrest among workers. As the war progressed, inflation escalated and grievances spread. The cost of living allowance granted to most workers in 1942 proved inadequate as the cost of goods and services continued to mount. In 1945, workers claimed that the cost of living had gone up by 200 per cent, without a corresponding relief in wages. The African Civil Service personnel took the lead in demanding a 50 per cent increase in the cost of living allowance and a minimum wage of 26 kobo per day. The poor response of the government to these demands led to the general strike of 1945 in which 17 trade unions with a total membership of about 30,000 workers went on strike for 37 days.[98]

Intensive and extensive economic activity had to await the end of the war. During the immediate post-war years the Nigerian governments resumed colonial economic activities at a rapid rate. Their projects included the construction and improvement of roads, bridges, port facilities, electricity installations, dams, railways, telephone and telegraph services, airports and water supplies. Between 1950 and 1962, transport and communications expenditure alone absorbed 20 per cent of current expenditure.[99] Whereas in 1946 there were 705 miles of tarred roads, by 1963

95. International Bank for Reconstruction and Development *The Economic Development of Nigeria* (Baltimore Maryland: John Hopkins Press, 1955), p. 666.
96. *Ibid.*
97. *Ibid.*
98. J. S. Coleman, *op. cit.*, pp. 256–258.
99. G. K. Helleiner, *op. cit.* p. 301.

there were 7,500 miles of such roads. Most of this expansion was in the South where from 1953 to 1963 the total mileage rose from 10,675 to 28,000 miles.[100] Close to 400 miles of existing rail track was completely relaid during the decade between 1949 and 1959.[101] A further 400 mile railway extension into Bornu province was completed in 1964 with a loan of ₦20 million from the World Bank.[102] This increase in economic activities was also reflected in a fourfold growth in foreign trade cargo handled at Nigerian ports between 1946 and 1963, and in the tenfold increase in electricity generated between 1947 and 1964.[103] Such intensive economic activities contrast very sharply with economic life during the period of the depression and the Second World War.

The inevitable consequence of the pervasive scarcity of the period of the Depression and the Second World War was the intensification of competition among individuals for the scarce socioeconomic resources. Although the resources in the urban areas got scarcer nothing had changed in the rural areas to motivate people to return there to enjoy better livelihood. The deplorable rural economic condition continued to prevail. In many cases, the situation worsened. The artificial scarcity induced in the area of cash crop farming caused a number of the cash crop farmers to abandon the enterprise and move to the cities. Those retrenched in the urban areas continued to hang around there in search of new jobs and opportunities because a return to the village was not a meaningful alternative. A cut-throat competition ensued among the urban dwellers which had no parallel during the previous years. It was no longer a question of fighting to secure a job; many had to fight to retain their jobs, to prevent their already unenviable and dwindling standard of living from slipping below a tolerable threshold.

Three major developments regarding the voluntary communal associations took place in reaction to the insecurity generated by this competition. First, many more people sought solace in them. This period witnessed a tremendous growth in their number and membership. Although no accurate count was made it is clear that between 1928 and 1948 the number of such associations had grown about sixfold and the number of Nigerians who were

100. *Ibid.*
101. *Ibid.*
102. *Ibid.*
103. *Ibid.*

members had increased more than tenfold.[104] As more and more people came face to face with socioeconomic insecurity they opted for membership in one or more of these organisations. This increased membership and the proliferation of the unions in turn attests to the success of the early associations in providing the individual with a meaningful degree of socioeconomic security. By the way these organisations carried out their functions, they demonstrated beyond any doubt that they were the only institutions capable of ameliorating the individual's insecurity in the colonial urban setting.

Second, a parallel development led to the formation of communal associations of language groups. As more people joined the competition for resources, the spatial area of their search for resources widened considerably to include, not only members of different clans, villages, and districts, but increasingly, members of different linguistic groups. Hence, although as early as 1908 a member of the Legislative Council spoke in favour of reconstructing the boundaries of Yorubaland so as to have all Yoruba together, it was not until 1942 that the first Pan Yoruba association was formed, the Yoruba Literary Society. In 1944, the *Daily Service* justified the need for an all-inclusive multipurpose association of the Yoruba as follows:

"we anticipate ... an era of wholesome rivalry among the principal tribes of Nigeria ... while they must guard against chauvinism and rapid tribalism the great Yoruba people must strive to preserve their identity."[105]

In 1945 a pan-Yoruba Union, the Egbe Omo Oduduwa, was formed in London by Yoruba students in the United Kingdom including Obafemi Awolowo. Similarly, during the period under consideration, the Ibibio Welfare Union (later Ibibio State Union) was formed in Ikot Ekpene in 1928, the Urhobo Brotherly Society (later Urhobo Progress Union) was set up in Warri in 1931, and the Ibo Union (later Ibo Federal Union, and much later Ibo State Union) was established in Lagos in 1936. Later this formation of all-inclusive ethnic unions spread to previously inarticulate groups such as the Idoma, Tiv, Birom and Bakweri.

---

104. Estimates were arrived at on the basis of my own survey and information in E.P.O. Offodile, "Growth and influence of Tribal Unions," in *West African Review*, Vol. XVIII, No. 239 (1974), pp. 937–941.

105. *Daily Service*, Lagos, 17 October 1944, quoted in J. S. Coleman, *op. cit.*, pp. 345–346.

The functions of these communal associations betrays the socio-economic basis for the emergence of ethnicity and the contemporary boundaries of Nigerian ethnic groups in the colonial urban setting. They met the individuals demands for socioeconomic security in the new environment. In the rural areas, the village unit offered socioeconomic security. Psychological security was also provided by the certainty of the norms, customs, and traditions. In the city, the migrant was no longer assured of the minimum goods and services. Entry into the colonial system invoked the spectre of unemployment for a group that was landless. Although the migrants still retained rights to land in their home villages this land was, in most cases, quite irrelevant to their immediate economic needs. They depended for their livelihood on the sale of their labour-power. The communal associations helped them to adapt to this insecure urban life. They provided economic, social and, when the time came, political solidarity among persons from a given village, district, or language group.[106]

Some of them were, in effect, savings clubs called "esusu" by the Igbo and "adashi" by the Hausa. Members made occasional payments at times of marriages or burials. Also, they made periodic monetary contributions in rotation to enable the recipient member to purchase capital goods or to utilize as a small credit. The institution served as a self-creating banking facility. In some instances, credit was so emphasised over solidarity that the savings group did not meet at all. Its members were only known to the organiser.[107] In their function of providing social services, the ethnic (linguistic) associations were as important as the government, and probably more relevant.

In the urban area, the new migrant was faced with different

106. Immanuel Wallerstein, "Voluntary Associations" in J. S. Coleman and Carl G. Rosberg, Jr. eds., *Political Parties and National Integration in Tropical Africa* (Berkeley, California: University of California Press, 1966), pp. 318–339; E. P. O. Offodile, "Growth and Influence of Tribal Unions," in *West African Review*, Vol. XVIII, No. 239 (1947), pp. 937–941; Kenneth Little, "The Role of Voluntary Associations in West African Urbanization", in *American Anthropologist*, Vol. LX, No. 3 August 1957), especially pp. 591–594.

107. S. G. Ardener, "The Social and Economic Significance of the Contribution Club Among a Section of the Southern Ibo," *Proceedings of the West African Institute of Social and Economic Research (WAISER) Annual Conference – Sociology Section* (Ibadan: WAISER, March 1953), pp. 128–142, For an analysis of Adashi see M. G. Smith, "Cooperation in Hausa Society" in *Information*, Vol. X, No. 1 (January, 1957), pp. 1–20. On credit facility, see M. P. Banton, *West African City* (London: Oxford University Press, 1957), p. 188.

bases for social relations. A parochial frame of reference adequate in the village was inadequate in the city. His kinsmen and other village acquaintances were too few in the city to be useful socio-economically. It became necessary to identify with those who spoke the same language even though they might have been the former rivals or enemies of his village. His boundaries of both the ingroup and outgroup became extended. It was no longer the neighbouring village or clan but a culturally and linguistically distinct group which dominated his conception of these boundaries. Ethnic identity thus became an issue for the urban migrant when it probably had no meaning for his more parochial parents.[108]

During the period of the Depression and the Second World War the colonial government virtually withdrew from the realm of employment and the provision of welfare amenities. This withdrawal heightened the importance and significance of the communal associations. They became the only institutions in which the individual could realistically expect to solve some of his most pressing problems. This transfer of responsibility for socioeconomic welfare from the Government to the communal unions, and the greater cohesion of the latter, contributed significantly to the emergence of ethnicity and the creation of ethnic identity.

108. Leonard Plotnicov, *Strangers in the City: Urban Man in Jos* (Pittsburg: University of Pennsylvania Press, 1967).

Chapter 4

SOCIAL DISTANCE AND THE EMERGENCE OF ETHNICITY

The Myth of Cultural Diversity

Among Nigerians, ethnicity is very closely associated with a strong belief in a perceived cultural and linguistic diversity of the country. It is often regarded as the inevitable consequence of sociocultural differences. References to Nigeria as a "mere geographical expression", a "heterogenous" society, or as having a "federal character" reflect this belief in the pervasiveness of these differences. Indeed many Nigerians regard ethnicity as a biocultural phenomenon arising from the mere existence of various cultural groups within the same polity. By this definition, ethnic groups are groups whose members share similar sociocultural and linguistic characteristics distinct from those shared by members of other groups. Ethnic groups exist and are unchanging. They have maintained their precolonial features and boundaries.

The difficulty with this attitude to ethnicity and this definition of ethnic groups lies in its unscientific nature. Attempts to identify the differences among the so-called ethnic groups degenerates to sheer subjectivism. The extent of diversity tends to vary with the analyst's whim, caprice, and momentary interest. At one time, an indigenous Nigerian way of life ("Nigerianism") is identified which must be protected against foreign ideology (usually limited to socialism) and alien influences (whatever foreign trait the analyst opposes). An African personality is even accepted. In both cases the sociocultural situation is seen as so similar or even identical that a certain homogeneity and concensus can be attributed to it. At another time, the Nigerian peoples are perceived as significant only in their differences. They are claimed to be as different as the various nations of Europe, that only their common colonial experience holds them together, and that only sectional, rather than national perspective, is possible.

This unscientific approach is reflected in the tendency at varying times to treat sociocultural differences within the same "ethnic group" as minor and at other times as major differences. Again, no consistent criteria are used as the basis for this assessment, just as no independent yardstick is used for deciding whether the differences among the groups are major or minor. It is completely subjective. For example, linguistic differences among the Igbo which, in many cases, prevent communication are assumed to be insignificant compared to those between the Igbo and Yoruba, and for no valid reason. Similarly, differences in music, song, art forms, and diet within and among ethnic groups are subjectively interpreted. What is more, when ethnicity is under discussion, hardly any mention is made of what is common among these groups.

Therefore, whether or not diversity as opposed to similarity is emphasised varies with the individual analyst, particularly his interest at the moment. Certainly a strong case and, probably a stronger case than diversity, can be made for concensus and homogeneity among the various sociocultural groups in Nigeria. It is generally recognised, for example, that at this historical junction and, especially during the precolonial times, the extended family system, with its emphasis on welfare and social responsibility rather than individualism, and its ethic of an individual as his brother's keeper, is common to all Nigerian peoples. Also religion is a pervasive aspect of all the cultures, as is the fact that production was organised to statify definite biosocial needs rather than being dictated by the desire for the expanded reproduction of private capital.

These precolonial societies of Nigeria were all more interested in utilising their local resources, including labour power, for satisfying their immediate needs for food, shelter and clothing in accordance with their habits and traditional consumption patterns than in the desire for profit. This very low priority given to the profit motive in precolonial Nigerian societies is also reflected by the fact that, in many cases, production was determined more by social and religious reasons than by economic reasons. Also individuals in these societies did not operate on the basis of the sale of their labour power for profit. Labour power was not a commodity to be bought and sold in the market like any other object of exchange as during the colonial times. There was no dichotomy between those who worked and those who owned the means of production. Most people owned their own means of production and not a minor section of society. Therefore there had not emerged a class such as workers in factories for whom the sale of their labour power is the only source of livelihood.

The precolonial systems were all dominated by independent peasant and handicraft production where the peasant and craftsman owned their implements of production and undertook the sale of their own food. There was no divorce between ownership and work. It was the purchase and sale of inanimate wares, not human labour power, that was of primary concern. Similarly, in social life, priority went to the interest of the collectivity, age group, or obligation to the ruler rather than to the individual and his interests. Even the famed Hausa merchants who operated throughout much of West Africa subordinated their individualism and desire for monetary gain to the demands of clientage, the desire to get ahead in society through climbing the social apron strings of the Emirs.

The overwhelming majority of Nigerians shared a common experience of colonial oppression and capitalist exploitation, poverty, ignorance and disease, poor diet, and basic similarities of race, dance, music and art. In all these societies, people thought in collective terms. Such collective thought enabled them to maintain bonds of kinship even with those who were not generally included in the family unit. Consequently, good fortune and misfortune were associated with the kinship group as a whole rather than with the individual alone. Kinship governed all social relations, binding together the life of the entire community.

This collectivism made marriages in these societies different from the atomistic European type. Precolonial Nigerian marriages involved the union of individuals as well as their families and communities. In fact, prospective husbands and wives had little or no choice in their marriage. Usually the two families arranged the union. Marriage was a sacred institution through which individuals contributed offsprings to the community. The idea of celibacy was, therefore, revolting. There was the sacred obligation to marry and bear children. Polygamy was common and raised the status of the family concerned.

As deeply religious individuals, precolonial Nigerians believed in the Supreme Being, the Creator and Controller of the universe, the Creator of heaven and earth, the Omniscient and Omnipotent, Who is eternal and beyond human knowledge. All things originated from Him and bear witness of His power and glory. At least in the south of the country, belief in the ancestors was also common. A person was not just an isolated individual with complete freedom and personal moral responsibility. He was a member of the family, clan, village, or group of villages in a particular chain of ancestory. He had a complex set of moral and religious obligations to his ancestors. The living and the dead were interdependent and capable of communicating one with the other.

Again, land was owned by the community. The individual procured farm and residential land through the community land allocation system. Most of the occupations were hereditary, often centering in particular lineages of or compounds. All societies practised slavery and engaged in active slave trading in the nineteenth century. In spite of this slavery, there were some opportunities for the slaves to better themselves economically, socially, and politically. Status mobility was common. Among other similarities is the respect for elders.

The truth of the matter is that, as in many other spheres of national life, Nigerians have merely followed in the footsteps of their erstwhile colonial masters without fully appreciating the latter's motives, or they have appropriated the colonial heritage for their own personal and class interests. It is pertinent to note that Tanzania consists of at least one hundred and fifty cultural-linguistic units. Nevertheless, no one ever hears Tanzanians talking of their heterogeneity, diversity, or federal character; and they are not organising themselves into a federation with a proliferating number of states. Tanzania is a unitary state; so are Ivory Coast, Mozambique, Zambia and many other African states which consist of a multiplicity of cultural-linguistic groups. They do not celebrate this diversity in their national anthem either or conceive of and define their problems essentially in ethnic terms.

The assertion of the importance of cultural-linguistic differences and their divisive tendencies ignores the assimilationist streak in the precolonial relations of the Nigerian peoples. In the North the Islamic religion and Hausa language were creating a common socioeconomic and political culture for the various peoples of the area. Even the victorious Fulani had become Hausa-speaking by the end of the nineteenth century. At the boundaries between the Yoruba and Edo-speaking peoples, Igbo and Igala, Igbo and Idoma, Igbo and Efik-Ibibio, and Efik and Ijaw peoples, a growing intermixture of culture and language was clearly evident. The case of assimilation between the Ibo and Ijaw of the Niger Delta has already been mentioned.[1]

1. See Chapter 3 first paragraph.

Lacking a sense of history and an historical perspective to social phenomena, Nigerians fail to realise the colonial origin of this emphasis on what is different among them to the neglect of what is common. Colonial racism was in need of justification. Its myth of the superiority of European culture relative to African culture needed empirical referents. Hence, colonial anthropoligists focussed on the exotic aspects of Nigerian cultures identifying their "primitive" character. Any evidence of similarity with British culture was surpressed. In this way, anthropology served the function of colonialism to inferiorise the population. Later, this approach to the study of cultures, based first on the denial of African culture and then on hierarchies of them, was replaced by that of cultural relativity. All cultures were unique in themselves. Emphasis was, therefore, placed on what made them unique, the differences. This perspective served both the function of inferiorisation, since British culture was still assumed to be the ideal, and that of dividing the colonised at the same time. A legacy of analysis of Nigerian cultures characterised by its emphasis on what was different was left behind by the colonial anthropologists. This was the major contribution of analysts like C. K. Meek, Daryll Forde, Amaury Talbot, Margery Perham, P. C. Lloyd, Simon Ottenberg, M. G. Smith and others to the understanding of the Nigerian peoples. And it is these colonial "experts" that Nigerians now depend on for their understanding of the various Nigerian precolonial social formations.

These agents of colonialism were instrumental in perpetuating the myth of cultural diversity among Nigerians. They successfully shaped the perceptions of the latter in the direction of recognising only differences among members of different communal groups. As M. Rockeach has argued, the social distance between individuals and members of different social groups varies with perceived, rather than objective, similarity.[2] It is confirmed empirically by M. B. Brewer's study of East Africa which shows that social distance toward outgroups varies with perceived dissimilarity to the ingroups,[3] and by Richard Brislin's study of nine ethnic groups at the University of Guam.[4]

2. M. Rockeach, *The Open and Closed Mind* (New York. Basic Books, 1960).
3. M. B. Brewer, "Determinants of Social Distance Among East African Tribal Groups," *Journal of Personality and Social Psychology*, Vol. X, No. 3 (1968), pp. 279–289.
4. Richard Brislin, "Interaction Among Members of Nine Ethnic Groups and Belief Similarity Hypothesis," *Journal of Social Psychology*, Vol. LXXXV, (December 1971), pp. 171–179.

This virtual exclusion of intercultural similarities from the perceptual map of most Nigerians was functional for colonialism. It diverted attention away as much as possible from colonial exploitation, oppression, and domination. Instead, Nigerians focussed on relations among themselves, interpreting them as inherently conflictual because of these assumed differences. Such a diversion helped the colonial system to survive as long as it did. Also, the emphasis on differences worked against Nigerian solidarity against colonialism and its attendant national underdevelopment. As Nigerians increasingly internalised this view of the country as a heterogenous entity, it became more and more difficult for the resultant ingroup-outgroup sentiments to be overcome, and for class consciousness to emerge. Therefore, dangerous bases for organising the national population against colonialism were preempted.

The most dangerous pattern of agitation against imperialism and capitalism is that which runs along lines of relations of production. It has consequences for the complete destruction of these systems which mobilisation along communal lines does not have. By manipulating the assumed cultural differences, the colonialist successfully divided members of the same classes, thereby preventing the emergence of strong, revolutionary movements. It became difficult to think consistently along class rather than communal lines.

The Colonial Policy of Divide and Rule

The British colonial administration encouraged communal sentiments among Nigerians.[5] It seized every available opportunity to spread the myth and propaganda that they were "separated from one another by great distance, by differences of history and traditions, and by ethnological, racial, tribal, political, social and religious barriers".[6] In fact, in 1920, Sir Hugh Clifford, the colonial Governor of the country at the time, made it abundantly clear that his administration would seek to secure "to each separate people the right to maintain its identity, its individuality and its nationality, its chosen form of government; and the peculiar political and social institutions

5. J. S. Coleman, *Nigeria: Background to Nationalism* (Berkeley: University of California Press, 1958), pp. 193–194.
6. Quoted in *ibid.*, p. 193.

which have been evolved for it by the wisdom and the accumulated experiences of generations of its forebears".[7]

This encouragement was reflected structurally by the administrative systems of indirect rule and regionalisation. Indirect rule started out as an instrument for overcoming the pervasive financial, personnel, and communications problems of the colonial administration in Northern Nigeria and ended up as a means for reinforcing communal identity among Nigerians, creating a new sense of communal identity where none existed, and providing a new symbolic and ethnocentric focus for the urban population. In the view of James Coleman, "the overwhelming emphasis has been upon greater tribal integration . . . there can be little doubt that it has complicated the task of welding diverse elements into a Nigerian nation."[8] In summary, indirect rule widened the social distance among the communal groups in Nigeria, thereby reinforcing the ethnocentric factor in the emergence of ethnicity.

Indirect rule was first established in Northern Nigeria between 1900 and 1913. Then, during the period 1916–1919 it was extended to Benin and Yorubaland. From about 1927 it was transplanted to Eastern Nigeria; and by 1937 all parts of Nigeria were governed by it, except the municipalities of Lagos, Port Harcourt, Enugu, Kaduna, Kano and Zaria. It was abolished in the East by the Eastern Region Local Government Ordinance of 1950.[9] Initially, it was designed to overcome the problem of shortage of trained British personnel, and to limit expenses. Between 1900 and 1906, Frederick Lugard, the British Commissioner responsible for the administration of the North faced the same basic problems as those facing his counterpart in the South – lack of trained personnel, small revenues, and an absence of specific directions from Whitehall. But in addition, he had very little trade or cash crop production and no seaports to provide him with sources of taxation for revenues. Therefore, he had no real choice but to rely on the indigenous rulers.

In the North in 1906, there was only one British officer to 2,900 square miles of territory, and one to 45,000 Nigerians.[10] At the same time, there was a virtual absence of subordinate

7. Quoted in *ibid.*, p. 194.
8. *Ibid.*, pp. 52–53.
9. Margery Perham, *Lugard: The Years of Authority* (London: Collins, 1960), p. 142.
10. I. M. Okonjo, *British Administration in Nigeria, 1900–1950* (New York: NOK, 1974), p. 27.

clerical and technical staff and artisans needed by the colonial administration. In the midst of these difficulties, Lugard was face to face with a comparatively well-established bureaucracy which he only had to convert to his own purposes. The ruling emirs ran an efficient administrative system whose highly centralised authority extended over a vast territory and a considerable number of people. It was founded on a common adherence to Islam, responsible for the collection of taxes, the maintenance of order, and the administration of justice. Lugard, therefore, decided to impose his authority on the emirs and to use their administrations and officials as agents of Britain.

In an attempt to do this he met with fierce resistance from the emirs. Eventually, however, the latter bowed to British military superiority. The victorious colonialists had to station a garrison of troops at every provincial centre to protect British officials and to discourage the emirs from seeking to disturb the new order. Nevertheless, the requirements of indirect rule dictated that the colonial government adopt a policy of magnanimity and conciliation towards the defeated rulers. Therefore, an alliance was struck between the emirs and the British which bound the former more closely to their new masters and rallied them to the British cause in return for a guarantee of non-interference with the moslem religion, the fundamental ideological basis of emirate power, and consolidating and, in some cases, extending this power. This alliance offered Lugard the best hope of pacifying the defeated leaders, reconciling them to "permanent British presence, and winning and retaining their confidence and loyalty, while harnessing their undoubted administrative skills to British interest."[11]

A British resident was stationed in each emir's court, but he interferred only to a minimal degree. Indirect rule meant two levels of government, the foreign and local administrations. The former was divided into provinces run by the resident who was expected to conduct the delicate political relations with the paramount chief. The latter was headed by the local ruler but subject to the resident's control and supervision. It maintained law and order, prevented crimes, arrested criminals and vagabonds, made and enforced orders relating to good sanitation and public health. It recruited its own staff for these purposes. The complicated local tax system was reduced to a single tax on villages levied by the resident. The tax was still collected by the same

11. *Ibid.*, p. 36.

officials and all of it was paid into the emir's treasuries and accounted for to the resident. Once in the local treasury, at first a quarter and later a half of these revenues were transferred to the colonial treasury for colonial administration. Similarly, native courts existed side by side with colonial courts, the latter dealing with non-Africans. The former recruited its own personnel and followed local laws and procedure except where the British felt these to be unacceptable.

It was essentially this pattern of administration that was exported to the south. There, it ran into serious difficulties. Among the Yorubas, the Oba was less autocratic than the emir and, therefore, could not pacify his people for colonialism the way the emirs did. In the East where the precolonial situation was radically different because of the absence of chiefs who ruled over wide areas, the introduction of indirect rule was even more turbulent than in the West. It was marked by the colonial creation of a new class of chiefs hitherto unknown, the warrant chiefs. The majority of them did not have any traditional claim to the role which the British expected them to play. Hence, indirect rule contributed to one of the worst riots in the country, the Aba riots of 1929.[12] But it worked sufficiently well in the West and East to maintain some precolonial traditions and institutions.

One of the important consequences of indirect rule for the emergence of ethnicity concerned the Land and Native Rights Ordinance of 1910. It formally proclaimed all land in the North (with certain exceptions) as native land to be controlled and administered by the governor. He used it to limit the activities of Southern traders, businessmen, and especially lawyers and missionaries. The Northern authorities believed that the liberal ideas of the Southerners were capable of undermining the authority of the emirs, and, therefore, destroying that alliance between the Fulani ruling class and the colonial administration which Lugard regarded as crucial for colonial exploitation. The Ordinance assisted indirect rule by discouraging the free and uncontrolled immigration of Southerners to the North who might undermine the traditional authority. Those Southerners who crossed this barrier were forced to live in housing areas segregated from the indigenous population. In Zaria, for example, colonial policy led to several different settlements: (a) the walled city, housing the indigenous population, (b) Tudun Wada created by the British to

12, A. E. Afigbo, *The Warrant Chiefs* (London: Longmans, 1972), pp. 59–77.

house Northerners who were not indigenous to the town, and (c) Sabon Garis for what the colonial administration called "native foreigners." These were mainly Southerners.

In this and various other ways, indirect rule helped to perpetuate the powers of the emirs and the other precolonial rulers. It supported to the utmost the authority and prestige of the chief. It impressed on the masses that the chief was the effective ruler, and that as long as he administred his people to the satisfaction of the colonial masters, he had the whole might of the British colonial government fully behind him. The net effect of the increased influence of the paramount chief was a greater cohesion of the local population around the traditional bureaucracy and authority of the chief, and, therefore, a much greater inward orientation of the population toward their precolonial way of life or what was left of it following the colonial impact. Where new chiefs were created or old ones made to look after a wider area than before, a much larger population was integrated into this traditional way of life, thus strengthening the importance of local ties, norms, values and customs in the life of Nigerians.

As this happened, members of each chiefdom tended to look more toward their parochial local group for cultural, spiritual, social, ethical, and linguistic satisfaction. Members began to share common experiences in relation to others and, therefore, common history, tradition, and interest. This strengthened their feelings of exclusiveness and, consequently, their perception of a social distance as separating them from other chiefdoms. Under these circumstances conflicts of interest between chiefdoms further increased their social distance in economic affairs, security consideration, and ideology. The inevitable consequence was a greater salience of the ethnocentric component of ethnicity. Urban migrants then found it difficult not to be involved in the affairs of their communal homelands. For example, the Egbado Union pressed successfully to consolidate the native authorities operating in its rural area and to change the name of the division from Ilaro to Egbado. This involvement in turn reinforced and heightened the parochial and communal sentiments of the Egbado people resident in urban areas. Hence, it was easy for their alignments in the new urban centres to continue along communal lines rather than lines of relations of production.

At the level of ideology, indirect rule was anchored in white racism. Underlying it was a myth regarding the incapacity of the

African to rise beyond his traditional heritage; that it was mischievous to prepare him for life other than within his own native commmunity, and, therefore, African progress, if any, would be an inordinately slow and painful process likely to take several hundreds of years. This belief coincided with the marginalisation of the vast majority of the population by colonial capitalism, and the consequent creation of vast labour reserves in the country. In these reserves, the population was allowed and even encouraged to remain at the subsistence level of economic activity. In this way they would remain for a very long time a source of cheap labour for the few and scattered colonial enclaves where the European financial oligarchies carried on their economic activities. Certainly, the belief that the Nigerian could not break out of his heritage contradicted the empirical situation in the urban enclaves where Nigerians produced goods and services for the financial oligarchies and adopted to the European way of life.

Only as much education as was sufficient to run the various colonial enterprises was given. Its spread, therefore, varied with the spread of these enterprises. Hence, the South received more of this education than the North. Too, indirect rule made its impact more keenly felt in the latter than in the former, causing a differential in the introduction of Western education in the country. Such education was deemed capable of subverting the authority of the emirs, especially since its major harbingers were the Christian missionaries. Also, in the South more than in the North, recruitment into the ruling bureaucracy was related to performance in European schools.

Educationally, therefore, the one section of the country differed from the other. Initially all education in the country was under the direct control of Christian missionaries. Lugard's official policy excluded these missionaries from the North.[13] The muslim rulers of the area were hostile to them. Although in 1903 Christians opened a school in Nupeland at the invitation of the Emir of Zaria, the missionaries were only permitted to work in the non-Muslim Middle Belt. Thus, in 1947 the total secondary school enrollment in the North constituted only 2.5 per cent of the total for the country, although the area contained 54 per cent of the population.[14] By 1937 there was only one Northerner in the Yaba Higher College, and as late as 1951, the 16 million people of the

13. *Ten Year Educational Plan*, Nigerian Sessional Paper No. 6/1944, p. 11.
14. J. S. Coleman, *op. cit.*, p. 132.

North had produced only one person with a full university degree.[15] In 1953, primary school enrolment in the North was only one-eight that of the South.[16] In 1952 only 8.5 per cent of the total population of those over seven years were literate in Western script in Nigeria. Out of these 16 per cent came from the East, 18 per cent from the West and only 2 per cent from the North.[17] Within the North itself, the figure is much higher for the non-Muslim Middle Belt than for the muslim provinces.[18]

TABLE 4.1   *Number of schools in pupils in the north and south of Nigeria 1906–1957*

Year	Primary school		Secondary school	Primary pupils	Secondary pupils
1906	South:	126	1	11,872	20
	North:	1	0	Unknown	0
1912	South:	150	10	35,716	67
	North:	34	0	954	0
1926	South:	3,828	18	138,249	518
	North:	125	0	5,210	0
1937	South:	3,533	26	218,610	4,285
	North:	539	1	20,269	65
1947	South:	4,984	43	538,391	9,657
	North:	1,110	3	70,962	251
1957	South:	13,473	176	2,343,317	28,208
	North:	2,080	18	185,484	3,643

Source: J. S. Coleman, *Nigeria: Background to Nationalism* (Berkeley: University of California Press, 1958), p. 134, Table 14.

TABLE 4.2   *Regional variations in literacy in Nigeria, 1952*

Region	Percentage of population with 4 or more years of formal education	percentage of population with 1–3 years of formal education
East	10.2	5.4
West	10.7	6.6
Non Muslim North	1.4	1.8
Muslim North	0.7	0.7

Sources: J. S. Coleman, *op. cit.*, p. 134, Table 15.

15. *Ibid.*, p. 139.
16. D. Abernethy, *The Political Dilemma of Popular Education: An African Case* (Stanford: Standford University Press, 1969), p. 139.
17. J. S. Coleman, *op. cit.*, p. 132.
18. *Ibid.*, pp. 137–138.

During the period 1910–1929, a carefully controlled pro-gramme of education was sponsored in the North by the colonial government. The model was not the system in the South but that of Sudan. Its aim was to ensure that schooling did not radically disrupt the traditional feudal social order. The primary schools were constructed and run by the emirs. Islamic religion and Arabic were their prominent subjects. Also, these schools empha-sised training in health, native arts and crafts, gardening, carpent-ary, indigenous metal and leather works, and motor repairing. Character training was supervised by the traditional teachers, the "mallams". In all matters of dress, behaviour and traditional forms of salutation, including prostration, the pupils were required to conform to local customs.[19] These differences in the systems of education not only created an educational imbalance between the North and South but, as far as the emergence of ethnicity was concerned, widened the social distance between the peoples of the two parts of the country.

At the political level, the various parts of the country did not share a common experience for a long time. The North was excluded from the area of the legislative competence of the Legis-lative Council set up by the 1922 constitution. In fact, from the time of the amalgamation of the North and South in 1914 to 1946 the two parts of the country maintained only a tenuous linkage in law through the person of the Governor. They retained their dis-tinctive political identities and maintained separate administra-tions. The opportunity provided by the Nigerian Council set up in 1914 for a common legislative experience among the representa-tives of the various regions of the country was vitiated by the con-sistent absence of the Nigerians, particularly the chiefs, from the Council's deliberations.

The 1922 reforms set up only one Legislative Council in the country. But its powers to make laws were limited to the Colony of Lagos and the Protectorate of Southern Nigeria. The Governor alone was empowered to make laws for the Protectorate of North-ern Nigeria. The only link between the two halves of the nation was the participation of the Lieutenant Governor of the North in the Legislative Council by virtue of his membership of the Execu-tive Council, together with the Senior Residents of the Northern Provinces and the representatives of the Kano Chamber of Com-merce, and the mining industry which was found mainly in the

19. *Ibid.*, p. 138.

North. The operation of a common budget for the North and South also had the unintended effect of bringing debate on policies for the North under the competence of the Council. Again, although the Richard's Constitution which came into operation in 1946 provided for one Legislative Council for the whole country it provided for a House of Chiefs and House of Assembly in the North but just a House of Assembly each in the East and West. However, under it and for the first time Northern and Southern leaders sat side by side in the Legislative Council to discuss political affairs.

Elections took various forms in different parts of the country. Under the 1951 Constitution, the indirect system of elections prevailed throughout the nation. But while in the East and West there were three stages, the primary, intermediate, and final electoral colleges, in the North there were four stages, the town or village, district, emirate, and provincial levels. In order to ensure the election of persons sympathetic to the views of the natural rulers, the emirs and the Native Authority System in the North dominated by them were permitted to nominate a number of contestants equal to 10 per cent of the final (provincial) electoral college. Among these were the choices of the emirs. Various pressures operated on the college to elect the emirs' favourites. Thus, in Kano Emirate in 1951, none of the twenty successful candidates for the Northern House of Assembly had been elected at a lower stage. In fact, ten of the elected members had been defeated in earlier ballotings.[20] For the federal elections of 1954, the regulations were altered to permit any ten members of the final electoral college to nominate non-members as candidates. In Kano Emirate, sixteen of the eighteen nominated in this manner were elected.[21]

In Nigeria, direct universal adult suffrage was first introduced in the Lagos Town Council election of 1950. Outside the capital it was first used in 1954 in the Eastern Region to elect members to the Federal House of Representatives. It was again used for the 1957 election to the Eastern House of Assembly. Direct and quasi-universal and quasi-tax payer suffrage was first used in the West for the federal elections of 1954. Universal franchise emerged in that region in 1956. In the North, on the other hand, direct

20. Richard Sklar, *Nigerian Political Parties* (Princeton, N.J.: Princeton University Press, 1963), p. 30.
21. *Ibid.*, p. 30.

elections based on tax payer suffrage were only introduced in 1956 for the election to the regional House of Assembly. And even then it was limited to nineteen specified urban electoral districts.

The federal election of 1959 was concluded on the basis of universal adult suffrage in the East, West and Lagos. In the North, on the other hand, only male persons were eligible to vote or be voted for. Similarly, by 1958, local government elections in the East, West and Lagos were carried out, as during parliamentary elections, on the bases of direct election and universal adult suffrage. But in the North, tax payer suffrage prevailed in subordinate local councils including districts, village and town councils. In all parliamentary contests, local government elections in the East, West, Lagos, and in town councils in the North, voting was by secret ballot. But in the rural areas of the North open voting prevailed, with voters grouping behind the candidates of their choice.

These sectional differences in the political process divided Nigerians along communal lines, rather than lines of relations of production and, therefore, increased the social distance among members of the various groups. The same effect was produced by the attempt of the colonialists to divide the people along communal lines, as a mechanism for maintaining domination over them. As a political line the colonialists used sectionalism to curb African nationalism and to maintain their power. For example, in 1920 Sir Hugh Clifford effectively dampened the emergent West African nationalism by preying on the communal sentiments of the Nigerian members of the National Congress of West Africa when the latter called for reforms of the colonial order:

"I am entirely convinced of the right, for example, of the people of Egbaland ... of any of the great Emirates of the North ... to maintain that each one of them is, in a very real sense, a nation ... It is the task of the Government of Nigeria to build and fortify these national institutions".[22]

The impact of this colonial machination was disastrous. A local faction emerged which repudiated the Congress and undertook to organise a pro-government Reform Club. By 1934 the Congress movement in Nigeria had become moribund. Nigerians channelled their political attention toward their communal homelands.

22. J. S. Coleman, op. cit., p. 194.

Again, the colonialists tried to check the march of Nigerian nationalism by identifying with and sponsoring reactionary communal interests in the country, particularly in the North, and preying on their communal sentiments and animosities. For example, before the Second World War, the Yoruba and Hausa dominated petty trade in Jos. Igbo traders came during the war and concentrated in a part of the "Native Town" which the Hausa had a sentimental and possessive attachment to. The result was tension between the Hausa and Igbo.

The war ended in the midst of high hopes and expectations by the people, but scarcity, inflation, and the rationing instituted during the war prevailed. In addition, the general strike of 1945 hit the supplies of food to the North by rail. This action caused a severe shortage of food and consequently, serious anxiety for the population. Each morning for several weeks, a long line of people waited outside the market to receive their fixed ration of grain from the District Officer. The British blamed the strike and the resultant difficulties on the leading Igbo anticolonialist of the time, Nnamdi Azikiwe, and the Igbo. They prevailed on Northerners to boycott the strike. What is more, they exploited the situation to incite the Hausa against the Igbo in Jos. In the prevailing atmosphere of intercommunal trade competition and the animosities arising from the settlement of the Igbo in the "Native Town," the Jos communal riots of 1945 became inevitable.[23]

The colonialists even resorted to the manipulations of elections along communal lines. In the 1951 elections in Kano, for example, the colonial administration tried very hard to frustrate Northern allies of Southerners opposed to the candidates of the emirs. These allies were not allowed to hold public meetings, and acts of intimidation and victimisation against them were not investigated. In spite of these harassments, the NCNC-NEPU alliance swept the polls in the primaries in the Kano metropolitan area. That no single candidate of the emirs was successful, shocked the colonial authorities not only in Kano, but also at the regional capital, Kaduna. As a result, the office of the Chief Commissioner in Kaduna instructed his Residents to aid the efforts of the Native Administration in the remaining rounds of the elections:

23. Leonard Plotnicov, "An Early Nigerian Civil Disturbance: The 1945 Hausa-Ibo Riot in Jos," *Journal of Modern African Studies*, Vol. IX, No. 2 (August 1971), pp. 299–300.

"In the Primary Elections in certain areas there have been outstanding examples of the ability of political parties commanding a minority of popular support succeeding, by organising voting arrangements, in securing a disproportionate degree of representation. It is apparent ... that this aspect of electoral practice is becoming more widely realised ... His Honour feels that it is important that adequate steps should be taken to ensure that the necessity for preelection discussion and agreement takes place where the majority of candidates and electorate are faced by well organised opponents, although those opponents may be in the minority".[24]

It is an open secret that British officials in the North were very sympathetic to the Native Administration. Most of these officials were ultra-conservative elements who were frustrated by the liberal changes in Britain that undermined the powers of the British aristocracy. They found in the aristocratic system in the North a nostalgic haven where they could protect and promote the way of life which they saw disintegrating in their home country. They strongly believed that the emirate system would not be able to protect itself from what they considered to be the demagogic rhetoric of the radical Southern nationalists and their Northern allies. The system of electoral colleges was designed so that "a handful of volatile, politically conscious urban dwellers do not swamp the vast mass of rural voters".[25] Within the emirates, neither the returning officers nor the masses they called upon to vote or stand for election saw themselves as doing anything but carrying out the lawful commands of the British and local authorities.

This colonial manipulation of elections poisoned relations between the North and South with a consequent increase in the social distance between members of their populations. In fact, when Nnamdi Azikiwe, the second Lagos Member of the Legislative Council, complained of official election malpractices in the 1951 elections, the Northerners regarded it as a slur on the colonial regime in the North and the Native Administration. Later Azikiwe even sent a cablegram to the British Secretary of State for the colonies to intervene and ensure a free and fair election in the North, a move which was highly resented by Northerners.

24. Quoted in C. N. Ubah, "The Indirect Elections at Kano, 1951," (unpublished mimeo) (Nsukka, Nigeria, 1976), pp. 13–14.
25. Quoted in *ibid.*, p. 21.

The Lack of Economic Unity

In the colonial economy there was virtually no unity across the communal homelands of the Nigerians. Its dominant sector was import-export and, therefore, externally oriented rather than being internally oriented toward the integration of the various communal homelands. In reality, there was no such thing as a national economy. Instead, there existed in the country foreign-owned economic activities which were directed at external needs or run in the interest of external financiers for whom national economic integration was not part of the economic calculus.

As indicated earlier, three major areas of economic activities emerged, the Kano-Kaduna-Zaria-Jos complex, the Lagos metropolitan area, and the Port Harcourt-Aba-Enugu-Onitsha axis and their surrounding rural environments. Investments in marketing, transport, and export services associated with the dominant colonial economic activities of cash crop production and mining, gravitated overwhelmingly to these three core areas. Similarly, investment in manufacturing industries was attracted to the same areas for marketing, transport, employment, and political reasons. But these areas remained isolated one from the other with hardly any salient economic exchanges between them. Instead, salient economic exchanges existed between each area and the advanced capitalist countries of Europe and America.

Thus, the colonial economy was made up of core areas which were relatively juxtaposed. The density of flow of their exchanges with the outside world was much greater than that of exchanges among them. Each was on its own, strongly linked with economic entities whose centres of gravity lay in the centres of the capitalist world. A consequence of this false, disarticulated and non-structured economy is that it could be broken up into microeconomies without serious danger to the various economic activities, a situation which, under normal conditions, would create an intolerable economic retrogression. The weakness of national cohesion is a reflection of this disarticulated economy. Such an unstructured economy is also a source of micronationalism. The area interested in the export economy has no need of the rest of the country, which may indeed seem a burden upon it. It may therefore contemplate establishing a micro-independence.[26]

26. Samir Amin, *Accumulation on a World Scale* Vol. I (New York: Monthly Review, 1974), pp. 288–289.

An extensive development of equitable and mutually rewarding economic exchanges tends to create a good basis for the establishment of friendly neighbourly relations among peoples. It also fosters peace and an atmosphere of mutual understanding among peoples by promoting higher living standards, increased employment, and more rapid economic progress. It is like a barometer which indicates the direction of good will; it is a messenger of peace and unity. Karl Deutsch insists that a wide range of transactions is essential to the growth of "security communities," characterised by cooperation, peace, and political integration.[27]

The statement, "The helpfulness of economic ties may be largely in the extent to which they function as a form of communication and as visible sources of reward"[28] hits the crux of the problem. If economic transactions are a form of communication, then communications theory would suggest that information contained in such transactions can be dissociated, and recombined in different ways with material from memory, and used in different contents.[29] Such a recombination process enables economic transactions to be important for issues which do not affect them in any immediate sense. An exporter is likely to have a general interest in the well-being of his market, an interest that transcends the marketing conditions narrowly defined for his products. As a result, he may become attuned to the needs of the importing area or country over a wide range of non-economic matters such as politics, cultural activities, and social affairs which may have only a very remote influence on his trade. For example, Daniel Lerner has found from a study based on a sample of French business leaders, that their support for the European Defense Council as opposed to the maintenance of the French national army varied directly with the importance of export trade to the businessman's firm.[30] Only in a very few cases could any of these businessmen be said to have a direct economic interest in the decision.

If the groundnut, cotton, tin, and columbite produced in the North were converted into manufactured products in the East and

27. Karl Deutsch, *et al.*, *Political Community and the North Atlantic Area* (Princeton, N.J.: Princeton University Press, 1957), p. 53.
28. *Ibid.*, p. 157.
29. Karl Deutsch, *The Nerves of Government* (Glencoe, Ill.: Free Press, 1963).
30. Daniel Lerner, "French Business Leaders Look at E. D. C.," *Public Opinion Quarterly*, Vol. XXI, No. 2 (Spring 1956), p. 220.

West, the cocoa of the West transformed into chocolate and other manufactured goods or simply processed for export in the East and North, and the palm produce of the East turned into soap and other secondary products in the West and North, the problem of national unity would have been less difficult than it is. Significant members of the country's population would thus acquire vested economic interests in other regions than those of their communal homelands. At least for selfish economic reasons they would be compelled to pay attention to activities in other parts of the nation in order to encourage a greater understanding between the people of their area and those of areas with which their economic activities are linked. They would be forced to take an interest in and appreciate the way of life of these other peoples at least in order not to alienate them to the ruin of their businesses. In general, they would have to cultivate the friendship of others and promote good neighbourliness among the relevant peoples. The livelihood of people in the various regions of the country would be tied together and made mutually interdependent. The workers in the soap making factories of the North would realize that without the palm produce from the East the source of their livelihood would dry up. They would have a vested interest in maintaining a positive relationship between the North and East. Thus, there would exist countervailing forces to those of secession, disunity, and micronationalism. People of different areas would have a basis for seeing their destinies as tied together, and would have a vested interest in peace, friendship, and coopera-tion with one another. The tendency under peripheral capitalism for some Nigerian leaders to neglect the development of areas other than those of their communal homeland would become irrational, and so would any tendency to think that one part of the country can go it alone without the support of the other parts. National unity could then be assured. For obvious selfish reasons, the colonialist did not establish such an internally integrated economy. They were more interested in an economic structure which would help to create, reinforce, and perpetuate the exploita-tion of the labour-power and the resources of the local area for the benefit of metropolitan private capital.

This fragmentation of the economy along with the reluctance of migrants to venture far away from their communal homelands reinforced the ethnocentric component of ethnicity. The same effect was produced by the situation which characterised the fringes of the colonial urban centres. Here the local labour force commuted daily from the village to the town for work. Some of the workers resided in villages within walking distance of their place of wage labour. This enabled them to cultivate land in the village while, at the same time, working in the town. In addition, it helped to avoid the high cost of housing, the trauma of urban life, and to supplement their low wages. This confinement of the labour force to colonial activities in the communal homeland, together with the unintegrated nature of the colonial economy, meant that the labour force, and even the other classes, were fragmented along regional lines. Intraclass solidarity was thus made more difficult, the social distance among individuals increased and this social distance became salient along communal lines.

The Relevant Precolonial Differences

In spite of the similarities across the various precolonial societies of Nigeria, certain differences among them have affected the social distance among their members. In the intensely competitive atmosphere of colonialism it could not be otherwise. Under conditions of pervasive emphasis on differences rather than similarities it was inevitable. However, the tendency to associate all the differences among the groups with ethnically relevant social distance is far-fetched. In fact, only three major differences are significant: those associated with language, religion, and deference to authority. These differences were relevant for behaviour in the new colonial order.

Of these variations, that of language has been the most significant. Language is the major means of communication among humankind. Therefore, it is the essential precursor of social interaction and behaviour. Without such a symbolic medium of communication shared by individuals, frustration, stress, anxiety, lack of trust and insecurity characterise social relations. The situation is complicated and worsened when such a lack of communication takes place in an atmosphere of intense socioeconomic competition and communal exclusiveness. In societies where different and mutually unintelligible languages are spoken, there is a tendency for the individual initially to confine his pattern of communication and, therefore, his social relations to members of the same language group, at least until he is able to learn the other languages.

Nigeria is a multi-lingual society. Bamgbose suggests that there are about 400 different languages in the country[31] and with the exception of the three major languages, Hausa, Igbo, and Yoruba, each occupies a very restricted area. As a result, many Nigerians encounter a different language just twenty miles outside their communal homeland.[32] Therefore, migrations of more than local scope bring divergent local languages into contact. However, only about ten major languages may be identified. In the 1950s, the percentage of the population for whom these languages were mother tongues were: Yoruba – 16.6 per cent, Edo – 1.5 per cent, Igbo – 17.9 per cent, Ibibio-Efik – 2.7 per cent, Ijaw – 1.1 per cent, Hausa – 18.2 per cent, Fulani – 9.9 per cent, Kanuri – 4.2 per cent, Nupe – 1.1 per cent, Tiv – 2.3 per cent.[33] The diversity is further ameliorated by the use of Hausa as a lingua franca in the North. Too, the colonial period saw pidgin English develop as a widely spoken language in the urban areas. And, of course, English has been the official language since the onset of colonisation. There has been a considerable linguistic mixing arising from precolonial contact along linguistic boundaries.[34]

Religion was another divisive factor in the social relations among Nigerians arising from precolonial differences. In this respect, the relevant distinction is between Muslims and non-Muslims. Islam was introduced into Northern Nigeria about five hundred years ago. However, its effect on the population was greatly intensified and its area of dominance expanded after 1804 when the Fulani religious leaders in the town of Sokoto waged a holy war that brought most of Hausaland under the orthodox Islamic leadership of the Sultan of Sokoto. In the South, on the other hand, only a portion of Yorubaland came under islamic influence. The rest remained animist. During the colonial period many of them embraced Christianity, in some cases with enthusiasm, even fanaticism.

Religious differences have a high potential for separating people from one another. Throughout history these differences have been the basis of tension, animosity, hostility, and even war.

31. Ayo Bamgbose, "The English Language in Nigeria," in John Spencer, ed. *The English Language in West Africa* (London: Longmans, 1971), pp. 35–48.
32. Olasope O. Oyelaran, "Urbanisation, Migration and Language in Nigeria: A Note on Research," a Paper presented at the Conference on Social Research and National Development in Nigeria, September-October 1975, p. 11.
33. J. S. Coleman, *op. cit.*, p. 15.
34. *Ibid.*, pp. 15–17.

Many times a certain fanaticism is associated with religious beliefs which excludes social relations with people of different religion, or hampers mutual trust and confidence when such relations happen to exist. This is because religion tends to define what constitutes appropriate social behaviour. When this definition is at crosspurposes with another, normal relations become difficult. For example, the orthodox Islamic doctrine in the North which confines married women to the purdah makes moslem men uncomfortable when they interact with non-Moslems accompanied by their wives, who do not even wear veils.

Religious beliefs and feelings have historically been among the strongest and most enduring factors compelling human beings to cluster together in exclusive communities sharing strong bonds of association. The social obligations, concensus, and expectations which create the social bonds that unite the people in the community and which facilitate the inevitable interactions of community life, become strong integrative forces when they derive their meaning and sacredness from religion. The level of sanctity and sacredness with which the attendant values, rules, norms, and customs of daily life are commonly held and expressed, tend to determine the strength and cohesion of such societies. By purporting to provide divine answers to the ways people should behave in life, religion assumes a tremendous importance in shaping the life, ways, and thought patterns of human groups.

Every society develops an ethos or a collective understanding of the nature of things and of man's relationship to man and his surroundings. This ethos provides the basic guidelines for the definition of the rights, duties, obligations, and responsibilities of members of these societies and their institutions. It defines the fundamental structures, systems, and channels of interaction for the members, as well as the belief systems which embody the internalised values that, in part, propel action. When the ethos is legitimised by a unique religious faith, it tends to become a strong moral and social force which gives ultimate cohesion and an aura of exclusiveness to the group.

Such exclusiveness increases the social distance between members of different religious groups. In Nigeria, this fact is reinforced by the distinction which Islam makes between the believer and the unbeliever. This distinction explicitly discourages serious mutually rewarding interaction between members of the two groups. It conceives of their relationship as essentially a struggle in which one will inevitably prevail over the other and in the conduct of this struggle, the jihad or holy war is a self-fulfilling instrument. The infidel who eats pork, is given to excessive drinking of alcohol, and does not accept Mohammed as the true prophet of Allah, is only good as an object for conversion to the faith. One of the consequences of this distinction is the tendency for a long time of the Moslem North to be oriented to Mecca and the Arab world in general. This is reflected in the tracing of the people's history to the Arab North, the emphasis on Koranic schools in which Arabic is the medium of teaching, the fashioning of the early school curriculum on the model of the Arab peoples, and the institutionalisation of the Sharia judicial court system. The inevitable consequence of this external orientation is the increase in the social distance between the North and South of Nigeria.

Again, differential precolonial deference to authority adversely affects the social distance among Nigerians. This fact becomes clear with a comparison of the attitude to authority on the part of the Hausa, Igbo, and Yoruba. The precolonial Hausa-Fulani political system was a theocracy organised along essentially feudal lines. It was organised around the emirate ruled by a monarch, the emir. The emirate was a vassal state in the Sokoto empire. Its ruler was appointed by the Sultan of Sokoto, the spiritual and temporal head of the empire. A new emir had the power to relieve a number of political officers of their posts and to replace them with his own protégés as a reward for the latters' loyalty.

Most offices carried with them fiefs, or geographical areas, under an officer who collected taxes from these areas, part of which he transmitted to the emir while keeping the rest to himself. The structure of authority was a vertical hierarchy of ranked officials extending from the least powerful to the emir and then to the sultan. Commands flowed from the top downwards while loyalty and obedience flowed in the opposite direction. Deference to authority was such a strongly held value that disobedience, even by the emir, could be punished by removal from office. In cases of armed conflicts, office holders raised soldiers for the emir and were rewarded with booty and captive slaves. It was in the interest of the official to cultivate and retain the favour of the emir through frequent demonstrations of loyalty and obedience. This was the easiest and quickest path to a disproportionate share of the society's surplus. Therefore, the authority relations were despotic in character emphasising relations of power and dependence between subordinates and their superiors.

The society itself was highly stratified. At the top were the hereditary Fulani nobility who were favoured for office, particularly the ruling dynasties. Slaves occupied the lowest rung of the social ladder. In the middle were the freemen usually occupationally ranked in this order: the mallams and wealthy traders were at the top, cloth workers, silversmiths, commission agents, and farmers in the middle, and butchers, tanners, eulogists, hunters, and blacksmiths at the bottom. Ascription was, therefore, a pervasive aspect of the authority structure. However, a man's fate was not entirely determined by blood. Social mobility was possible through becoming the obedient client or loyal follower of the privileged. High office led to personal enrichment. Thus, authority roles were a source, not only of immense prestige, loyalty and respect, but also the most important means of acquiring wealth and status, overshadowing other alternatives. The emir was at once the wealthiest and most powerful person in the emirate.

Obviously, this structure of authority put a high premium on deference to authority, loyalty, obedience, and sensitivity to the interests, opinions, views, and demands of one's superiors. It strongly favoured qualities of servility, respect for authority, allegiance to the powerful, and submissiveness. Such a system frowned on the self-assertiveness of the individual. Success in an independent occupational and other non-ascriptive roles, or individual initiative and self-instigated actions towards goals not sanctioned by one's superiors were negatively evaluated or at best irrelevant. The first and foremost social commitment was loyalty to the emir. This allegiance was demonstrated by gifts, obedience, and sometimes prostration before his presence, as well as by the prompt execution of his orders and wishes. It was a grave sin to fail to discharge duties assigned by one's superior. Subservience and unquestioning obedience were inescapable aspects of social life in precolonial Hausa-Fulani society at the time of contact with colonialism.[35] This was given sacred sanction by Islam.

On the contrary, the precolonial Igbo authority structure was highly diffuse. It lacked any political centralisation. With few

35. Information about precolonial society has come from Robert A. LeVine, *Dreams and Deeds* (Chicago: University of Chicago Press, 1966); M. G. Smith, "The Hausa of Northern Nigeria," in J. L. Gibbs, ed., *Peoples of Africa* (New York: Holt, Rinehart and Winston, 1965); M. G. Smith, *Government in Zazzau* (London: Oxford University Press, 1960).

exceptions, decision-making in an Igbo society was performed not by a single leader but by a council of elders which was highly responsive to the popular will. In fact, the polity was republican in character. There was virtually no rigid stratification of individuals by blood or occupation. The only major ascriptive hierarchical distinction was between freeman and slave. The later were either secular or religious. Otherwise, age grades, title societies, and other universalistic criteria provided the basis for social status and influence in the society. For example, in many villages the title society such as the Ozo society operated as a political oligarchy controlling decision-making even at public meetings at which all men had a right to speak.

Deference to authority was very low. Wealth conferred authority and social status. A man gained prestige and power by accumulating the foodstuff required to join title societies and perform other ceremonies. The ability and opportunity to engage in this process of accumulation were not limited by blood ties. The societies were open to all freemen. Social mobility, wealth and power were independent of performance in authority roles. Therefore, loyalty and obedience to superiors, so important in Hausa-Fulani society, was virtually unknown to Igboland. In a general sense, obedience and respect were accorded only to the elders. Authoritative individuals were significant as objects of emulation rather than as recipients of loyalty and obedience. They were to be competed with rather than deferred to. Self-assertiveness and individual initiative were highly valued.

Thus, Igbo society looked down· on people who accepted superiors, depended on them, or relied on them for their progress. Subservience and unquestioning obedience signified weakness and a lack of masculinity. It placed a premium, instead, on occupational skill, enterprise and initiative. The man who was respected, powerful and influential was the one who was sufficiently self-motivated to work hard and to successfully compete with and challenge the power and wealth of his superiors. His success was basically self-made rather than attained through climbing the socioeconomic and political apron strings of his superiors. Occupational achievement in pursuit of one's interest was the primary basis for positive social evaluation, the most highly esteemed and reawarded personal quality.[36]

36. On the Ibo society refer to: C. K. Meek, *Law and Authority in a Nigerian Tribe* (London: Oxford University Press, 1937); M. M. Green, *Ibo Village*

The Yoruba authority structure tended to strike a balance between the opposite extremes represented by the Hausa-Fulani and
Igbo systems. It was hierarchical in form but not authoritarian in
content. Command did not flow down from the king to the
ranks of obedient officials. On the contrary, power was widely
dispersed among partly self-governing units. There was relatively
little concentration of power at the centre. However, the Yoruba
Oba was a divine king whose prestige and ritual status far exceeded
his political power. In fact, as a result of this divinity, he rarely
ventured outside his palace. In spite of this religious aura which
surrounded him, one or more councils of state, consisting of
hereditary chiefs and representatives of major territorial groups in
the kingdom, were the main decision-making organs. While the
Hausa emir could only be deposed by his overlord, the Sultan
of Sokoto, the Yoruba Oba could be deposed and ordered to
commit suicide by his council. The latter then appointed a
successor from a large pool of members of several royal lineages
who could inherit the throne. Obedience to him was not total and
loyalty was not unquestioning.

Yoruba kingship operated in a social structure containing
strong independent units characterised by lineage, territory, and
associational ties based on such criteria as age, religion, and
occupation. Most commonly, each of these groups selected its
leader as a counterweight to the authority of the Oba. An ascriptive ranking of groups in the society existed. At the top were the
several royal lineages which could inherit the throne. They were
followed by the non-royal lineages capable of taking and inherit-
ing chieftaincy titles, then by commoners whose lineages had no
hereditary claims to title. Among the commoners there were hereditary craft occupations of unequal status. Finally, the slaves
occupied the bottom rank in the hierarchy.[37]

Affairs (London: Sidgwick and Jackson, 1948); Simon Ottenberg, "*Ibo
Receptivity to Change.*" in W. R. Bascom and M. J. Herskovits, eds., *Continuity
and Change in African Cultures* (Chicago: University of Chicago Press, 1958);
Daryll Forde and G. I. Jones, *The Ibo and Ibibio-speaking Peoples of South
Eastern Nigeria* (London: International African Institute, 1950).

37. On slavery in Yoruba society see: P. C. Lloyd, "*The Yoruba of Nigeria*," in
J. L. Gibbs, *Peoples of Africa, op. cit.*; W. B. Schwab, "Kinship and Lineage
Among the Yoruba," *Africa*, Vol. XXV, No. 2 (1955), pp. 352–374; Daryll
Forde, *The Yoruba-Speaking Peoples of Western Nigeria* (London: International
African Institute, 1950).

Although the Oba was lavishly provided for economically, cheftaincy in Yorubaland did not involve fief holding. Access to personal wealth by the rulers was very limited; they could not use their political position to exploit the kingdom's resources for their personal enrichment. In fact, through trade and other activities, a commoner could make himself wealthier than a chief. Membership of the Ogboni title society and the opportunity to take chieftaincy title by the wealthy commoners accorded political power and prestige to men of proven occupational achievements rather than those with acceptable ascriptive credentials. Thus, the Yoruba Oba and officials had much less control over their subjects than the Hausa-Fulani emir. Hereditary previleges and duties lived side by side with opportunities for individual initiative and self-assertion. At the same time, an individual could attain high status and prestige by royal favours. For example, the Oba's favourite slaves and eunuchs could be raised by him to positions of greater importance and affluence than those of titled men in the society.[38]

Finally, and closely related to the differences in their authority structures, these three precolonial societies varied in their pattern of social behaviour. They required different personality characteristics. The Hausa pattern idealised disciplined behaviour guided by respect for the collective arrangement of the social order and with due regard for the sensibilities of all in the society. Emphasis was placed on winning the social and political favours and friendship of others, particularly those of higher social and political status. Anarchic and selfish aggressive behaviour, especially when it was dictated by the pursuit of wealth and other economic interests, was rejected. Faithfulness to and solidarity with others were cherished ideals as was inoffensiveness in social relations. An excessively independent spirit was frowned upon. The Hausaman who displayed energetic and industrious qualities was not necessarily admired. In fact, if these qualities were associated with the pursuit of personal wealth he would be prevented from winning the favour of the office holders who controlled access to the major social resources.

Clientage was an ideal manner of social advancement in the society as well as an inescapable aspect of social life. It involved an obedient followership of a man's patron in the latter's struggle for political office. In such a system the commoner without a pat-

38. *Ibid.*

ron was not merely a deviant but a rebel, since he admitted of no personal allegiance. Such individuals occupied a disadvantageous position in the society, and were disapproved of on moral grounds. The Hausa status system was politically oriented; political office led to wealth.

In contrast the Igbo pattern of social behaviour idealised egalitarian, selfish and anarchic pursuits, with due respect, of course, to age and tradition. It emphasised the independence of the will, leading to the amassing of wealth. The struggle for wealth was the central dominant feature of social life. It was characterised by fierce individualistic struggle. The gaining of friends was not as important as the acquisition of material resources. A certain boisterousness and aggressiveness was expected in social relations. The energetic and industrious person, who achieved wealth and, therefore, fame through his occupation, was admired. He was expected to be sufficiently motivated to work hard and well. It was morally permissible for him to manipulate others in his accumulation of wealth. Status mobility was essentially determined by economic performance clearly untied to political office.

Among the Yoruba, however, the prevalent pattern combined elements from both the Hausa and Igbo features. Social relations were determined by both political and economic motives. The system of social mobility contained two major strands. One conformed to the Igbo pattern of emphasis on occupational excellence and attainment which could be politically recognised. The other was identical with the Hausa mode of putting premium on political clientage in the royal court and in military adventures. Although hereditary restrictions were much greater among the Yoruba than the Igbo, it was much less than among the Hausa. Generally, the Yoruba enjoyed greater opportunities for social mobility than the Hausa. More specifically, change in social status through occupational performance was much greater than among the Hausa. Social incentives inclined towards both the authoritarian political virtues of subservience and obedience and the occupational ideals of diligence and individualism. But the Hausa was more authoritarian and the Igbo system more individualistic. The value of making friends and influencing people lived side by side with anarchic pursuit of economic objectives. It ought to be iterated that these value and behaviour patterns are ideal types. In reality, all societies are mixed types.

These objective differences in the precolonial socioeconomic and political life at the time of contact with colonialism by themselves do not constitute a necessary and sufficient condition for the emergence of ethnicity. In the light of the various precolonial acculturation and assimilatory processes among the groups, and the existence of differences within the groups, they do not even constitute a necessary prerequisite, their salience and significance being low. These differences assumed a tremendous significance only because of the colonial atmosphere of peripheral capitalism which divided groups, regions, institutions, structures, and individuals into fiercely competing units, and in which, by colonial design reinforced by petty bourgeois, commercial bourgeois and comprador bourgeois interests, emphasis was placed on differences rather than similarities in intergoup interaction. A myth of unbridgeable differences was propagated which the population internalised. The perceptual map of the individual was transformed into a system totally incongruent with the objective reality of the unity of the various Nigerian peoples. Under these circumstances, the emergence of ethnicity on the basis of precolonial sociocultural differences running along linguistic lines was inescapable.

The Resultant Ethnic Identification

This excessive and unrestrained manipulation of communal differences had two major consequences for the emergence of ethnicity. First, it made communal differences among groups the essential basis for group alignment by, secondly, focussing attention away from differences running along lines of relations of production, and class differences. With the society perceptually disaggregated into disparate ascriptively defined units, it was no longer possible to observe even minimally the mutual adaptation to one another's ways which characterised the relations among individuals in the Niger Delta of the precolonial times and in the various boundary areas of the various cultural-linguistic systems. Individuals began to relate to one another on the basis of the prediction, expectations, and definitions of the situation informed by the internalised myth of intercommunal differences. Self-fulfilling prophecy was the consequence. Under this frame of mind, individuals inevitably focussed attention on, and consequently, observed actions compatible with this internalised myth. This further reinforced the belief in the reality and significance of the diversities.

This emphasis on differences tended to paint a static picture of precolonial Nigerian societies. The sociocultural differences at the time of contact with colonialism are abstracted and more or less reified. The motion of society prior and subsequent to colonial contact is ignored and, with it, changes in these differences. For example, the obfuscating impact on the precolonial societies of the colonial exploitation of the farmers and workers of all Nigerian communal groups, is not apparent. This creates an attitude of permanent and mutual exclusiveness of individuals along communal lines. Because individuals were different they must continue to be so, irrespective of any changes which objectively tend to unite them. Under these circumstances, interactions across communal lines were selective and guarded. Mutually rewarding relationships were possible only with members of the same ascriptively defined group.

Similarly, class consciousness was stultified. As communal factors became increasingly salient in social life, class relationships became correspondingly insignificant. In fact, the Northerners refused to participate in the 1945 general strike essentially on communal grounds. They perceived it as the activity of Southerners which, in any case, had negative consequences for them. Later of course, labour actions received wisespread support. For example, the 1964 general strike was endorsed by most workers irrespective of communal origin. But such class actions were confined to sporadic and isolated cases of clearly intolerable provocations. They have not been generalized into most social, economic, and political relationships. Soon after the 1964 strike, workers voted along communal lines in the federal elections of that year and took active part in the intercommunal disturbances of 1966 which culminated in the civil war.

It is not correct to argue that the low level of class consciousness and, therefore, the tendency of ascriptive criteria to be the salient factor of identification, stemmed from the underdeveloped nature of the economy and the low level of social differentiation.[39] As is clear from the origin of the myth of communal differences, the subjective consciousness of class interests does not need to be congruent with the objective reality of a significant development of classes. It can be deliberately created and manipulated. However, it was not in the interests of the colonialists and their

39. I argued in this fashion in Okwudiba Nnoli, "Socioeconomic Insecurity and Ethnic Politics in Africa," *The African Review*, Vol. IV, No. 1 (1974), pp. 1–23.

Nigerian heirs to sponsor class consciousness. The most dangerous form of consciousness for colonial and neocolonial exploitation and oppression is that which runs along lines of relations of
production. Such consciousness leads logically to a revolutionary
attack against the ownership of the means of production, the
basis of colonial and neocolonial domination. Its inevitable end
product is a scientific socialist transformation of the peripheral
capitalist society foisted by imperialism. But such a transformation is anathema to the chief priests of imperialism and their
local lackeys. Hence, it was in the interest of the exploiting classes
to discourage the emergence of class consciousness. Objectively
the sponsorship of, and emphasis on, communal differences
served this function.

Under these circumstances, alliances, necessitated by individual
insecurity arising from divisive socioeconomic competition in the
colonial urban setting, could not take class lines. Alliance theory
suggests that a successful alliance tends to emerge when the partners share identical or complementary concrete interests within
a wider community of shared interests, ideology, values, ethics,
norms, and symbols. In the colonial urban enclaves, the existence
of identical or complementary interests among prospective
individual alliance members was always out of the question.
It is clear that inter-individual socioeconomic competition was
a pervasive feature of these enclaves. In fact, it was the central
motive for the alliance. As Frantz Alexander has correctly pointed
out, the resulting alignment is characterised by the psychological
paradox reflected in Sumner' s concept of "antagonistic cooperation."[40] Ingroup members in urban Africa are still hostile to
each other; they have not abandoned their individual interest and
the corresponding hostile aggression toward each other. They
have only renounced a part of their hostile impulses directed
against each other probably primarily out of utilitarian motives
because life in the group increases security. However, cohesive
group ties are permanently countered in colonial, post-colonial
and, in general, capitalist societies by disruptive forces of antagonism. Everyone remains nearer to himself; the identification of
the group members with each other is only a partial one. Egoistic
interests remain the most powerful motives and are only somewhat mitigated by group solidarity.

40. Frantz Alexander, "Discussion of 'Hostility and Fear in Social Life'", in
Social Forces, Vol. XVII, No. 1 (October 1938), p. 27.

Therefore, the more significant basis for alignment in the colonial and post-colonial enclaves is the community of shared interests. This community was manipulated to run along communal lines by the continual emphasis on the real and assumed differences among the various communal groups in the country. It is within this context that perceived dissimilarity along linguistic and sociocultural lines impeded intercommunal alignment. Instead they encouraged communal associations and gave the various emergent communal alliances cohesion against their neighbours. Ethnicity was the consequence. The new ethnic group was a unique creature of the urban setting. Its members usually had not met each other prior to their residence in the city. They were held together solely by the real and assumed linguistic and sociocultural similarity, as well as by the need to overcome urban insecurity. The internal cohesion of these groups, in turn, prevented them from merging with others, but rather encouraged them to retain their own identities.

The individual's subjective perception of communal differences made him exclude members of different communal groups as allience partners. There was neither any concrete identical or complementary interests binding him to others nor any shared community of expectations, orientations and attitudes to life. Only a mutual feeling of exclusiveness united them. This feeling was continually reinforced. In this way, when individuals are conscious solely of differences along communal lines they form groups whose interests become interwined with ethnic identity and both are reinforced. This was the basis of the impact of social distance on the emergence of ethnicity in Nigeria.

Chapter 5

THE POLITICISATION OF ETHNICITY

The Role of Factionalism within the Privileged Classes

As the communal associations proliferated and urban dwellers increasingly flocked to them, intraclass and inter-individual socio-economic competition began to be translated into competition among communal unions. The pervasive scarcity and inequality of the peripheral capitalist society fully challenged and stretched the resources and functions of these unions. The apparent withdrawal of the government from the realm of employment and social welfare amenities also heightened the importance and significance of these associations for the individual. They became the only institutions within which he could meaningfully expect to solve some of his most pressing problems. Socioeconomic action shifted from the individual to the group. At the same time, the rapid extension of the activities of the unions contributed to their greater cohesion and the greater identification of the individual with them. Inevitably, therefore, intergroup dynamics intruded into the ethnic scene.

With the increasingly greater salience of the union than the colonial state for the satisfaction of the socioeconomic needs of the individual, the member gave these unions his loyalty at the expense of the state. This trasfer of loyalty was reinforced by the rewards accruing to him from the activities of the communal association. A sense of solidarity in group membership, together with pride in the successes of the union, also increased his identification with it. As the associations competed with one another, the members enjoyed a sense of shared history and experience which, among other things, deepened their sense of belonging to, and their identification with the ingroup. They learned to fight their socioeconomic battles together. The outgroups became more clearly defined and "appropriate" negative stereotypes were imputed to them. Perceived appropriate norms and behaviour patterns to govern relations with outgroup members began to emerge in all spheres of life, particularly housing and marriages. Thus, a certain inward orientation characterised the ethnic group. Further conflicts arising from interethnic competition strengthened this orientation. These conflicts also increased the social distance separating the various ethnic groups. As a result, the loyalty of the members to the group and the group's cohesion increased. With the increasing social distance, it was becoming clearly probable that groups would not attempt to satisfy the needs of outgroup members. In fact, the logical tendency would be to exclude them from sharing in the social and economic resources of the society. Since the individual's welfare could not be adequately satisfied unless the ingroup was triumphant in interethnic competition, the cohesion of groups was easy to achieve. Conflicts among communal groups within the ethnic ingroup were never allowed to adversely affect the ability of the ingroup to compete successfully with the other groups. Inward orientation and cohesion of the group were also encouraged by the existence of a bureaucratic machinery of sorts which organised the activities of the ethnic unions. The various activities which marked Igbo Day celebrations outside Igboland reflect such integrative endeavours. By combining the loyalty of its members with ingroup cohesion the ethnic group mustered enough power to successfully challenge any superethnic institution.

This growing power of the ethnic groups and its negative consequences for the development of a common national consciousness were recognised by a few nationalist leaders and organisations of the time. In 1945, Eyo Ita, sensing the negative trend that was emerging as a result of the growing power of these parochial associations warned that "the greatest need of Nigerians today is to become a community ... to evolve a national selfhood."[1] He urged Nigerians to "seek coordination among them [ethnic unions] in a way that will help to build a strong national consciousness."[2] In its charter published in 1938, the Nigerian Youth Movement (NYM), the first nationalist movement in the country founded in 1936, called for the unification of the ethnic groups through the search for a common ideal.[3] As a part of its efforts to achieve this national unity, the movement organised branches in key centres throughout the country. In 1938, new branches were opened at Ibadan, Ijebu Ode, Warri, and Benin in the West, Aba,

---

1. *West African Pilot*, Lagos, 2 June 1945, p. 1.
2. Quoted in J. S. Coleman, *Nigeria: Background to Nationalism* (Berkeley and Los Angeles, California: University of California Press, 1958), p. 219.
3. *Ibid.*, p. 224.

Enugu, Port Harcourt and Calabar in the East, Jos, Kaduna, Zaria and Kano in the North. By the end of 1938 the NYM claimed to have more than 10,000 members and nearly 20 provincial branches in all parts of Nigeria.[4]

In spite of its good intentions, however, the NYM could not escape the inevitable consequences of the inexorable power of ethnic clanishness generated by the activities of the ethnic unions and their fundamental underlying basis, the objectively determined factional competition among the emerging petty bourgeoisie and comprador bourgeoisie. It became the first major political casualty of interethnic hostility and strife. In June 1938, Ernest Ikoli, a founder member and an active leader of the NYM, became the publisher and editor of the Lagos-based *Daily Service* which claimed to be the organ of the NYM.

Meanwhile, Nnamdi Azikiwe, another leader of the organisation, owned other newspapers. One of them the *West African Pilot* had consistently and unequivocally championed the cause of the NYM. As a result of the journalistic skills of Ikoli, the *Daily Service* became a very keen competitor of the journalistic enterprises of the financially-limited Azikiwe. Both papers served the same small reading public. Azikiwe's enthusiasm for the NYM immediately began to wane. A split occurred within the movement which ushered in ethnic politics in Nigeria. Azikiwe soon resigned from the executive committee of the organisation. Later, pleading preoccupation with business activities, he resigned his membership of the movement as well. Although he later retracted the latter resignation he ceased to be an effective member of the organisation.

This conflict of economic and professional interest helped to set the stage for events which propelled the country irretrievably into the politicisation of ethnicity. In February 1941 Dr. K. A. Abayomi, a former President of the NYM, resigned his seat on the Governor's Executive Council. A struggle for succession ensued within the movement between Ernest Ikoli, the then President, and Samuel Akinsanya, the Vice-President. Both were founding members of the organisation. Ikoli eventually emerged successful. His business enemy, Azikiwe, was not happy, and neither was the defeated Akinsanya. Both, along with their respective Igbo and Ijebu-Yoruba supporters, rationalised their defeat as a manifestation of ethnic prejudice against Ijebu and Igbo peoples. But

4. *Ibid.*, p. 225.

Ikoli was an Ijaw, not a non-Ijebu Yoruba and he was supported by a prominent Ijebu-Yoruba, Obafemi Awolowo. Adamantly, Azikiwe and Akinsanya, along with their supporters, withdrew from the movement. A press war ensued between the *Daily Service* and the *West African Pilot* in which appeals to ethnic sentiments and arguments were dominant. Azikiwe and the Igbo never rejoined the NYM which, after 1941, was composed mainly of the Yoruba. The Southern Nigerian political scene has ever since been dominated by the cleavage between these two communal groups.

This fateful Ikoli-Akinsanya political conflict is quite illuminating of the social basis of politics in Nigeria in general and ethnic politics in particular, the major class interests which dominate the political struggle and underly ethnic politics. It shows that although many interests are involved in the political process, it is only certain of them which dictate the direction and nature of political developments. In this case, it is interesting that the split in the NYM was not associated in anyway with the conflicting interests of farmers or members of the working class. Rather it involved the ownership and monopoly of the nationalist press.

Nationalism services the interests of all strata in the society but it services some interests more than others. The development of nationalism, nationalist movement, and political parties depends first and foremost on the dynamics of the interests of their leaders and only peripherally, if at all, on those of the followers. The character of a movement is, therefore, determined by the interests of its leadership. Finally, ethnic politics arose from the rationalisation of the failure of a faction of the leadership to achieve its economic interests. The failure of Azikiwe to prevent the establishment of a rival journalistic enterprise lay behind the Ikoli-Akinsanya affair and its political consequences. The interests of factions of the emerging privileged classes became generalised and mystified as the interest of the communal group and indeed that of the ethnic group at large.

Thus, politics, during the era of the nationalist struggle for independence from colonialism, was dominated by the conflict arising from the assertion of the interests of the Nigerian petty bourgeoisie and comprador bourgeoisie against the dominance of the interests of the financial oligarchies of Britain in particular and Europe in general. Benefits accruing to the other local classes were merely incidental to this conflict. The leadership of the nationalist struggle was dominated by the emerging petty bourgeoisie and comprador bourgeoisie reared in the colonial system of production with its accompanying educational programme, and playing a role in the production process that was totally dependent on the activities of the British and other European financial oligarchies.

A careful examination of the aims and election manifestoes of the nationalist parties shows their overwhelming emphasis on relations of distribution (the historical area of emphasis of these two classes) and the superstructure of society, such as the principles of social interaction and the political process, rather than on the infrastructure, the relations of production. Uppermost in the mind of the nationalist leaders was the battle against the racism of colonial ideology. They dug into the corpus of bourgeois writings to pick up ideas such as liberty, equality and fraternity, and opposed these values to the racism, racial inequality, the colour bar, and racial political domination characteristic of colonialism. As in Europe at the time of the bourgeois revolutions, these leaders confined these concepts to the level of abstraction. However, in Europe before the French revolution of 1789 when these values were popularised by the capitalists, the capitalist class had already gained dominance over the local economy and was using these principles to enable it to dominate the political process as well. Hence, its emphasis was on the superstructure and its abstract principles.

No equivalent development had taken place in Nigeria. Nevertheless, this fight against racism had an objective basis. The nationalist leaders and members of their classes were the ones most directly affected by racial discrimination, in terms of salaries, opportunities for contract work, and business in the professions and various other fields of their direct involvement. Their struggle was, however, progressive in that it was waged against the injustice and domination of colonialism, particularly those arising from its racist ideology. The veteran father of Nigerian politics, Herbert Macaulay, became politically pre-eminent as a result of his campaigns against the compulsory acquisition of lands at Apapa by the colonial government in 1921, as well as his pursuit of the interest of the Lagos Market Women's Guild.

The origin of the Nigerian Youth Movement (NYM) lay in the fight against a colonial scheme to increase the number of Nigerian technical and medical assistants through vocational education of a sub-professional quality. The NYM emerged to propagate ideas on educational policy contrary to what many educated Nigerians of the time correctly interpreted as a racist educational policy of educating Africans along inferior lines, and to demand government scholarship to finance the education of Nigerians in the United Kingdom. This political organisation and its successors placed an emphasis on the freedom of Nigerians to control the realms of political and economic power. Hence, Africanisation and later Nigerianisation occupied an important position in their programmes of activities. In the field of administration the NYM was represented by the effort to abolish the differential salary structures for Europeans and Africans, and the demand for Africans to be represented in the top positions in the military, police, judiciary and civil service. Politically, the call was for Nigerians to hold cabinet, ministerial, and parliamentary positions. In the field of economics, efforts were geared towards breaking European monopolies to provide opportunities for local traders, contractors, transporters and others who wished to control the market of their nation and to dominate its economic positions.

The class character and interests of the nationalist parties were most glaringly reflected in their activities when Nigerians assumed political positions of authority. They immediately embarked on the use of the political machinery to pursue their class interests of amassing wealth and privileges against the interest of the majority of the country, the workers and peasants. Oblivious of the conditions of their people and the inherent injustice of the situation they quickly moved into the white salary scales and GRA residential areas to break racist monopoly of these privileges. Thus, the Nigerian leaders were more desirous of imbibing the life style and privileges of colonialism than in abolishing its injustice and oppression of the Nigerian masses. Their interest was petty bourgeois in nature, focussed on relations of distribution. They were not interested in the creative production that characterised the metropolitan bourgeoisie, only in the perquisites of the colonial political stratum.

Both the Foster-Sutton Tribunal and the Coker Commission of Inquiry exposed the selfish and class interests of the nationalist leaders.[5] They used the public as a source of financial capital for their economic interests and those of the aspiring local commer-

5. *Report of the Tribunal Appointed to Inquire into Allegations Reflecting on the Official Conduct of the Premier of, and Certain Persons Holding Ministerial and Other Public Offices in the Eastern Region of Nigeria, Cmnd. 51,* (London: HMSO, 1957). *Report of Coker Commission of Inquiry Into the Affairs of Certain Statutory Corporations in Western Nigeria* 4 Vols. (Lagos: Federal Ministry of Information, 1962).

cial and industrial classes. The Foster-Sutton Tribunal of Inquiry into the affairs of the African Continental Bank (ACB) revealed how the family of a nationalist leader, Nnamdi Azikiwe, sustained a financial empire through the use of public funds.

According to the report of the inquiry, the colonial government had made it clear that unless the ACB could raise its liquidity from 8 to 30 per cent and inject fresh capital to restore solvency, it would not renew its licence. The bank was in a severe financial crisis. If it were to collapse, the Zik Group Companies, which depended on its huge overdrafts, would, as a whole, have collapsed also and Azikiwe would have been ruined financially.

In response, Azikiwe, through the Eastern House of Assembly which he led, created the Eastern Region Finance Corporation. In 1955, ₦4 million of public funds, raised by the Eastern Region Marketing Board from the sweat of the peasants, was paid to the Finance Corporation to invest part of it in buying shares in the ACB. ₦1,600,000 was so invested, thereby restoring the bank's solvency, salvaging the Zik Group Companies and providing Azikiwe and his family dividends which otherwise would not have been forthcoming.[6] This highly dubious class transaction was rationalised as intended to break foreign banking monopoly in the country and liberalise credit facilities to Nigerians. Of course, such credits were not intended for the workers and peasants but the emerging petty bourgeoisie and comprador bourgeoisie. In reality, however, it was motivated by the "shoddy way and manner the Manager of the Marina Branch of the Bank of British West Africa limited"[7] treated Azikiwe when the latter approached him in October 1943 for a loan to improve his journalistic enterprise, which made Azikiwe determined to be a banker as well.[8]

Similarly, the Coker Commission of Inquiry in Western Nigeria in 1962, highlighted this mingling of politics and personal and class economic interests in the activities of the nationalist movements. It revealed that the publicly owned National Investment and Properties Company Ltd. (NIPC) was controlled by members of the nationalist party, the Action Group (AG). The directors of the NIPC were party leaders. They "loaned" some of the public funds pumped into the company to the party and its rich industrialist and commercialist supporters in the region. The directors

6. *Ibid.*
7. Richard Sklar, *Nigerian Political Parties* (Princeton; New Jersey: Princeton University Press, 1963), pp. 167–168, footnote 53.
8. *Ibid.*

of the company made loans to themselves through other companies of which they were directors or owners. The major beneficiaries of these loans were professionals, chiefs, merchants, industrialists, and contractors who supported the nationalist party. In this way, the National Bank of Nigeria and the NIPC both controlled by the party were used by the new political class in the region to accumulate capital.[9]

What is even more despicable is that the funds thus squandered by the petty bourgeoisie and the comprador bourgeoisie were generated by the peasantry. These funds came from the Commodity Marketing Boards set up at the end of the second World War to purchase cocoa, palm produce, groundnuts, and cotton from producers at fixed prices for sale abroad. They paid the peasants subsistence wages both during lean and bumper years and kept the surplus for the purposes of agricultural development and research.

In 1954, the new Regional Marketing Boards, which replaced the commodity boards, were authorised to invest the huge surpluses they had exploited from the peasants over the years, not in agriculture alone, but in development and research generally. This was a licence secured by the emerging privileged local classes for the looting of the peasants' money. It provided the funds which went to the rescue of the ACB and which the NIPC shared out to the political leaders in Western Nigeria. The peasant creators of the wealth suffered in silence. Credit liberalisation for Africans, promotion of economic opportunities for Nigerians, and the encouragement of Nigerian businesses to them remained hollow-sounding and incomprehensible cliches. They were not part of the socioeconomic calculus of the dominant local classes. In fact, in his address to the University of Nigeria during the launching of its Endowment Fund in 1976, Nnamdi Azikiwe saw fit to thank "humble palm oil" rather than the peasants for the resources that built that University.[10]

Nigeria's politicians and bureaucrats became the nation's new men of wealth, having acquired their riches through holding public office. In this practice, they allied with the local businessmen, contractors, transporters, industrialists, commercialists and professionals who, under conditions of peripheral capitalism,

9. *Report of the Coker Commission of Inquiry, op. cit.*
10. Nnamdi Azikiwe, "The Reorientation of Nigerian Ideology" (Endowment Fund speech), *The Sunday Observer*, December 19, 1976, p. 2.

constituted the petty bourgeoisie and comprador bourgeoisie. These classes were aware of the importance of wealth as a means of acquiring power in the capitalist world, the reciprocal relationship between political power and wealth. It is no wonder that the politicians and bureaucrats of the civil regime are today among the wealthiest members of the society, and, indeed, none of them is not a man of substance today. The political parties wanted to control the banking system in order to consolidate their political power and build up their economic power. The party in power used the bank to build up its rich potentates. State-controlled banks such as the ACB and the National Bank of Nigeria served as instruments for advancing credits to these classes to build their economic power. Import and export licences monopolised by foreign firms were liberalised to encourage these classes to venture into fields formerly beyond their reach. This was the true meaning of their nationalist struggle for independence.

Thus, the search for petty bourgeois and comprador bourgeois fortunes dominated the nationalist struggle for independence. Its inevitable consequences were the regionalisation of politics and the politicisation of ethnicity. Objectively, the petty bourgeoisie and the comprador bourgeoisie of Nigeria were regionalised, and one major ethnic group dominated each region demographically. As has been indicated earlier, the colonial economy was disjointed and fragmented into three major enclaves corresponding roughly to the Northern, Western and Eastern regions.

Consequently, the pattern of migration in Nigeria was quite different from that in the rest of West Africa. In the colonial economy of much of the rest of West Africa disarticulation and disjointedness arbitrarily created complementary interests between the interior and the coast. Most of the colonial economic activities were located along the coast, while the population predominated in the interior. Therefore, the people of the interior needed the jobs and other activities at the coast to eke out a living in the colonial situation, and the coast needed the working population of the interior to help to supplement its sparse manpower. Hence, there has been such a migration from the interior to the coast that the population ratio of the interior and the coast shifted from $\frac{2}{3}$ and $\frac{1}{3}$ in 1920 to $\frac{1}{2}$ and $\frac{1}{2}$ in 1970 respectively, representing a reduced growth rate of the interior of 0.4 per cent a year and an increased growth rate of the coast of 0.5 per cent per year.[11] No

11. Samir Amin, *Modern Migration in Western Africa* (London: Oxford University Press, 1974), p. 73.

148

such imbalance exists as a result of migrations within Nigeria. The flow of migration in Nigeria was also much weaker than in the rest of West Africa. For example, in 1952, Nigerian provinces had a non-original population of 5 per cent compared with 20 per cent for the rest of West Africa.[12]

Under these circumstances the relatively national outlook and consciousness of the petty bourgeoisie and comprador bourgeoisie in the other parts of West Africa were absent in Nigeria. The alliances between the traditional rulers, bureaucratic officials, petty bourgeoisie and comprador bourgeoisie from different parts of the country which could be observed elsewhere, was hardly viable or rewarding in Nigeria. In Nigeria, each section of these classes was quagmired in economic activities of its regional enclave. The members of each region exploited the local advantages accruing in their own regions from the production of palm oil, groundnut, cocoa, and other cash crops, the transportation of these crops to the metropole, the sale of manufactured goods from the metropole, white collar jobs in the foreign firms and colonial bureaucracies, and petty contract work and trading. In the process, they acquired a regional economic outlook which limited their horizon, hampered their venturing out to the other regions economically, and encouraged them to view the regional economy as their own preserve or empire, their sphere of influence, an undisputed area of their economic supremacy. This parochial attitude was reinforced by the divide and rule policy of the colonial power, its propaganda on behalf of ethnic differences and exclusiveness, its encouragement of the fear of ethnic domination by exploiting the regional socio-economic imbalances created by its economic activities, and its choice of administrative units and political constituencies which ran along regional geographical lines.

The petty bourgeoisie and comprador bourgeoisie of each region perceived their needs and interests as unconnected with those of their counterparts in the other regions. They felt that once their needs, wants, and interests were satisfied, the rest of the country could suffer. Unfortunately they could get away with this attitude. Since the various regions were economically self-contained units, hunger, poverty, disease, dissatisfaction, and disgruntledness in any of them would hardly have serious repercussions in the others and the country as a whole. For example, neither the boom nor the later slump in the price of cocoa pro-

12. *Ibid.* pp. 73–74.

duced in the West had any noticeable economic impact in the other two regions, the North and East. Lacking in any shared activities and common cause, the regional sections of these classes were devoid of any feeling of class solidarity and national class consciousness. They perceived one another as significant essentially as objects of divisive competition and conflict rather than those of peaceful competition and cooperation. Any attempts by members of the same class from one region to carry on economic activities in another region were resented by the indigenous members of the same class in the latter region. Mutual exclusionism prevailed.

Instead, solidarity was achieved among the various noncommunal factions of these classes within each region. These factions included a tradition-oriented section which wielded economic power and social influence as a result of control over certain traditional activities. This section's interests contradicted those of the section dominated by men whose economic power and social prestige depended on the new colonial activities. Among this section there was distinction between those who manned the bureaucratic apparatus of state and whose interests diverged from those who were outside the employ of the state. Among the latter there was the difference between those who served as middlemen or go-between in the service of foreign companies and the independent entrepreneurs. Regionalism submerged the contradictions among these various factions of classes within the same region, rendering the incipient conflicts among them secondary and insignificant. Therefore, it was not valuable for political alignments within a region to emerge on the basis of these differences.

The isolated and autonomous nature of the regional enclaves rendered alliances of these factions across the country hardly viable or rewarding. For example, in a situation of competing regional bureaucracies, the economic interests of the bureaucratic factions of the various regions did not necessarily coincide. Under these circumstances, a national political party of that faction would be pointless. Similarly, national alliances of the other factions were unrealistic. If these intraclass differences had formed the basis of political alignments, the resultant political parties would have found it difficult to enunciate an intelligible and easily identifiable basis for their necessary mobilisation of the masses. National politics hinged on the single issue of wresting power from foreign hands. On this question there was little that distinguished these various factions. In this struggle none was oriented toward the relations of production.

Initially, some nationalist political parties emerged in Nigeria and built up a truly nationalist movement, the regionalisation of the petty bourgeoisie and comprador bourgeoisie notwithstanding. Mention has already been made of the national orientation and nationwide activities of the National Youth Movement between its inception in 1936 and the Ikoli-Akinsanya episode of 1941. Both the NYM and the National Council of Nigeria and the Cameroons (NCNC) were able to mobilise a considerable national following by exposing the exploitation, racism, and injustices of colonial rule. In fact, in 1945, following Azikiwe's story of a plot by the colonialists to assassinate him, the leader of the NCNC became a national hero throughout most of the country including many previously inarticulate linguistic groups such as the Cameroonians, Nupe, Tiv, Igbirra, Birom and Idoma, indeed most of the Middle Belt, and a growing number of Hausa, Fulani and Kanuri.[13] Soon, however, the contradictions among the regional factions of the petty bourgeoisie and comprador bourgeoisie asserted themselves.

It was difficult for any of these factions to effectively challenge the existing leadership of the nationalist movement without appealing for support along regional and ethnic lines. No such faction could form a political party on the same platform of popular nationalist demands such as independence, equality, more and better social amenities and, at the same time, justify its separate existence. On the other hand, a new political party could not base its existence on a policy of mere oppositionism to the existing party. It must adopt the same popular nationalist programmes but still justify its separate existence on the basis of some important and visible indicator. Regionalism and ethnicity were the most convenient and appealing of such criteria.

The conditions were ideal for the use of regionalism and ethnicity for establishing a political base. Prior to the formation of the nationalist political parties, ethnic consciousness was already well developed. In fact, at its inauguration on 26 August 1944, the NCNC provided for organisational membership. Among the inaugural members were 2 trade unions, 2 political parties, 4 literary societies, 8 professional associations, 11 social clubs and 101

13. J. S, Coleman, *op. cit.*, p. 290.

ethnic unions.[14] It had earlier been demonstrated that ethnicity and ethnic loyalty serviced the interests of the colonial urban dwellers. Therefore, the urban population and, through it, the rural communities were favourably predisposed to appeals based on ethnicity. The low level of industrialisation and the rudimentary development of occupational and other non-communal associations also made ethnic appeals very likely to succeed politically. In addition, the political constituencies were geographical in nature and ethnically homogenous. Therefore, to win the support of an ethnic group was to win a political constituency. Since in Nigeria, the ethnic group homelands were quite large geographically and demographically, a strong political base was guaranteed.

Under the condition of congruence between the interests of the political parties and the ethnic associations[15] increased political

14. *Ibid.*, pp. 264–265.
15. In terms of class interests, the leaderships of the nationalist political parties and the ethnic associations largely coincided. The inaugural officers of the Egbe Omo Oduduwa and their professions were as follows: President, Sir Adeyemo Alakija (lawyer); Vice Presidents: Yekini Ojikutu (businessman), S. A. Akinfenwa (businessman), I. O. Ransome-Kuti (educator), Alhaji Shoye (businessman), Dure Adefarakan (businessman), Chief Otun Akinyede (businessman), S. O. Gbadamosi (businessman), Dr. Akinola Maja (medical doctor and banker); Treasurer Dr. K. A. Abayomi (medical doctor); General Secretary, Obafemi Awolowo (lawyer) Legal Advisers: Bode Thomas (lawyer), and H. O Davis (lawyer). This list coincides with that of the inaugural officers of the Action Group (AG): President, Obafemi Awolowo (lawyer); Vice Presidents; Gaius Obaseke (businessman), Chief W. E. Mowarin (businessman), Chief Arthur Prest (lawyer), M. A. Ajasin (College Principal); General Secretary, Bode Thomas (lawyer); Assistant Secretaries, S. O. Shonibare (businessman), Anthony Enahoro (businessman and publisher); Treasurer, S. O. Ighodaro (lawyer); Publicity and Propaganda Secretary, M. A. Ogun (businessman); Administrative Secretary, S. T. Oredein (trade unionist); Legal Advisers, S. L. Akintola (lawyer), and M. E. R. Okorodudu.

The combination of political party post and post in the ethnic association is fully reflected in the Provisional Committee of the Ibo State Union elected in December 1948 and its relation to the National Council of Nigeria and the Gameroons (NCNC). President, Nnamdi Azikiwe (president of the NCNC); Deputy President, A. C. Nwapa (later NCNC Central Minister of Commerce); First Vice President, R. A. Njoku (later NCNC Federal Minister); Second Vice President, M. O. Ajegbo (later NCNC Attorney-General of Eastern Region); Third Vice President, H. U. Kaine (later a Federal Judge); Principal Secretary, J. A. Wachukwu (later NCNC Chief whip and secretary of NCNC Parliamentary Parties, Speaker of the Federal

activity led to the politicisation of ethnicity. The struggle for political power became interpreted in ethnic terms. It became a struggle for the hegemony of the various regional factions of the petty bourgeoisie and comprador bourgeoisie, first in the regional enclave, and then in the country as a whole. As the nationalist movement gathered momentum, contradictions within these classes became more manifest and their various communal factions focussed on creating a political base by appealing to ethnicity. This pattern was intensified with the introduction and expansion of elective politics of the Western parliamentary democratic type. Under this sytem where candidates for political office are not chosen for their commitment to the nation but can promise all manner of socioeconomic goods and services to their ethnically-conscious constituents because electoral constituencies are defined along spatial lines rather than lines of specialisation of functions, the politicisation of ethnicity is inevitable. Michael Parenti has observed that, in such systems, ethnically salient candidates tend to emerge and persist.[16] As ethnic consciousness thus increases in scope and intensity, the socioeconomic and political atmosphere becomes charged with tension. Those ethnic groups hitherto dormant in the socioeconomic competition are galvanised into action. This further separates the society in terms of identity and loyalty.

Of course, in their intraclass struggles, the hegemonic regional factions of these privileged classes paid lip services to the desirability of national unity, and condemned ethnic particularism. For all intents and purposes these declarations were not taken seriously and were never intended to be. The same people who

House of Representatives and Federal Minister); Permanent Undersecretary, B. O. N. Eluwa (later an executive with the Nigerian Broadcasting Corporation); Treasurer, M. I. O. Onwuka; Political Adviser, Nwafor Orizu (later NCNC nominee of the Eastern House of Chiefs and Federal Senator); Economic Adviser, Mbonu Ojike (later NCNC Minister in the Eastern Region and Second Vice President of the NCNC); Cultural Adviser, K. O. Mbadiwe (later Second Vice President of the NCNC and a Federal Minister); Medical Adviser, Francis Akanu Ibiam (later NCNC nominated Governor of Eastern Region) and Educational Adviser, E. I. Oli (later NCNC Minister of the Eastern Regional Government). See Richard Sklar, *Nigerian Political Parties* (Princeton, N.J.: Princeton University Press, 1963), pp. 68, footnote 78; 70, footnote 86, 106, footnote 43; and 108–110.

16. Michael Parenti, "Ethnic Politics and the Persistence of Ethnic Identification," *American Political Science Review*, Vol. LXI No. 4 (1967), pp. 717–726.

inveighed against ethnicity and ethnic identity simultaneously institutionalised them by making them a basis for economic participation within the regional enclaves and, to a lesser extent, for political participation at both the regional and national levels. Obviously, ethnicity served the objective interests of these privileged classes in important ways. In any case, ethnicity is one of the major antidotes against the development of class consciousness. It creates vertical links across classes and helps the political system of each regional enclave to maintain a level of integration quite out of proportion to objective class differences within the region.[17]

This politicisation of ethnicity and regionalisation of politics was encouraged by the colonialists. The Richard's Constitution of 1946 led to a political and budgetary regionalisation of the country. Designed in part to preserve the authoritarian system of indirect rule, it established a legislature in each of the three regions, the North, East and West, based on elections from the undemocratic native administrations. The regional legislatures, in turn, sent representatives to a central legislature.[18] The constitution was premised on the assumption that regional political integration was a necessary first step toward national political integration. Thereafter, the colonial administration made every effort to encourage regional thinking. The MacPherson Constitution of 1951 not only preserved the regions but increased their powers.

The Action Group (AG) was born in March 1951 to exploit this new constitutional development. Although in 1947, Obafemi Awolowo, its leader, had advocated ethnic constitutional regions, it was not until 1951 that he formed the political party to implement this idea. The new party was founded on the assumption that, under the prevailing conditions in the country, the only certain avenue to political power was through a regional political party. It was politically motivated by the desire of the anti-Azikiwe faction of the Nigerian petty bourgeoisie and comprador bourgeoisie, essentially Yoruba-speaking, to frustrate an NCNC government led by Azikiwe from coming into power in the

17. Claude Ake, "Explanatory Notes on the Political Economy of Africa," (Mimeograph copy) (Tanzania: University of Dar es Salaam, 1975), pp. 16–17.
18. Sir Bernard Bourdillion, "Nigeria's New Constitution," *United Empire*, Vol. XXXVII, No. 2 (March–April 1946), pp. 76–80.

Western Region. Accordingly, the main theme in the party's electoral campaign was common opposition to Azikiwe, together with the threat of Igbo domination under a unitary constitutional system. It was even suggested that a victory of the NCNC in the West would mean the use of that region's vast cocoa wealth to develop the "poor naked savages" of the Eastern Region, Azikiwe's home region.

Such parochial ideas and sentiments attracted the following of a significant proportion of the Yoruba petty bourgeoisie and comprador bourgeoisie, notably those in the professions, the old Lagos Yoruba families smarting under the ruthless economic competition from Azikiwe's chain of enterprises, and the rich cocoa farmers and traders of Yorubaland. The ideas also attracted the support of Yoruba intellectuals opposed to the NCNC on grounds of principle, and Yoruba chiefs who were the patrons of the Pan Yoruba cultural organisation, the Egbe Omo Oduduwa of which Awolowo was the General-Secretary. The membership of non-Yoruba groups in the West such as Edo, Ishan and Itsekiri was sought for cosmetic purposes. The party relied on the influence wielded by the former groups over the Yoruba masses for its electoral support and therefore its political power.

Thus, the Action Group became the first party of the Nigerian petty bourgeoisie and comprador bourgeoisie to be inspired by, founded on, and nourished by ethnic chauvinism and regional parochialism. For the first time, a nationalist group, desirous of wresting the reigns of national government from the colonialists, explicitly associated itself with the destiny of one ethnic group in the country, considering itself as merely the political wing of that ethnic group's cultural association. It based its appeals for mass support explicitly and implicitly on ethnic sentiments, sensibilities, and interests. This negative development marked the culmination of the process of the politicisation of ethnicity in the country which began in 1941 with the Ikoli-Akinsanya dispute. It further marked the beginning of the escalation and spiraling of interethnic hostility among the Nigerian masses which culminated in the ethnic massacres of 1966 and the consequent civil war.

This ethnic and regional origin of the Action Group forced the NCNC to increasingly assume an ethnic and regional character. The major determining factor in this process was the election of 1951. The MacPherson Constitution did not provide for direct election into the federal legislature. Instead, central legislators and ministers were to be selected from among representatives elected to the regional legislatures. The AG had won the election to the Western Legislature. But Azikiwe, the NCNC leader, had been elected to that Legislature from one of the constituencies in Lagos, then an integral part of the West. The AG-controlled House was expected to elect two of the five NCNC Lagos representatives to the House of Representatives. The AG used its majority to prevent Azikiwe from being elected. The elected officials, Dr. Olorun-Nimbe and Prince Adeleke Adedoyin, refused to step down for their leader. Therefore, the National President of NCNC was confined to the Western Region as the Leader of Opposition much against his wishes.

His absence from the centre created a dichotomy between his leadership of the party and its leadership of the parliamentary process. He was unable to control the activities of the NCNC parliamentarians at the centre. This anomaly led to the Eastern Regional political crisis of 1952/1953 in which a few of the parliamentarians came out in open defiance of the party's directives. The parliamentary crisis was finally resolved in early 1953 by the dissolution of the Eastern House of Assembly. Thereafter, Azikiwe resigned from the Western House, contested and won a seat in the elections to the reconstituted Eastern Legislature, and became its leader of Government. By this last act the NCNC capitulated to the vastly growing forces of ethnic chauvinism and regionalism generated in the parliamentary political arena by the Action Group. The NCNC had always relied on the Igbo as the bulwark of its support. During the period 1944–1947, the Ibo Union, Lagos branch, was one of the most active member organisation of the party. The Ibo Federal Union often took the initiative in organising receptions for the NCNC delegation during its famous tour of the country in 1946. After 1953 the ties between the Igbo and the NCNC became much closer than ever before.

Although between 1943 and 1948 Azikiwe had advocated the creation of ethnic protectorates in a federal Nigeria, the NCNC later preached a unitary form of government. At its third annual convention in Kano in August 1951, the NCNC reversed its position on federalism in favour of a unitary arrangement.[19] This change was not motivated by the "recent divisionist tendencies in the country and to accelerate the attainment of our goal for a

19. National Council of Nigeria and the Cameroons, *Forward to Freedom and Progress* (Yaba: NCNC, 1951), p. 26.

united Nigeria"[20] as the NCNC propaganda indicated. Rather, after 1948, it had become clear to the party that it would not gain the electoral support of the bulk of the Yoruba and Hausa, the ethnic groups that dominated the West and the North respectively. But the party felt that it would likely gain the support of the ethnic groups in the Middle Belt, in the non-Yoruba areas of the West and in the East and the Cameroons. Only a unitary system promised the NCNC a chance of winning a national majority whereas regionalism contained the possibility of an anti-NCNC Yoruba control of the West, and an anti-NCNC and pro-British Hausa-Fulani control of the North.[21] Finally, it had to accept the political reality of a peripheral capitalist society, that parliamentary political power under conditions of intraclass political competition among the petty bourgeoisie and comprador bourgeoisie flows from the geographic homelands of ethnic groups. This development completed the regionalisation of Nigerian politics and the politicisation of ethnicity.

In the North in October 1951 a reactionary regional political party was formed, the Northern People's Congress. It was formed for Northerners, by Northerners, and for the pursuit of objectives limited to the North and the Northerners. Its emphasis was on the region rather than the ethnic group. Although the North is ethnically more heterogeneous than the South, the integrative bonds of Islam and the Fulani Empire gave a large section of it a common identity. In its mobilisation of the political support of the masses, the Congress formented and made an extensive use of the widespread fear in the North of being dominated by the educationally more advanced peoples of the South. Its "northernisation" policy of preferring applicants from the North and even outside the country to Southerners for posts in the public service of the North was an important instrument in this process of mobilisation.

At the time of the formation of the NPC its aristocratic Fulani leaders were avowedly antinationalistic and opposed to social and political reform. The North lacked a significant crop of nationalist-minded petty-bourgeoisie and comprador bourgeoisie. Operating under the system of indirect rule in which wealth carried prestige but not necessarily political power, members of these latter classes in the north sought political influence through

20. *Ibid.*
21. James Coleman, *op. cit.*, p. 324.

accommodation with the local aristocracy, not revolution. In the process they became so reactionary as to oppose agitation for national independence.

Interethnic Struggle for Political Power

Thus, by 1953 the major political parties in the country, the NCNC, AG, and NPC had become associated with the three major ethnic groups, Igbo, Yoruba and Hausa, and the three regions of the country, East, West and North respectively. Hence, the 1954 Constitution, which the Nigerian nationalists, organised in these various political parties, participated extensively in formulating, was the first to transform the structure of Nigerian government from unitary foundations to those of federalism. This regionalist document was hailed by the nationalist leaders as most likely to preserve national unity. In a reference to it, K. O. Mbadiwe gleefully noted that it "marked the first time in our history when Nigerian political parties acting through their various leaders decided on the type of constitution under which Nigeria should be ruled."[22] But it was this same constitution which, for the first time, created regional Premiers, regional governors, regional public services, judiciary and marketing bodies, and provided for separate regional progress toward the full attainment of self-government. It fully institutionalised regionalism in the country. It reflected a successful attempt by the regional factions of the emergent privileged local classes to carve out spheres of economic influence for themselves. Politically these factions set about mobilising the masses in a bid to control the governmental apparatus in these regional empires as a means of maximising their economic benefits.

In the process, these regionalists succeeded in creating the false impression that the various political parties were the champions of the interests of various ethnic groups, and that struggles of these parties for political dominance in the country represented the struggles of the various ethnic groups for political ascendency in the society. They covertly and even openly used emotive ethnic symbols and played on alleged ethnic conflicts of interests as a means of mobilising mass support for their own selfish class interests. In competition for the limited numbers of positions and scarce resources within the regions and at the feder-

22. Quoted in J. S. Coleman, *op. cit.*, p. 371.

al level the regional parties generated antagonism and hostility among the major linguistic groups in the country. Their propaganda often emphasised some alleged conflict of interests among these groups with each party claiming to be protecting and advancing the interests of one of the ethnic nationalities or the other. The inevitable consequence was the intensification of the politicisation of ethnicity.

Essentially, the strategy of these various parties for winning political power in the country was similar. First the strategy called for the intensive mobilisation of the ethnic homeland to ensure its monolithic support at times of elections. Second it sought the widening of the political base from the ethnic homeland to include the whole region. This meant obtaining the support of the homelands of the minority ethnic groups within the region. For example, at the formative meeting of the AG it was "felt that the Yorubas should first weld themselves together so that it might be difficult for other tribes to break through them. It was therefore finally decided that for the time being, we should ensure that the Yorubas were first strongly organised and that the Benins and Warri and other non-Yorubas could be drawn in later. These were the reasons why the Benins and Warri have not yet been invited."[23] Third, it aimed at winning elections in the region of ethnic supremacy and consequently controlling the region's governmental power.

Fourth, the strategy emphasised the use of governmental power in the region of its control to eliminate all forms of opposition in the area and to ensure maximum support of the region's population for the party during elections to the federal legislature. Fifth, it encouraged agitation by minority ethnic groups in regions under the rival political parties against their governments and in support of regional status. This tactic was designed to weaken the competing parties in their regional spheres of influence, and to ensure electoral support during federal elections. Sixth, it sought to control the federal government by winning the majority of seats at federal elections, or failing in this, to join any possible winning coalitions that will guarantee socio-economic rewards to its regional faction of the petty bourgeoisie and comprador bourgeoisie. It is illuminating that, after the 1959 federal elections, the AG sent emissaries to both the NCNC and NPC in search of a winning coalition to form the

23. Quoted in Richard Sklar, *op. cit.*, p. 104, footnote 40.

government. The NCNC entered a coalition with the NPC rather than the AG essentially for personal and regional material gains.[24]

Seventh, the strategy aimed at using federal governmental power to (a) divert national resources to the privileged classes in the region of its control, particularly those of its major ethnic group, (b) increase its influence in its region of pre-eminence, and weaken the influence of the competing parties in their respective regions of dominance. It is illustrative that the crisis in Western Nigeria in 1962 attracted a state of emergency from the NCNC-NPC coalition in Lagos while a more intense and violent crisis in the same region in 1965 did not lead to a similar measure. In 1962 the federal coalition had an interest in weakening the AG, hence the state of emergency and the subsequent creation of the MidWest State. In 1965, however, the two parties to that coalition had divergent interests in the imposition of a state of emergency. Eight, it subordinated the unity of the country to the interests of the party in control of political power in the region or at the centre, as the case may be.

On the question of the separation of Lagos from the West the subordination of national and even regional interest to party political advantage by the AG and the NCNC was clear. The AG's major interest in the unity of the two lay in the burning desire to undermine Azikiwe's strong national base by bringing the largely NCNC-controlled municipality under the dominance of an AG-controlled regional government. For the same reason the NCNC opposed the merger of the West and Lagos and supported the separation. Although the possibility of a separation evoked a threat by the AG to lead the West in a secession out of the federation, and the party refused to accept the separation of 1954 until the constitutional conference of 1957, Obafemi Awolowo, in his autobiography, conceded that Lagos was a financial liability to the West and that its merger with that region was not in the regional interest.[25]

Again, on the question of the creation of states, considerations of national unity assumed secondary importance. For example, while the NCNC supported the creation of the Mid West

24. Bill Dudley, *Instability and Political Order* (Ibadan: University of Ibadan Press, 1973), pp. 61–63.
25. Obafemi Awolowo, *Awo: The Autobiography of Chief Obafemi Awolowo* (Cambridge, England Cambridge University Press, 1960), p. 247.

state in the West and actively worked for its fruition it fiercely opposed the creation of the Calabar-Ogoja-Rivers state as persistently demanded by the COR State Movement. It felt that the creation of the latter state would undermine its regional power base. Finally, the petty bourgeois and comprador bourgeois leaders of the various political parties threatened to lead the regions in secession from the Federation whenever their political interests were thwarted.

A similar tendency was exhibited by the AG and the NPC. In fact the ethnic and regional origin and character of the AG arose from the failure of Yoruba nationalists like Awolowo and Bode Thomas to break Azikiwe's political hold on Lagos, and their inability to carve out a national following for themselves. They therefore sought their political fortunes in the politically virgin fields of the Western Region. There the relatively obscure national leaders allied with natural rulers and mobilised the peasantry to become big-time politicians in their small regional enclave. This pattern of fragmentation of the political structure has been repeated many times ever since then. The most ardent advocates of new states or regions have always been aspirants to high positions in the political, administrative, professional, and business fields who have failed to attain positions of pre-eminence at the national, regional or state levels, and who hope to attain such heights in smaller constitutional entities. They rationalise their inordinate ambitions by pleading reasons of national unity.

The AG's attitude to the minority ethnic groups in the country was also politically motivated. This party developed to be the chief spokesman of those minority groups outside the Western region. The motive here, of course, was to undermine and weaken its rival political parties in their regions of preeminence and, therefore, in the nation generally. Within its own region of control the AG carried out a concerted policy of repression of minority opinion, sentiment and interest articulated and expressed outside its framework. In 1955 the Western House of Assembly unanimously adopted a resolution favouring the carving out from the West of a separate state for the Benin and Delta provinces. However, that decision was meant for public political consumption and to be confined to the realm of political rhetoric. Of course, in the event of disunity within the AG in 1962 the NCNC and NPC used it as a basis for the creation of the Mid-West Region, essentially to spite the Action Group. This action could not have been implemented without the internal difficulties of the party.

The NPC also carried on similar practices. Prior to 1957 it consistently opposed national independence, and internal self-government for the North. Its expressed reasons included the fear that, following independence in a united Nigeria, the Southerners would rule the North.

"It is the southerner who has power in the North. They have control of the railway stations, of the Post Offices, of Government Hospitals, of the Canteens; the majority employed in the Kaduna secretariat and in the Public Works Department are all southerners; in all the different departments of Government it is the Southerner who has power."[26]

Its major reason, however, was the party's lack of confidence in its ability to dominate the national political process without the support of the colonial authorities. In the absence of this control, the NPC was deeply apprehensive of its ability to ensure the transfer of power in the North progressively into the hands of a conservative coalition of the traditional aristocracy and the emergent petty bourgeoisie and comprador bourgeoisie identified with the ruling Fulanin gida who would be interested in maintaining the traditional system of appointing emirs and in carrying out local government reforms within the emirate system.

According to Abubakar Tafawa Balewa, "we shall demand our rights when the time is ripe. We want independence and we shall fight for it if necessary ... "[27] Hence, the introduction on 31 March 1953 of a motion by Anthony Enahoro of the Action Group that Nigeria be granted independence in 1956 precipitated a crisis during which the NPC made a veiled threat to lead the North in secession out of the federation and masterminded the Kano riots of May 1953. Later in 1966, when the privileged classes of the North again felt politically insecure they threatened secession and organised rioting against southerners.

Similarly, the NPC's policy of regionalisation stemmed from its inability to attract any significant following outside the North and, therefore, to dominate national politics. In fact, for the greater part of its life, the party confined its activities to the

26. Quoted in J. S. Coleman, *op. cit.*, p. 361.
27. Quoted in Richard Sklar, *op. cit.*, p. 98, footnote 25.

North and openly pursued policies that were regional in character. It championed the cause of the regionalisation of the political process. The political motive behind this championship is reflected in Balewa's

"it is true that we are now trying an experiment never tried in any part of the world, that is the devolution of authority from the centre to the Regions, but I take it that this is merely temporary up to the time when the Regions in Nigeria reach equality. We may have to reverse it when the North can really march with the East and the West, we may have to reverse the recommendation of a regional autonomy and to strengthen the centre and weaken the Regions, but we want a strong regional autonomy for a temporary measure, that is all and nothing more".[28]

Following the 1953 motion for independence in 1956 opposed by the NPC, the party announced an Eight-Point Programme of regionalisation endorsed by an NPC-controlled joint meeting of the Northern House of Assembly and the Northern House of Chiefs. Among other things this document demanded that: (a) there shall be no central legislative body and no central executive or policy making body for the whole of Nigeria; (b) the services of the railway, air services, posts and telegraphs, electricity and coal mining shall be organised on an inter-Regional basis; (c) all revenue shall be levied and collected by the regional governments except customs revenue at the port of discharge which shall be separately cleared and charged to duty according to the region of consignment by the central agency for the regions in charge of defense, external affairs and customs.

Mention had already been made of the role of the NPC-NCNC federal coalition in carving out the Midwest from the West. This action may better be understood when it is realised that the NPC was fiercely opposed to the creation of states in the North in spite of the intense demand for the Middle Belt State. Of the three main political parties, the NPC was the most regional in outlook. The party sought to control political power in the Region as a whole and resisted all attempts to introduce a wedge into this regional unity. But equally, for political reasons, they were not averse to the exploitation of minority sentiments in order to weaken the other rival political parties.

On the question of the intensive mobilisation of the ethnic homeland, the evidence is clear from the nature of the leadership

28. Quoted in *ibid*., p. 99, footnote 26.

of the parties, the involvement of ethnic groups in their organisational activities, and the pattern of ethnic support which they
received. Most of the leaders of those parties were drawn from
the corresponding dominant ethnic homeland. This fact is
reflected in the following Table 5.1. The homelands in turn
represented the areas of dominant interest of the parties.

The participation of ethnic associations led by the same
privileged classes in party activities was important in the NCNC
and the AG. For the NPC the role of ethnic associations was comparatively absent. The common bond of the Islamic religion and
the multi-tribal span of the traditional Fulani empire, have
created a regional rather than an ethnic outlook in the upper
North. Nevertheless, the traditional leadership of the emirate system operated through the native authorities to ensure mass
support for the NPC, particularly in the Hausa areas of the North,
but even in the other areas of the region. In the East, the Igbo
State Union is the dominant ethnic arm of the NCNC, ensuring
Igbo support for and solidarity within the party. It attempted to
resolve quarrels between Igbo politicians before they reached
the party level. For example, in April 1953, a meeting of Igbo
leaders was convened in Port Harcourt by Dr. Azikiwe in his
capacity as the President of the NCNC to reconcile the parties to
the Eastern Regional dispute. The recalcitrant Ministers were
asked to resign from the Executive Council in the best interests of
the Igbo people and the Eastern Region. This involvement infur-
iated the non-Igbo NCNC men in the East who thereafter joined
the opposition charging the NCNC with serving the purpose of
Igbo domination. In 1958, K. O. Mbadiwe and his supporters

TABLE 5.1   *Ethnic distribution of leaders of the major Nigerian parties in 1958 as
percentage of total*

Party	Igbo	Other eastern groups	Yoruba	Other western groups	Hausa Fulani	Other northern groups	Others
NPC	—	—	6.8	—	51.3	32.4	9.4
NCNC	49.3	9.9	26.7	5.6	(2.8	)	5.6
AG	4.5	15.2	68.2	7.6	(3.0	)	1.5

Sources: Richard Sklar and C. S. Whitaker, Jr, "Nigeria" in J. S. Coleman and Carl
Rosberg, Jr., *Political Parties and National Integration in Tropical Africa* (Berkeley, Cal.:
University of California Press, 1966), p. 612, Table I; Richard Sklar, *Nigerian Political
Parties (Princeton, New Jersey: Princeton University Press, 1963)* p. 324, Table I.

tried to use the Igbo State Union to apply pressure on Nnamdi Azikiwe but failed. The latter's suggestion of the use of the Igbo method of reconciliation, "Igbandu," to settle his dispute with Mbadiwe within the party, reflects the same reliance on ethnic instruments in the conduct of party activities.

At the lower political levels, the Igbo State Union worked tirelessly to identify the NCNC with the cause of Igbo advancement and welfare. In many cases the town, village, district and clan unions affiliated with the Igbo State Union filled in the gaps left in the official party organisation. In fact, certain branches of the party such as the strong NCNC branch in Port Harcourt derived their strength and drive from various units of these associations which were affiliated with the Union. These local units of the ethnic unions provided mass support for the party's causes as they obviously did in favour of Nnamdi Azikiwe during the time of the official inquiry into his dubious financial deals with the African Continental Bank in 1957, and at the time of his dispute with Mbadiwe in 1958.

Much of the support for the NCNC in the East arose from the widespread tendency of most Igbo to identify the party with their collective interests. This is reflected in their block vote which enabled the party to win all the 50 constituencies in Igboland during the 1959 federal elections. Such overwhelming support was never enjoyed by the AG. Hence, while the NCNC could afford formally and rhetorically to draw a clear line between the party and the Igbo State Union the AG could not. The latter never equivocated on the partisanship of the Egbe Omo Oduduwa, the leading ethnic association aligned with it. Unlike Nnamdi Azikiwe who resigned his Presidency of the Igbo State Union because of the embarrassment it caused to the NCNC, Obafemi Awolowo remained the General Secretary of the Egbe. Dr. Akinola Maja, "Father of the Action Group" and Chairman of the Board of the National Bank succeeded Sir Adeyemo Alakija as the Egbe's President. S. L. Akintola, Premier of the Western Region was at the same time a legal adviser to the Egbe.[29] Akintola once pointed out that the interests of the party and the Egbe were inseparable.[30] In 1958, Akinola Maja openly urged the Egbe to work and vote for the party in the 1959 federal elections.[31]

29. *Ibid.*, p. 464.
30. *Ibid.*, p. 464.
31. *Ibid.*, pp. 464–465.

The Egbe used its influence in Yorubaland and worked vigorously to smooth the relationship between the AG, the chiefs, other men of influence, and the urban and the rural masses in the implementation of party policies. Often it operated through the Obas who, as patrons, supported it on grounds of Yoruba patriotism. The Egbe settled disputes between Yoruba political leaders and chiefs that might otherwise embarrass the AG. For example, in 1954, it settled the long-standing dispute between the Awujale of Ijebu-Ode on one side and certain chiefs and people of Ijebu-Ode on the other. In 1958, it tried unsuccessfully to settle the breach between the Oba of Lagos and the Action Group. In its search for Yoruba solidarity behind the party, the AG occasionally used it to coerce recalcitrant traditional rulers as was done to the Alafin of Oyo in the early 1950s. The AG's ability to mobilise rural mass support for the party rested on the virtual inseparability of cultural and political matters in the eyes of the rural folks.

The pattern of electoral support for the three main political parties demonstrates their emphasis on, mobilisation of, and alignment with, the major ethnic groups in their respective regions of pre-eminence. The NCNC and the NPC consistently swept the polls in Igboland and Hausa-Fulaniland respectively. In Yorubaland, the AG proved electorally dominant even through it always shared the Yoruba vote with the NCNC-Mabolaji alliance. Quite illustrative of this ethnic pattern of support was the voting behaviour during the 1959 Federal election. This preindependence election was keenly contested by the parties because it was expected to provide the government that would lead the country into independence. It was widely interpreted as a struggle among the various ethnic groups for the control of the post-colonial state. The various ethnic groups closed ranks in support of their traditional political parties. The aim was to have a member of their group emerge as the Prime Minister. The results were illuminating.

In the Western Region, the Action Group won thirty-three out of a total of sixty-two seats contested. Thirty of these victories were won in Yoruba constituencies. The AG's traditional rival in the region, the NCNC, won only eight seats in Yorubaland. Its share of the Yoruba vote had dropped from 41.9 per cent in 1954 to 17.4 per cent in 1959.[32] However, in its traditional area of

---

32. Kenneth Post, *The Nigerian Federal Election of 1959* (London: Oxford University Press, 1963), p. 360.

support in the East, the NCNC won fifty-eight out of the seventy-three seats, capturing all the fifty constituencies in Igboland. Even the independent candidates that in the past robbed the party of total victory in Igboland failed to win a seat. In the West, two of the independents were victorious; they later declared for the AG. In fact, in sixteen Igbo constituencies the NCNC received over 90 of the votes and in eleven others it received between 80 per cent and 90 per cent of the votes.[33]

In the North, the Hausa-Fulani areas voted solidly for the NPC. The party won 134 seats in the area or 77 per cent of the total number of seats for the region. It won a third of its seats in constituencies where it received more than 80 per cent of the total votes. Forty-two out of forty-five of these constituencies were located in Bornu Division, and Kano and Sokoto provinces. Also, the party was strong in Bida and Abuja emirates, northern Katsina emirate, Minna division, and in a number of constituencies which included the local native administration headquarters, such as Adamawa Central and Katagum West.[34] The traditional rival of the NPC in the Hausa-Fulani areas, the Northern Elements Progressive Union (NEPU) won only a handful of seats in the area. It won eight seats.

More than any other factor, the interparty struggle for political power politicised ethnicity and spread ethnic thinking to the most remote areas of the country. During times of election campaign, workers penetrated all areas of the country in search of votes. Their invariable ethnic messages and innuendoes spread to all parts of the country. Many rural inhabitants who had neither come in contact with members of other ethnic groups nor heard stories about them from relatives that visited periodically from the urban centres began to form images, attitudes, and stereotypes of other ethnic groups, to develop ethnic interests, and to associate their achievement with one or the other of the political parties.

This development further polarised the country into ethnic compartments separated from one another by increasing divergence of political beliefs and interests, political experience, and history of political struggle. Violence attendant on the electoral campaigns became associated with interethnic relations. Under the circumstances, political disputes over the census, elections, constitutional reforms, and the distribution of social amenities

33. *Ibid.*, p. 364.
34. *Ibid.*, p. 367.

aggravated interethnic tension and hostility which further politicised ethnicity. Those political parties adversely affected in the struggle for power, threatened several times to pull their ethnic supporters out of the federal arrangement. The consequent truncation of political aims and the recruitment of political leadership caused serious difficulties for national integration and the development of the productive forces of the country. It also created the problem of the ethnic minorities.

Politics and the Ethnic Minorities

In the prevalent atmosphere of ethnic consciousness and the struggle for political power among the major ethnic groups, the less numerous language groups were inevitably drawn into ethnic politics. The dynamics of their involvement resembles that of the major groups. It is illustrated by certain political developments in the Eastern Region in 1952/53 which split the Igbo and Efik leaders of the NCNC in a manner reminiscent of the Ikoli-Akinsanya affairs of 1941. In 1952, Nnamdi Azikiwe, the NCNC President, had tried unsuccessfully to persuade Eyo Ita the leader of the NCNC government in the Eastern Region and a director of several companies in the Zik Group of companies to influence the deposition of local government funds in the African Continental Bank in which Azikiwe and his family had controlling shares. In the power struggle within the party later that year Azikiwe retaliated by rudely expelling Eyo Ita from the NCNC: "Your behaviour on the question of your resignation is a shame to you and your race. It is obvious that no self-respecting party can associate with a person like you. You are hereby informed that you have been expelled from the party with ignominy and for life."[35]

Thereupon the Efik-speaking leaders of the NCNC from the communal homeland of Eyo Ita together with other party leaders from the neighbouring Ibibio communal homeland including Dr. Udo Udoma, President of the Ibibio State Union, resigned from the party. By so doing, they protested the treatment meted out to Eyo Ita. They deeply resented the aspersion which they perceived was cast on the Efik people by the letter expelling Eyo Ita from the party. Later, the expelled members of the NCNC, along with the other former leaders of the party who had resigned

35. Quoted in *ibid.*, p. 123, footnote 78.

in protest over the expulsions, formed the new political party, the National Independence Party. Eyo Ita became its first President. The new party became the embryo movement of the ethnic minorities in the Eastern Region, charging Igbo domination of the region and demanding regional status for the homelands of these ethnic minorities.

Similarly E. O. Eyo turned from being the NCNC Government Chief Whip in the Eastern House of Assembly and chairman of the strategic Eastern Region Development Corporation to a fierce opponent of the NCNC and an ardent champion of the interests of the ethnic minorities of the region. The genesis of this *volte face* is to be found in the political quarrel in 1955 between him and Azikiwe over the latter's handling of the result of the public Commission of Inquiry into Bribery and Corruption which found Eyo's close associate, Mbonu Ojike, the regional Minister of Finance, guilty of wrong doing. Eyo accused Azikiwe of financial malfeasance in transferring massive public funds into the African Continental Bank, precipitating a tribunal of inquiry which found the NCNC leader guilty. Expelled from the NCNC because of this accusation he found a haven in the party for the ethnic minorities of the region.

Thus as was the case with the development of regional and ethnic political parties by the leaders of the privileged classes of the major ethnic groups, the petty bourgeois and comprador bourgeois leaders of the minor ethnic groups were unable to achieve or retain regional, political, and economic leadership. They, therefore, opted for the leadership of sub-regional entities. Only such leadership guaranteed the enormous socioeconomic benefits accruing from public service. Encouragement for this option was provided by the intense atmosphere of ethnic chauvinism, divisiveness and tension generated by the political activities of the leaders of the major ethnic groups in the country.

The increasing solidarity of each major ethnic group behind a political party, and the emphasis placed by Nigerian politicians on the pursuit of ethnic interests, raised fears among the leaders of the minority groups concerning neglect and domination by the leaders of the major groups. They perceived their opportunities for political leadership, contract, senior positions in the public service, and loans for business activities threatened by the tendency of the major political parties in government to secure these for the members of their classes from the major ethnic groups. By leading minority group agitation against "domination" and for regional status these leaders hoped to carve out a place in the Nigerian political sun for themselves.

The politics of the ethnic minorities was made possible by the enclave nature of the country's economy. Just as the regions constituted economic enclaves separated from each other and linked to Europe, the various minority ethnic homelands constituted economic enclaves of their own. The rubber and palm products of Efikland and Ibibioland were not used in the industries of Igboland. Similarly, the tin mined in Jos was sent to Europe rather than to other parts of the North. The dominant economic activities of the Midwest were not linked to those of the rest of the Western Region. The sub-regional economic enclaves provided the objective basis for empire building by members of the privileged classes from the area. By excluding their counterparts of the major ethnic group in the region from sharing in the surplus from the production in the enclave, the leaders of the minorities expected to maximise their benefits from the intraclass division of the national wealth. Again, no thought whatsoever was given to the creation of this wealth.

Finally, political activity by the minorities was prodded on by the major political parties as a means of generating and increasing their national following. In fact, the Action Group successfully projected a national image, contrary to its secessionist sentiments of 1955, by fighting the cause of ethnic minorities in the Eastern and Northern Regions. In 1951, Chief Enahoro of the AG called a conference in Sapele which demanded a Benin Delta state. In 1952 and 1953 this demand was reaffirmed by the AG. In 1955 the AG controlled Western House of Assembly passed a resolution supporting the creation of the state renamed the Midwest State. Simultaneously, it made similar demands for the creation of the Middle Belt State in the North, and the Calabar-Ogoja-Rivers (COR) state in the East.

In the elections held in the South in 1954, 1956, and 1957, the NCNC and the AG competed for the support of the minority ethnic groups by identifying with their aspirations for statehood and promising to fight their cause at the 1957 Constitutional Conference. Therefore, at the 1957 London Conference, the two Southern parties were committed to the creation of additional states. Only the NPC was free of this ethnic minority vice. It repeatedly rejected the creation of new states in the North. Instead, it began to redress the grievances of the minorities in the region by: (a) granting increased power to the provincial administrations, (b) sending a delegation to Libya, Pakistan and Sudan to study their systems of administration with particular reference to how they had solved the problem of ethnic diversity, and (c) attempting to win leaders of the minority groups over to its fold; in 1956 it was sufficiently successful to capture 28 of the 43 Middle Belt seats in the Northern regional elections. But although the NPC refrained from supporting the agitation of minority groups in the East and West, it joined with the NCNC to carve out the Midwest State from the West in 1963/64 to spite the AG, and during the 1959 elections it allied with the Niger Delta Congress in the East which favoured the creation of a separate Rivers State and won a federal seat in Brass Division.

Political gain rather than principles lay behind the support of minority demands by the major parties. This is illustrated by the fact that each party either opposed the creation of new states in its region of control or imposed unattainable conditions for creating them while urging the creation of states in the rival's region of dominance. Hence, the NCNC, while accepting the creation of new states in principle and the creation of the Midwest State in practice, was consistently opposed to the creation of the COR state, rationalising its objection by the argument that the new state was solely motivated by an anti-Igbo sentiment, and suggesting separate statehood for the Calabar, Ogoja and Rivers peoples. The AG tied the creation of the Midwest, to which the Western House was committed, to the simultaneous creation of states in in North and East.

Indeed, for the Action Group and the NPC the only support outside their region of dominance came from the minority areas of the regions of control of their rivals. In the East, the AG only won the votes of sections of the Ibibio, Efik peoples and the people of Enyong division. In the North it was supported by the Bornu people of Bornu division, the Chamba of Adamawa, all the peoples of Numan division with the exception of the Kanakuru, the Birom of Jos, the Tiv, the Arago of Lafia division, the Jarawa and Sayawa of Bauchi division, and the Ekiti, Igolo and Igbomina Yoruba of Ilorin Division. The only support for the NPC in the south came from the Ijaw of Brass division in 1959. Only the NCNC managed to win parliamentary seats in the areas of the major ethnic groups that supported its rivals. In the West it was supported by Illa, Ibadan, Ilesha district Yoruba and the Oyo Yoruba of the Madakeke ward. But it always won majority votes in the Midwest particularly among the Igbo, Edo and

Urhobo peoples. In alliance with the NEPU it won some seats in Hausaland.

Thus subregional factions of the local privileged classes asserted demands for separation from the dominant cultural-political

TABLE 5.2 *Eastern house of assembly elections 1957: Party strength in minority areas*

Area	NCNC	AG-UNIP	Total
COR state			
Ibibio-Efik	7	11	18
Non Ibo areas of Ogoja	2	4	6
Non Ibo areas of rivers	3	3	6
Total	12	18	30
Ogoja state			
Non Ibo areas	2	4	6
Ibo areas	7	0	8
Total	9	4	14
Rivers state			
Ijaw	3	3	6
Ibo	5	0	5
Total	8	3	11
Ibo areas	52	0	54

Source: J. S. Coleman, *Nigeria: Background to Nationalism* (Berkeley and Los Angeles, Cal.: University of California Press, 1958), p. 392, Table 26.

TABLE 5.3 *Western house of assembly elections 1956: Party strength in the minority areas*

Area	AG	NCNC	Total
Midwest state			
Avocates	0	11	11
Opponents:	4	3	7
Western Ijaw	0	2	2
Total	5	16	20
Yorubaland	44	16	60
Regional Total	48	32	80

Source: J. S. Coleman, *Nigeria: Background to Nationalism* (Berkeley and Los Angeles, Cal.: University of California Press, 1958), p. 389, Table 25.

TABLE 5.4   *Northern house of assembly elections 1956: Party strength in the minority Areas*

Area	NPC	NCNC-NEPU-BYM	UMBC-AG	Total
Middle belt state				
Non-Yoruba areas	27	1	10	38
Yoruba areas	1	0	4	5
Total	28	1	14	43
Rest of the region	78	8	2	88
Regional total	106	9	16	131

Source: J. S. Coleman, *Nigeria: Background to Nationalism* (Berkeley and Los Angeles, Cal.: University of California Press, 1958) p. 395, Table 27.

groups in the regionalised system of 1954. These factions did so essentially for intraclass factional reasons. But during political campaigns for elections to the regional and federal legislatures, at politcal rallies, on the pages of newspapers, in petitions, at constitutional conferences, during elections, and even in private conversations, these regional leaders spread minority ethnic sentiments, chauvinism, and exclusiveness in an effort to mobilise mass political support for their cause. In the process they formented hatred and hostility toward the majority ethnic groups of the various regions throughout the urban and rural centres of the minority areas. As a result, those ethnic groups which were politically dormant were galvanised into political activity in furtherance and pursuit of ethnic interests.

Intolerant policies of the parties in power in the various regions exacerbated interethnic hostility, fanning the embers of ethnic emotions, sentiments and feelings. Often the ruling party employed strong-arm tactics such as arbitrary arrests by the native authority police and similar agencies of the law, police harassment, threats of withdrawal of social services, threats of arrest, and the muzzling of opinions to intimidate recalcitrant minority groups and their leaders into supporting the regional government. When these failed, policies of victimisation were implemented. Equipment already purchased and deployed for projects were allegedly withdrawn after the elections. Areas voting for the regional opposition were deliberately starved of social amenities as a form of punishment. The net effect was the increased politicisation of ethnicity.

A similar effect was also produced by the activities of the

Minorities Commission of Inquiry into the fears of the ethnic minorities set up in 1957 by the Colonial Office. It was to ascertain the facts about the fears of minorities in parts of the country and to propose means of allaying those fears. For several months, the Commission toured all parts of Nigeria, receiving memoranda and taking oral evidence in public and private from individuals, ethnic associations, minority groups, political parties and government officials. This tour generated much interest, opinion, and discussion of ethnic problems in the country, thereby heightening ethnic awareness, one component of ethnic consciousness. The hope of some and the fear of others that the inquiry would result in the creation of more states in the country helped to politicize this consciousness. When the Commission recommended safeguards for minorities other than the creation of states, an ethnic political storm was raised which kept ethnicity alive as a political issue. The NPC and the NCNC accepted the report while the AG and the various minority movements rejected it as unrealistic and disappointing. The matter did not rest until a complex procedure for the creation of states in the future was provided by the preindependence Nigerian constitution.

Thus, by the time of national independence in 1960, Nigerian politics had become synonymous with interethnic struggle for power, as far as Nigerians and non-Nigerians alike were concerned. Political power was widely perceived as being important and instrumental in the struggle among the ethnic groups for the division of the national wealth. At both the regional and national levels, politics was interpreted in terms of the sending of representatives into positions of power that will enable them to transfer regional or national resources to the ethnic homeland. Politicians were judged by their constituents with the criterion characterised by how much of such wealth they were able to transfer to the homeland, and acted accordingly. Under these circumstances, the internalisation of ethnic political attitudes was assured.

The media of socialisation such as the family, press, and private as well as public conversation had become infected by the ubiquitous malaise of ethnicity. Ethnic political beliefs, stereotypes, loyalty, hostility, and identity were passed on to successive generations through the process of socialisation. This development intensified the polarisation of the society into sub-national ethnic cultures further separated in terms of identity and loyalty. The only significant point of contact among them was confined to the market place but this was becoming increasingly characterised by interethnic competition and conflict. Consequently, the ethnic factor assumed a self-fulfilling and self-sustaining dynamic of its own which daily reinforced the individual's internalised ethnic sentiments. The persistence and growth of ethnicity in Nigeria had become inevitable.

Chapter 6

POLITICS AND INTERETHNIC SOCIOECONOMIC COMPETITION

The Regionalisation of National Wealth

Superficially, Nigerian politics have presented an image of a struggle among the various ethnic groups for a division of national resources. Most Nigerians have come to believe that unless their "own men" are in government they are unable to secure those socio-economic amenities that are disbursed by the government. Hence, governmental decisions about the siting of industries, the building of roads, award of scholarships, and appointments to positions in the public services, are closely examined in terms of their benefits to the various ethnic groups in the country. In fact, there has emerged a crop of "ethnic watchers" who devote much of their time and energy to assessing the differential benefits of the various groups from any government project. There is even talk of instituting an ethnic quota system in the admissions of Nigerian students into the country's universities.

This image of Nigerian politics is reinforced by contemporary bourgeois definitions of politics which view it as the authoritative allocation of values. Although "values," as used in the definition, is not restricted to resources but refers widely and generally to choices or decisions, in practice it has been interpreted to mean resources. It is clear, however, that those resources available for allocation must first be produced and that the process of production is as important, if not more so, than that of distribution. In any case, the two are so closely interrelated that no meaningful discussion of one in isolation from the other is possible. Their apparent separation in Nigerian political life is explained by the dominance of the political process by the traditional aristrocracy, petty bourgeoisie and comprador bourgeoisie. Historically, these classes have never been oriented toward the productive aspects of social life. They emphasise the distributive dimension.

Unable to increase production they depend on the manipulation of distribution for the benefits which they derive from society.

In Nigeria, one of the instruments for this manipulation has been ethnicity. By presenting politics as an interethnic struggle for socioeconomic resources, these classes camouflage intraclass struggles for the division of the national wealth that is inimical to the interest of the underpriviliged classes, the working class, and the poor farmers who constitute the vast majority of the population.

It is evident from the analysis so far that the central determining factor in Nigerian politics has been the regionalisation of the colonial economy with its consequent development of various regional factions of these privileged classes. In reality Nigerian politics was the struggle among these various factions first to dominate the wealth in their region of origin and, second, to use this regional dominance as a springboard for the acquisition of some of the nonregional wealth. In the pursuit of these objectives, these petty bourgeois and comprador bourgeois leaders elicited the support of the various other classes by an appeal to ethnicity. Such support enabled them to control the various regional governmental apparatuses. Since this control was not an end in itself, it was employed in the service of the leaders' underlying political motivation, the use of political power to achieve intraclass economic dominance. How was this possible?

In 1951 when the various regional factions of these privileged classes assumed power in the regions, public wealth was the chief source of capital for Nigerians. Private indigenous investors were almost nonexistent. The traditional aristocracy, petty bourgeoisie and comprador bourgeoisie that came into political power lacked investible funds with which to achieve their aim of economic transformation into the bourgeoisie proper, the national bourgeoisie. The only way these two classes could effect this change was to use public funds for investment in their private enterprises, as well as to use governmental power and resources to create investment opportunities for themselves. It is not surprising, therefore, that the vast majority of the businessmen in every region supported the party in power in the region. For example, the Northern Amalgamated Merchants' Union and the Northern Contractors' Union were closely connected with the NPC; the Union of Niger African Traders at Onitsha and the Eastern Nigeria Civil Engineers and Building Contractors of Enugu were strong backers of the NCNC. Action Group influence was dominant in the Federation of Civil Engineering Building Contractors of Yaba, the African Contractors' Union, the Nigerian Produce Buyers Union and the Nigerian Motor Transport Union. Both the AG and the NCNC were supported by various wings of the market women.[1]

Public funds provided investment and loan capital to private firms and individuals. Commercial contracts were awarded by the government and their statutory corporations, and it was good business to have the right political connections. According to Richard Sklar during the period 1951–1957, the Western Regional Tenders Board awarded building contracts exceeding ₦5,000,000 each to 12 African contracting firms, all of which were owned and managed by members or supporters of the Action Group.[2] Commercial patronage such as government loans, licensing and contracting were channelled through public agencies that were political in character. In all regions, these agencies served the economic interests of the regional faction of the privileged classes.

Many of the benefits that accrued to the various factions depended on the share of the national wealth which the regional government controlled. Hence, an intergovernmental struggle ensued for the regional control of certain sources of national wealth. This was the objective class basis of the interethnic struggle for socioeconomic resources in Nigeria. The regional governments mobilised ethnic support on behalf of this struggle which it rationalised in ethnic rather than intraclass terms.

Some of the relevant sources of national wealth were the Marketing Boards. These marketing institutions were created immediately after World War II around the country's principal export crops. There was the Cocoa Marketing Board, the Oil Palm Produce Marketing Board, the Groundnut Marketing Board and the Cotton Marketing Board. The major function of these Boards was to stabilise local cash crop prices well below their world market equivalent in order to accumulate public capital. Other functions included the appointment of licensed agents to purchase and transport the crops to the ports, the control and regulation of the activities and the remuneration of those engaged in export trade, the control over the local processing

---

1. Richard Sklar, *Nigerian Political Parties* (Princeton, New Jersey: Princeton University Press, 1963), pp. 450–452.
2. *Ibid*.

of produce, the making of grants to the regional production development boards, the financing of research, the regulation of buying for export, the determination of periods during which buying for export was possible, the fixing of producer prices, carrying out of price support and stabilisation policies, and the regulation of the quality and grading of produce. Regional Development Boards were set up to administer marketing board grants for research and agricultural development.

At the beginning of 1953 Nigeria's sterling balances in London exceeded ₦300 million.[3] Of this amount ₦50 million was contributed by the marketing boards.[4] The Nigerian political leaders sought to repatriate portions of these sterling balances for the purposes of local economic activities. At the London Constitutional Conference they applied pressure to this effect. In addition, the Action Group strongly urged the regionalisation of the activities and assets of the marketing boards as the AG was more specifically representative of the interests of the petty bourgeoisie and comprador bourgeoisie than the NCNC and the NPC. Within this party was to be found a business group of impressive size and influence in Western Nigeria. This group constituted probably the largest and wealthiest compact business community of black Africans in Africa.[5] Many of them were entrepreneurs, merchants, and bankers who had experienced economic and social frustrations under colonial rule. Their interest lay in a government that would provide them with funds and opportunities to expand their business.

Therefore, following the decisions of the 1954 Lagos Resumed Constitutional Conference in favour of political and economic regionalisation, the system of marketing boards was changed, providing for a central board and regional boards. Each region created one all-purpose marketing board to fix, stabilise, and support prices for all crops in the region, and to perform all the other functions of the commodity marketing boards. The central Marketing Board would serve the region in a consultative capacity on questions of price fixing, support, stabilisation, the appointment of buying and ginning agents, local processing, research and development, and other matters referred to it by the regional

3. The International Bank for Reconstruction and Development, *The Economic Development of Nigeria* (Baltimore: Maryland: The Johns Hopkins Press, 1955), p. 17.

4. *Ibid*.

5. *Ibid*., p. 18.

boards. It would prescribe the grades and quality of produce, appoint agents for bulk storage at the ports and for produce, arrange for shipping and sales abroad, keep a separate commodity account for each region, and share out the proceeds of sales to the regions in proportion to the purchases from each.[6]

The four commodity marketing boards were dissolved and their assets were distributed among the regional marketing boards according to the principle of derivation. The new institutions were authorised to make grants for development and research generally rather than for agricultural purposes alone as before. The West benefitted most from this sharing of assets on the basis of derivation. It received ₦68.8 million while the North obtained ₦49.6 million, the East ₦30.2 million and Southern Cameroons ₦4 million.[7] Cocoa produced in the West was the most lucrative cash crop at the time because of the prevailing boom in its world market. It was, therefore, the chief revenue earner among the export crops of the country, giving the West per capita and national incomes that were substantially greater than the national average.

Even during the period 1954 to 1961, the West continued to earn the greatest trading surpluses. During that period, another ₦43.6 million was added to the resources of the marketing boards by their trading surpluses.[8] Although this was less than one-quarter of the profits of the previous seven years it remained quite sizeable. Earnings on reserves accumulated over the years yielded a net surplus of ₦19.0 million. The Western Region earned ₦28.6 million of the trading surpluses with cocoa contributing ₦19.4 million of this earning. The region's wealth also produced a net income of another ₦10.6 million mainly from interest on securities held by its investment portfolio.[9] The Western faction of the privileged classes was triumphant.

The class character of this regionalisation of the funds of the marketing boards is clearly reflected in the pattern of disbursement of their surpluses. In this context it is noteworthy that the farmers who created this wealth were left out of its distribution. Instead, they faced a monopolistic situation in their dealings with

6. E. O. Awa, *Federal Government in Nigerian* (Berkeley and Los Angeles: University of California Press, 1964), pp. 228–229.
7. Richard Skelar, *op. cit.*, p. 163, footnote 41.
8. G. K. Helleiner, *Peasant Agriculture, Government, and Economic Growth in Nigeria* (Homewood, Illinois: Irwin 1966), pp. 164–165.
9. *Ibid.*

the boards. The latter were controlled by petty bourgeois and comprador bourgeois politicians who had interests in some of the companies acting as licensed buying agents, or who wished to establish such vested interests, or were protective of the members of their classes who had such interests. These buying agents bought the farmer's produce and sold it only through established channels to Britain, thereby restricting the flexibility and manouverability of the farmer in the sale of his produce. The privileged ruling classes also continued the inherited practice of fixing the prices at which the farmer would sell his crops at levels well below the prevailing international market prices. The farmer was denied the full benefit of his endeavours. The rationale for this exploitation was that the accumulated surpluses would be used for general development in the regions. In other words, as a class, the farmers had to pay for the general development of the regions including the transformation of the petty bourgeoisie and the comprador bourgeoisie into the wealthier and more economically powerful bourgeoisie.

In every region, each governing party maintained an extensive system of patronage that was financially anchored in the funds and activities of the regional marketing board. These funds provided investment and loan capital for the regional statutory corporations including those which undertook agricultural and industrial development projects independently or in partnership with other governments or with private companies. Some of the funds were also channelled into regional loans boards and finance corporations which made grants to local government authorities, private firms, and individuals. In all, political factors within the regions determined the personnel composition as well as the financial and other activities of these corporations.

All the members appointed to the Western Region Marketing Board at its inception in 1954 were politicians sympathetic to the ruling AG.[10] Between 1954 and 1962 the board had disbursed ₦128 million. Out of this amount ₦62 million was granted to departments of the regional government, ₦20 million had been invested in various Nigerian companies and ₦28 million was lent to the regional government and its other corporations. The only beneficiaries of the fund invested in Nigerian companies were the Agbonmagbe Bank, the Merchant's Bank, the Association of

10. John P. Mackintosh, *Nigerian Government and Politics* (London: Allen and Unwin, 1966), pp. 434–435.

Nigerian Exporters, the Cooperative Bank of Western Nigeria, the Nigerian Produce Marketing Company, the National Bank and the National Investment and Properties Company (NIPC). Of these, the Agbonmagbe Bank, the Merchants' Bank, the National Bank and the NIPC were controlled by AG politicians while much of the money lent to the other corporations was used to encourage businessmen sympathetic to the AG.[11]

The National Bank, a beneficiary of marketing board funds, handled the AG's accounts and gave it liberal overdrafts. It accorded similar treatment to the Amalgamated Press which published AG papers, and to leading party members.[12] When, in 1959 the Western Region Development Corporation was established to promote economic development, Alfred Rewane, a director of NIPC and the political secretary of Obafemi Awolowo, the AG leader, was appointed its Chairman. By 1962, the corporation had financial interests in fifteen companies, holding over 50 per cent interest in the Nigerian Plastics Companies, the Nigersol Construction Company, the Nigerian Water Resources Development Company and Nidogas. The Nigerian Water Resources Development Company and Nigersol obtained loans of ₦4 million and ₦2 million respectively for construction work, making the government and its agencies the largest source of contract work in the region.[13] Also, the corporation had undertaken the implementation of agricultural projects of ₦11.8 million, the construction of factories costing ₦3.0 million, and the building of a hotel at Ibadan valued at ₦266,000. When the Western Region Finance Corporation was formed, leading AG members were appointed to its board. It invested ₦4.6 million in six enterprises which were either on the verge of collapse or were bought at inflated prices. Practically all these enterprises belonged to members or sympathisers of the party.[14]

Indeed, the relationship between the marketing board and the indigenous banking institutions has been crucial for the embourgeoisement of the Nigerian privileged classes in the various regions of the country. This transformation has been the major cause and consequence of interethnic socioeconomic

11. *Ibid.*
12. *Ibid.*
13. *Ibid.*
14. *Ibid.*

competition. In 1958 there were three banks enjoying a close relationship with the AG. The National Bank of Nigeria was the most important of them. The major purpose of the National Bank was to give financial assistance to Nigerian businessmen. Its board chairman and general-manager were vice-presidents of the party, while most of its directors and major shareholders supported the party materially. The Western Region Marketing Board and the Western Region Production Development Corporation deposited their accounts with the bank. Also the marketing board made direct investments in the bank. For example, in 1955 the regional government deposited 45 per cent of its funds in the bank and the marketing board invested ₦2.0 million in the 4 per cent cumulative non-participating preference shares of ₦2 each.[15] In 1961 when insolvency and mismanagement threatened the bank, the marketing board converted its previous investment of ₦2 million into equity shares, made an additional investment of ₦4 million, and took over the bank.

The National Bank was a financial arm of the Action Group. The latter obtained unsecured loans from it, often using fictitious accounts, and concealing the fact from federal auditors.[16] The bank gave overdrafts to businessmen who habitually made considerable donations to the funds of the AG and the Egbe Omo Oduduwa.[17]

However, between 1959 and 1961, the major conduit for funds for the party was the Nigerian Investment and Properties Company. Its owners were four prominent AG leaders: Dr. Akinola Maja, Chief S. O. Gbadamosi, S. O. Shonibare and Alfred Rewane.[18] Between its birth in 1958 and 1961, the company obtained loans of over ₦12 million from the regional marketing board and another ₦4 million which the board had previously allocated to the Western Nigeria Development Corporation. It also received nearly ₦2 million for the sale of government property at inflated prices and by other dubious means. During this time, the company provided the AG with over ₦8 million.[19]

15. Richard Sklar, *op. cit.*, pp. 456–457.
16. *Report of Coker Commission of Inquiry into the Affairs of Certain Statutory Corporations in Western Nigeria* (Lagos: Federal Ministry of Information, 1962), Vol. I, pp. 55–58; Vol. II, pp. 1–8.
17. *Ibid.*
18. *Ibid.*
19. *Ibid.*

The National Bank financially controlled the party newspapers. But in 1960 these papers were taken over from the Amalgamated Press of Nigeria by the Allied Newspapers, substantially owned by NIPC. The Amalgamated Press was formed in 1953 through a merger involving the Service Press and the African Press. Obafemi Awolowo was the founder of the African Press and was an honorary director of the Amalgamated Press until 1955 when he resigned and sold his shares.[20]

Similarly, in the East, the regional government set up the Eastern Region Finance Corporation to serve as an intermediary for investing the regional marketing board's funds in an indigenous bank. The corporation had wide discretionary powers to stimulate economic activities through investment in business and financial enterprises, loans to other public bodies and investments in them, and loans to local businessmen. This corporation was inaugurated in 1955 with an outright grant of ₦4 million by the Eastern Regional Marketing Board. Thereafter, the corporation invested ₦1,578,600 in the African Continental Bank (A.C.B.) in 784,000 ordinary shares of ₦2 each and 93,000 preference shares of ₦2 each.[21] As has previously been mentioned, this investment, which was very advantageious to the bank's directors, salvaged the bank which was owned and controlled by Nnamdi Azikiwe, leader of the NCNC, and his family.[22] By virtue of this investment the regional government acquired 87.7 per cent of the ownership of the bank. Later the government took over total ownership of it. Consequently, most of the senior staff positions in the bank were filled by the leaders and members of the NCNC. For example, in 1958, A. K. Blankson was its Managing Director as well as the national auditor of the party and the Managing Director of the *West African Pilot*, the Associated Newspapers of Nigeria and the Comet Press which constituted the main publicity arm of the party and the Zik Group of Companies. F. S. McEwen was both the national secretary of the party and the General Manager of the *West African Pilot*.

20. *Western House of Assembly Debates, Official Report* (Ibadan: Western Regional Government Printer, December 1956), pp. 67–68.
21. *Report of the Tribunal Appointed to Inquire into Allegations Reflecting on the Official Conduct of the Premier of, and Certain Persons Holding Ministerial and Other Public Offices in, the Eastern Region of Nigeria* Cmnd. 51 (London: HMSO, 1957), pp. 22–23.
22. *Ibid.*

In 1957, the Zik Group was indebted to the African Continental Bank for ₦600,000 in debentures and overdrafts.[23] That year also, the NCNC itself owed the bank ₦194,518 in bank overdraft.[24] The ruling party used public funds invested in the bank for its party political activities. In addition, the bank served as a source of soft loans for the leading members of the party and those businessmen with party connections, notably to the licensed buying agents of the marketing board who purchased controlled crops from middlemen or directly from the producers at fixed prices. By 1957, African agents, supported financially by the A.C.B., supplied 49 per cent of all the palm oil bought by the Eastern regional marketing board.[25] In 1958, the marketing board withdrew the licence of one of its buying agents, L. N. Obioha, when the latter joined a newly formed opposition party, the Democratic Party of Nigeria and the Cameroons (DPNC) led by K. O. Mbadiwe, as the Vice Patron and principal financial backer. Indicative of this relationship between political and economic activities was the association of the DPNC with a new bank founded in Lagos by the party's Patron, and with a newly established newspaper.[26] Similarly, in 1960, the NPC set up the Bank of the North in which the Northern Regional Government had a controlling interest. The bank's nominal share capital ₦500,000 was subscribed to by the Northern Region Development Corporation, Northern Region Marketing Board, and individual supporters of the NPC[27].

The Eastern Region Finance Corporation also gave rise to other sources of patronage for the privileged classes. By 1956, four public boards and eight Corporations had been created. Ninety-two persons other than the chairmen had been appointed to them.[28] Apart from the emoluments paid out to their personnel, these institutions also provided opportunities for various types of lucrative contract work and services. Most of these contracts were awarded to those businessmen in the region with the correct political party connection. In 1958, the government terminated the appointment of O. N. Egesi as the Chairman of the Cinema Corporation because of his active involvement in the

23. Richard Sklar, *op. cit.*, p. 454.
24. *Ibid.*
25. *Ibid.*, 449.
26. *Ibid.*
27. *Ibid.*, pp. 458–459, footnote 58.
28. *Ibid.*

campaign of the Reform Committee against Azikiwe's leadership of the party.[29]

Thus, the regionalisation of the marketing boards which was embarked upon as a result of agitations guided by the ethnically-loaded slogan of West for the Westerners, East for the Easterners, and North for the Northerners, served the economic interest of the regions' privileged classes. Businessmen obtained contracts, traders secured trading licenses, and both received loans from banks whose solvency depended on money derived from the marketing board surpluses. Legal practitioners benefitted from the large amount of legal business which the various institutions established with some of these surpluses. Lecturers teaching in the new universities built with marketing board funds tended to advertise their party and ethnic loyalties.

Of course, some benefits accrued to the underprivileged classes, including government scholarships, roads, water supply and jobs. But these benefits did not have a class character similar to that of benefits accruing to the privileged classes alone. While one had to be a businessman to secure contracts and loans, all people and classes enjoyed the benefits of the scholarship, road, and educational programmes. The regionalisation of national wealth was not necessary for the attainment of those benefits which were general in nature; only a good government was necessary. On the other hand, in the intraclass struggle for wealth within the privileged classes, regionalisation was both imperative and inevitable. Ethnicity and regionalisation serviced the interests of many, but it serviced the interests of some more than others. In the pervasive atmosphere of ethnicity that prevailed, this differential was blurred. Interethnic rather than intraclass competition for the national wealth stood out.

While the business and commercial sections of the privileged classes were the major beneficiaries of the interethnic struggle for the wealth created by the marketing boards' exploitation of the farmers, the bureaucratic section of the petty bourgeoisie gained most from the interethnic struggle for posts in the Civil Service. In its struggle against colonialism, Nigerian petty bourgeois nationalism was strongly motivated by the exclusion of the Nigerian petty bourgeoisie from the perquisities of office in the colonial bureaucracy. Hence, the nationalists frequently demanded the Nigerianisation of that institution. Their emphasis was

29. *Ibid.*

on putting Nigerians in the senior posts in the governmental administration, paying them the same salaries, and providing them with housing in the racially segregated Government Reserved Areas (G.R.A.). Obviously, the emergent Nigerian bureaucratic petty bourgeoisie felt no qualms about enjoying benefits based on class and racial distinctions which excluded the vast majority of its compatriots. The most scandalous of these was the segregation in housing. In their desire to replace racial with class segregation in housing, these members of the privileged classes could ignore ethnicity. The Igbo bureaucrat residing at the GRA, Enugu, segregated himself from other Igbo residing elsewhere in the city. Worst still, he mobilised the latter to fight for this system of segregation under the banner of nationalism.

By 1945, Nigerianisation had become a serious political issue in the country. The post war economic expansion, together with the desire of the colonialists to intensify colonial economic exploitation of the country for purposes of the post war recovery of Britain, and the necessity to make some gesture toward economic development in response to the growth of the socialist world, impelled the colonial government to increase the size of the governmental bureaucracy. Its attempt to fill the new posts with overseas candidates from the demobilised services clearly demonstrated official reluctance to employ Nigerians in the senior posts. Hence the nationalists' demand for Nigerianisation.

In 1945, there were less than 1,300 expatriates and only 75 permanent local senior civil servants in Nigeria. But a total of 2,225 was needed. By the middle of 1948, the number had increased by 1,561 to 3,786, but nearly one-third of this total, 1,245, was vacant. Only 245 posts were occupied by Africans.[30] Such a situation in which so few Nigerians reached the senior ranks in spite of the availability of positions was clearly intolerable, and called for a change.

In reluctant reaction, the colonial government appointed a commission to ascertain ways to remedy the situation. This commission was headed by Sir Hugh Foot, the chief secretary to the Government and included Nnamdi Azikiwe. Among other things, it recommended that Nigerians should be appointed to senior Civil Service posts as fast as suitable candidates with the

---

30. I. F. Nicolson, *The Administration of Nigeria, 1900–1960* (London: Oxford University Press, 1969), pp. 258–261.

necessary qualifications came forward. In addition, it recommended the provision of more scholarships and training courses in order to ensure that the necessary qualifications were obtained.[31] This was the beginning of the scramble by the local petty bourgeois bureaucrats for positions and promotions in the public service. By 1954, this scramble had become involved in the process of the politicisation of ethnicity. It became an integral aspect of the interethnic struggle for national wealth. Ethnic forces were mobilised on behalf of those struggling for posts and promotions in the colonial bureaucracy. Consequently, the public service began to be regionalised even before the federal constitution of 1954 came into force. In addition to the nationalist struggle against the presence of expatriates in the bureaucracy, the various regional factions of the petty bourgeoisie also struggled for positions and promotions in the various regions.

For example, in 1952, the Nigerian Council of Ministers set up a commission to study the Nigerianisation policy. It reported in 1953, recommending steps to limit the appointment and promotion of non-Nigerians, and to encourage the appointment of qualified Nigerians.[32] A Nigerianisation officer was appointed to accelerate the process. In March, 1958, in response to further political pressure, the House of Representatives appointed a special committee to study the progress so far made and to suggest how to initiate further progress. Its report, published in 1959, denounced the existing programme of Nigerianisation and the perquisites of expatriates. It decried the fact that, of the 73 superscale posts in the administrative service, only 10 were held by Nigerians or other West Africans as compared with 63 held by expatriates. Nigerians held only 1 of 14 posts of Permanent Secretary, 6 of 35 posts of Deputy Permanent Secretary, and 6 of 34 posts of senior Assistant Secretary.[33]

At the same time, the Northern Region was apprehensive that Nigerianisation would mean the Southernisation of the

31. *Report of the Commission Appointed by his Excellency The Governor to Make Recommendations about the Recruitment and Training of Nigerians for Senior Posts in the Government Service of Nigeria* (Lagos: Government Printer, 1948).
32. Sir Sydney Phillipson and S. O. Adebo, *The Nigerianization of the Civil Service, Review of Policy and Machinery* (Lagos: Government Printer, 1954).
33. Taylor Cole, "Bureaucracy in Transition" in Robert O. Tilman and Taylor Cole, eds. *The Nigerian Political Scene* (Durham, North Carolina: Duke University Press, 1962) p. 104.

posts in the region if Southern Nigerians continued to replace expatriates. Therefore, in May, 1952, the Northern Regional Government resolved that suitable and qualified Northerners would be given preference over others in the recruitment of public service personnel, and that no Southerner would be appointed without prior consultation with the Northern Regional Executive Council. The Western Regional Government, while freezing the expatriation allowance, expressed serious misgivings over the appointment of Easterners to posts in the West, particularly in the Police. It became clear that with the politicisation of ethnicity, a national programme of Nigerianisation was doomed.

The situation was reinforced by the lack of the uniformity of educational and other policies in the North and South in the previous half century. The move toward Nigerianization in 1948 occured well before the creation of a federal structure of government and the resultant emergence of regional public services. Initially, the process was viewed as one of finding and training the best qualified Nigerians available and appointing them to posts in the unitary structure of the public service. Between 1948 and 1952 the number of Nigerians in the Senior Service had increased by 180 per cent, from 245 to 685.[34] Most of these had been promoted from junior posts. Nigerians now constituted 19 per cent of the senior section of the Service. With education in the North so far behind that in the South, Nigerianisation meant that the senior branches of the service would be occupied by Southerners who also dominated the junior posts. Practically all the students in institutions of higher learning both overseas and in Nigeria were from the South.[35] Educated Southerners pressed their demands for the admission of Nigerians to the Senior Service but the educated and uneducated Northerners alike were not prepared to see the Southerners replace the expatriates in the North and, therefore, called for the continuation of expatriates in the regional service. Under these circumstances, it was difficult to keep ethnic politics out of the Civil Service.

The statutory regionalisation of the unitary public service of Nigeria was the logical outcome of the federal arrangement ushered in by the 1954 constitution. On 1 October 1954, Regional Public Services were inaugurated with civil servants occupying

34. *Ibid.*
35. *Ibid.*

posts provided for in the regional budget. The regional legislatures discussed and decided provisions for new posts, salaries,
allowances, and conditions of service of the new regional bureaucracies. Recruitment, transfer, dismissal, and other forms of
disciplinary actions came under the control of the regional governor, with the regional Public Service Commission acting as his
adviser. Only the junior staff mourned this break-up of the old
unitary services. Their unions protested against this fragmentation. The senior civil servants were rather excited by the much
better prospects of promotion in the new regional departments,
ministries, corporations, and public companies. With more
bouyant revenues than before, the new regional governments
would spend lavishly on expensive cars, houses, and foreign
tours for Ministers and senior civil servants. Also, there was the
opportunity to award contracts and issue licences which could
attract commissions to them. Consequently, at the federal level
there was a serious loss of Nigerian officers offered promotion in
the home regions.

This regionalisation of the civil service enabled each of the
regional governments to manipulate political and administrative policies to suit each ruling party's urgent political and other
priorities, particularly service to the regional faction of the
privileged classes. Thus, the regionalisation of the public service
reflected the interethnic struggle for national resources; it also
released a pent-up energy for furthering this struggle. In the
West which benefited most from this regionalisation, the share-
out of the unitary "senior service" came to about 500 expatriates
and 300 Nigerians in 1954. By 1960, the Western region was able
to dispense with expatriates in key posts of the regional public
service. It immediately replaced the region's nine overseas
Permanent Secretaries with Nigerians.[36]

In the East, the replacement of expatriates with Nigerians also
accelerated. However, its pace was much slower than that in the
West. The region was much poorer and, therefore, could not
expand the public service as fast as in the West. Instead of setting
up new and expensive Ministries, the government turned the old
Secretariat under a Civil Secretary into the Office of the Premier
with responsibilities for coordinating the activities of the Ministries. The number of Ministries was fewer than in the West and

36. *Nigerianization of the Public Service of Western Nigeria* (Ibadan: Government
Printer, 1960), p. 2.

the government hesitated over the payment of the Gorsuch awards to the senior civil servants. In spite of this poor financial situation, the regional bureaucracy was forced to absorb Easterners displaced from the North by the Northernisation policy of the regional government. Although there was a mutual exchange of officers between the East and West, the Eastern Region registered a net gain of officers in this interchange. Positions had to be found for them in the regional service.

In comparison with the North, however, the similarities between the East and West were greater than the differences. By 1955, each had hundreds of qualified applicants for senior service posts returning from their studies abroad or graduating from the Nigerian institutions of high learning, from whom their Public Service Commissions could choose officers. It was no longer a case of taking all applicants who had the minimum qualifications. In the North, the situation was different. The Northerners were unprepared for the Nigerianisation of their regional service with Northerners. In the absence of qualified Northerners the implementation of such a programme in the North would have meant the domination of the regional Civil Service by Southerners. With the politicisation of ethnicity, the first political imperative of the new NPC government was the Northernisation of the machinery of the regional government.

By 1955, there was hardly a single Northerner in the "senior service" of the public service. In order to prevent the better educated ethnic groups of the South from securing the senior posts and associated benefits in the Northern bureaucracy, the regional party and government adapted and began to implement the policy of Northernisation. In 1957 the policy was defined by the Regional Public Service Commission as a system wherein "if a qualified Northerner is available, he is given priority in recruitment; if no Northern is available, an expatriate may be recruited or a non-Northerner on contract terms".[37] In 1958, Sir Ahmadu Bello, the Premier of the region and President of the NPC, referred to it as a policy which aimed to have "Northerners gain control of every thing in the country".[38] Its practical consequences extended beyond the public services. For example, pressure from a number of Northern commercial groups such

37. Quoted in B. J. Dudley, *Parties and Politics in Northern Nigeria* (London: Frank Cass, 1968), p. 220.
38. Quoted in *ibid.*, p. 220.

as the Northern Transporters and Contractors Company, the Northern Nigerian Contractors Association, the Northern Transport Owners Union and the Northern Amalgamated Merchants Union led to the reassessment of the procedure of the award of contracts by the Provincial Tenders Boards to the disadvantage of Southerners. In response to further pressure the government set up a commission to enquire into the retail trade in the region. Immediately afterwards most retail trade companies found it convenient not to have Southerners in their employment.[39]

With Northernisation, the insistence in the North upon the employment of only Northerners even at the expense of a generously interpreted minimum qualification increased year by year. In actual practice the policy has emphasised the exclusion of Southern Nigerians rather than foreigners. The replacement of Southerners in all posts took higher priority than the replacement of expatriates in higher posts. The privileged classes of the North perceived the expatriates correctly as a transient phenomenon but quite incorrectly as harmless and disinterested workers. They feared that Southern Nigerians employed in the region would bring their wives, children and relations and settle there, taking leases of land, exploiting the services of Northern peasants and using their official influence to give jobs and contracts to their brothers and cousins.

This fear was so strong and pervasive that the Northern Region Public Service Commission undertook to recruit and appoint personnel for even the lowest grades of public servant, heavily over burdening its office in the process. The heads of departments or Permanent Secretaries or Residents of provinces had no powers whatever to appoint civil servants. In 1955, Appointments Advisory Committees were established to make recommendations to the Public Service Commission about provincial recruitment. In 1959, a special Northernisation Implementation Committee was established to speed up the programme of Northernisation. The implementation of the policy began at the level at which "Southernisation" had gone furthest, notably the junior ranks, proceeding from there upwards right to the top. It relied on the British expatriate personnel to keep the machinery of the public service moving and to help in training Northerners to take over in the future. Nevertheless, by August, 1960, few Northerners had reached the upper echelons of the public service. Prior to that

39. *Ibid.*, p. 220.

date there was, indeed, no Northern Permanent Secretary. By 1961, of the thirty-seven senior posts of Permanent Secretary, Resident, and Head of Department, fourteen were held by Northerners, the remaining twenty-three by expatriates, eight of whom were about to retire.[40] Whereas in 1959 all thirteen Permanent Secretaries were expatriates, in 1963, of the sixteen posts of Permanent Secretary, only four were occupied by expatriates. Too, in the latter year eleven of the thirteen heads of provincial administration, Residents or Provincial Secretaries, were Northerners.[41]

However, the 1961 figures of 143 doctors and nine dentists in the region reflects the absence of strong popular pressures on the government for education. The only pressure available came largely from the ruling classes. It was inspired by the demands of interethnic competition for the national wealth, and the requirements of the policy of Northernisation designed to use governmental power to limit this competition in the North to the advantage of Northerners.

The teaching of administration at Zaria began in 1957, but its programme was ridiculous. It emphasised "senior service" etiquette and mores, a handbook on ceremonials, including photographs of how to wear uniform, how to attend functions such as school sports days, agricultural shows, polo matches, plays and military parades. Careful attention was given to the formal side of an administrative officers responsibilities such as official entertaining and semi-official hospitality.[42]

Although Northernisation was proclaimed in 1954, it was implemented with vigour in early 1958 when the Northern government discharged over 100 clerks of non-Northern origin from the regional civil service and 600 non-Northern daily-paid workers from the Public Works Department and replaced them with Northerners. By August, 1958, a total of 2,148 Southerners had been dismissed from the Northern public service since January 1954, leaving only 24 Southerners in the senior echelons of the permanent establishment.[43] Southerners were encouraged to seek employment in their regions of origin. The promotion

40. *Ibid.*, p. 221.
41. *Ibid.*
42. John P. Mackintosh, *op. cit.*, pp. 185–186.
43. Richard Sklar, *op. cit.*, p. 327; *Daily Times*, Lagos, 19 and 25 January, *West African Pilot, Lagos,* 10 September 1958; *Daily Service*, Lagos, 5 August 1958.

prospects of those who remained in the North were frozen. By October, 1959, only one Southern senior civil servant was left in the regions' public service. The pace of Northernisation was so rapid that, while in 1955 the percentage of Northerners in the civil service was negligible, by mid-1961 it had exceeded the 50 per cent mark.[44]

Northernisation also found expression in the regional government's land policy. The original land ordinance which excluded only persons not resident in the North, was reinterpreted to exclude all persons not born in the region from owning land outside the Sabon Garris, the residential areas of non-Northern Nigerians. Obviously Northernisation was bitterly resented by Southerners living in the North who enjoyed an advantage over the Northerners in socioeconomic competition within the area.

Northernization also served as an avenue for political party patronage for members of the privileged classes. For example, in 1963, four out of the twelve Permanent Secretaries who were Northerners were at one time or another active NPC party men.[45] Ibrahim Dasuki in Local Government and Ibrahim Argungu in Establishment and Training were once NPC members of the regional House of Assembly. Ali Akilu, the Secretary to the Premier and head of the region's Civil Service was an early member of the party and the convener of its Second Convention in 1950. Similarly, most of the Provincial Secretaries (Residents) were at one time or the other active members of the party. In fact, one of them, Yahaya Gusau, was, for a period, a member of the regional legislature. The Chairman and Permanent Commissioner of the region's Public Service Commission, Abubakar Imam and Dan Buram Jada, respectively, were, at one time, members of the regional House of Assembly. Dan Buram was even a regional Minister.[46] Also, in 1963, the Native Authority officials who were members of the traditional ruling oligarchy and, therefore, part and parcel of the privileged classes, occupied 62.5 per cent of the superscale posts, 63 per cent of the Permanent Secretary positions, and 81 per cent of the post of Provincial Secretary.[47] Of course, this politicisation of the Civil Service made nonsense of the concept of the impartial and neutral public service.

44. B. J. Dudley, *op. cit.*, pp. 221–222.
45. *Ibid.*
46. *Ibid.*
47. *Ibid.*, p. 222, Table 18.

As a result of the pervasive atmosphere of ethnicity prevailing at the time of the initiation of the policy of Northernisation, intra-regional struggle for public service positions were reflected in oblique references to Sokotonisation and Bornunisation. The Sokoto influence in the Service arose from the higher level of educated manpower from the area as well as the domination of the Native Authority personnel by individuals from the Sokoto emirate. Neither education nor service in the Native Authority system can explain Bornunisation. Bornu emirate had one of the lowest standards of education in the North, with a literacy rate 0.9 per cent. But 22.5 per cent of the superscale posts were held by Bornu men, 25 per cent of the posts of Permanent Secretary and 27 per cent of the position of Provincial Secretary.[48] The offering of public service posts to Bornu men was used as an instrument to counteract Bornu separatism. One of the consequences of this Sokoto-Bornu influence was intergenerational conflict within the bureaucracy. There was the factor of educational discrepancies. Only 16.6 per cent of the twelve Permanent Secretaries were university graduates. Most of those recruited from the Native Authority Service had no post secondary education. They were, therefore, resented by those recruited later who were university graduates and who tended to come from the lower North. For example, in 1962, 66.6 per cent of new entrants to the Ahmadu Bello University came from the Lower North; in 1963 the figure was 84 per cent.[49]

While Northernisation must be condenmed as inimical to national unity because of its tendency to engender ethnocentric outlook in the North, it must be pointed out that the East and the West could afford to demand Nigerianisation based solely on qualifications essentially because they were able to achieve *de facto* Easternisation and Westernisation without recourse to official policy. Even in the West, qualifications were secondary to the criterion of the region of origin of the civil servant. In the ongoing interethnic struggle for the national wealth by the regional factions of the privileged classes, Northernisation was the only alternative open to the Northern faction to maximise its share of national resources by preventing the Southern factions from appropriating some of the resources in the region of their pre-eminence under conditions in which the Northerners had no

48. *Ibid.*, p. 232, footnote 81.
49. *Ibid.*

access to similar resources in the South. A solution to the policy of Northernisation must be an integral part of the solution to ethnic politics in Nigeria.

Interregional Struggle for Federal Resources

Thus, Nigerianisation involved efforts by the ethnically-based ruling parties in the regions to secure the complete domination of the regional public service positions by the relevant regional functionaries, or, in their absence, to prevent rival ethnic groups from filling the relevant posts. The same strategy was evident in the interethnic struggle for positions in the federal public service. In 1954, following some losses of personnel from the central public services to the regional services, there were many vacant positions in the federal bureaucracy as well as in the public service of the Southern Cameroon Government which had been sequestered from the Eastern Region. Such vacancies were to be found also in nationwide departments such as the Police, Posts and Telegraph and Civil Aviation, Geographical Survey at Kaduna, Forest and Agricultural Research at Ibadan and Mines at Jos.[50] In 1955, there were 2,450 senior posts in the federal public service but only 550 Nigerians were employed in the service.[51]

In an attempt to fill these vacant posts with Nigerians the crucial question of the ethnic composition of the federal service, particularly Northern representation, was posed. There was an overwhelming predominance of qualified Southerners for the posts while electoral power placed the NPC of the North in the leading position within the coalition government. This situation created acute tension and strain in the Nigerianisation of the federal service. The Prime Minister, a Northerner, was effectively responsible for choosing the Chairman of the Federal Public Service Commission as well as the Permanent Secretaries. Hence, a Northerner was appointed the Chairman and several Northerners were appointed Permanent Secretaries whose qualifications would not have secured their appointment on the basis of merit.[52] Consequently, a slight increase in the number of Northerners in senior positions within the federal service has been evident since 1961. For example, in 1964, fourteen of the thirty-seven Nigerians

50. *Ibid.*
51. *Ibid.*
52. John P. Mackintosh, *op. cit.*, p. 197.

employed as High Commissioners, Ambassadors and Charge-d'Affairs were Northerners. Three out of the eight members of the board of the Nigerian Coal Corporation, four of the eleven of the Nigerian Railway Corporation and six of the sixteen Permanent Secretaries were Northerners.[53]

The Public Service Commission gave preferences to applicants from the North who possessed the minimum qualifications. In addition, officials in the North were encouraged and pressured to accept positions in Lagos. Otherwise, the Northern leaders were anxious to hold back the Nigerianisation of the federal service until enough Northerners were available to fill the relevant positions. A federal coalition government that obtained over 60 per cent of its parliamentary support from adherents of the NPC was inclined to resist speedy Nigerianisation at a time when less than 1 per cent of the higher posts in the federal service were filled by Northerners and when therefore, the posts to be vacated by expatriates would almost certainly be filled by Southerners.[54] It was to remedy this situation that preferences were given to Northerners.[55]

Mention has been made of Ahmadu Bello's interpretation of the Northernisation policy as the Northern control of the resources of the Nigerian federation. The attitudes of the leaders of the other ethnically based parties were similar. They all schemed to ensure that their region of political dominance and, therefore, their own ethnic groups, controlled the federal resources. This would enable them to appropriate a disproportionate share of these resources. The federal government was responsible for raising the bulk of the country's revenues and for apportioning them. It also controlled the police and the armed forces and through them, the maintenance of law and order throughout the federation.

The federal government was expected to give an economic leadership to the rest of the country. The necessity to exercise a general control over the price level, the balance of payments, and the rate of growth led it to take over the responsibility for the overall direction of the economy. Since 1958, the federal government has assumed control over the procurement of external loans

53. B. J. Dudley, op. cit., p. 227.
54. Federation of Nigeria, Annual Report of the Nigerianization Officer for the Year 1957 (Lagos: Government Printer, 1958), p. 7.
55. Federation of Nigeria, House of Representatives Debates April 13, 1960 (Lagos: Government Printer, 1960), p. 1516.

of over one year's duration. From 1959, it took charge of the floating of internal loans. The Banking Amendment Act of 1962 made it mandatory for the regional governments and their agencies to deposit part of their reserves with the Central Bank controlled by the federal government. This Act also empowered the Bank to regulate the minimum interest rates charged by the commercial banks, to approve their interest rate structure, and to fix the liquidity ratio by determining which of their assets would be accepted in assessing the holding of the banks. In this way, the federal government gained control over the operations of the regional marketing boards and, therefore, the regions' financial policies. Later too, the federal coordinating agencies such as the Council on Establishments, the Council on Natural Resources, and the National Economic Council gradually assumed a regulative rather than their usual advisory role.

As a result of decreasing revenues consequent on falling commodity prices, the increased volume of government activities generated by regionalisation led to the depletion of regional government surpluses and the suffering of deficits on current accounts. The position of the East relatively improved as a result of increased contribution of petroleum to the region's economy. Apart from the East, however, the regional governments successfully faced budgetary deficits which they made up by reliance on federal government disbursement.

Some of the regions relied more on federal resources than others. For example, the 1962–1966 Plan implied a transfer of federal resources to the North amounting to ₦58.2 million compared with ₦39.8 million to the West and ₦24 million to the East.[56] During the plan period, the North experienced rising recurrent expenditures, inelastic revenues and, therefore, recurrent budgetary deficits and depleted reserves. The regions's salvation lay in the control of the federal government, the remaining principal source of finance. The North expected 56 per cent of its total "internal" financial resources and 37 per cent of its overall total to come from the federal government.[57]

As far as the Plan was concerned, Northern control of the federal government had been very beneficial to the North. A large proportion of development spending was concentrated in the

56. Edwin Dean, *Plan Implementation in Nigeria* (Ibadan: Ibadan University Press, 1972), p. 247.
57. *Ibid.*

region. The Kainji Dam, estimated to cost ₦136.2 million, was to be located there, representing more than 10 per cent of the federal government's total spending. In the view of one economist, enough power could have been generated at less than one fifth of the cost of the dam by using natural gas.[58] But the gas was located in the South. Almost all of the ₦59.4 million allocated for defence was to be spent in the North. Apart from the federal institutions such as Ibadan University and Lagos University, including their teaching hospitals, most of the ₦78.4 million to be spent on health and education went to the North.[59] In 1963–1964, the North received over 50 per cent of the federal disbursement for agricultural expansion. Of the ₦20 million voted for this expansion ₦8 million was disbursed that year. The shares of the various regions were as follows: North ₦4.4 million, East ₦2.2 million and West ₦1.4 million.[60]

Much of the ₦94.6 million voted for transportation was also spent in the North. Out of this, the Bornu Railway Extension received an allocation of ₦24 million.[61] Between 1960 and 1962, the mileage of Trunk "A" roads belonging to the federal government which were constructed and tarred in each region were: North 149½ miles, West 19, East 85, and Lagos 3. In 1960–1961, estimated expenditure on roads was ₦6.6 million in the North, ₦4.8 million in the West and ₦3.4 million in the East. The costs of maintaining and building of aerodromes were ₦136,628 in the North, ₦48,812 in the West, and ₦53,084 in the East. Bridges planned in 1960 were as follows: North one each of 40 feet, 160 feet, and 240 feet span; East two of 40 feet span; and West one of 40 feet span.[62]

Also, by its control of the federal government the North ensured that in the struggle for federal resources there could be no policy which ran contrary to the interest of the leaders of that Region. Hence, it refused to allow the federal exploitation of the iron ore located in the region unless the ore-using industry was sited in the North. This attitude delayed the establishment of the proposed iron and steel industry in the country for three years during which intense political negotiations were carried on in the

58. I. M. D. Little, *Aid to Africa* (London: Overseas Development Institute, 1964), pp. 16–20.
59. B. J. Dudley, *op. cit.*, p. 277.
60. *Ibid.*
61. *Ibid.*
62. *Ibid.*, p. 293, footnote 47.

National Economic Council. Economically it was more lucrative to set up the industry near Port Harcourt in the East. By the time the negotiations were over Northern pressure had succeeded in forcing· through a decision to build two steel plants, one in the East and the other in the North, with the probability of a third being sited in the West. Instead of building one steel plant with a capacity for the production of $\frac{1}{4}$ million tons of steel, the decision meant the setting up of two plants each with half that capacity which would be less profitable to operate.[63]

The benefits accruing to the North as a result of these appropriations of federal resources become clearer within the context of the problems faced by the South at the time. By 1962, unemployment of pupils with school certificates and higher qualifications had increased by the alarming figure of 102 per cent from 1952. The corresponding figure for unemployment of primary school leavers and those with lower education was 89.8 per cent.[64] The average rate of urban unemployment in the South was more than twice the figure of the North, 28.9 per cent as against 13.1 per cent. Even in the South this high unemployment was unequally distributed among the component regions as follows: 38.4 per cent in Lagos 29.0 per cent in the East and 19.5 per cent in the West.[65] The situation becomes even clearer when it is realised that, with the increasing balance of payments difficulties at the time arising from a deteriorating terms of trade and an escalating governmental expenditure, oil production in the South was becoming the mainline of defense in the foreign exchange front. During the 1962–1966 plan period, oil alone was expected to contribute over ₦2 million in foreign exchanges.[66]

This disproportionate appropriation of federal resources was not a unique policy of the NPC. In fact, it pervaded the thinking and polices of the other major parties. The only difference, of course, lày in their capacity to carry it out. Since the NPC consistently dominated the federal government it was able to achieve its ambition in this regard. But even the NCNC was moderately successful in achieving the same goal. Although always the junior partner, it was consistently a member of the federal coalition

63. *Ibid.*
64. Federation of Nigeria, *Annual Report of the Federal Ministry of Labour for the Year 1961–62* (Lagos: Government Printer 1964), p. 12.
65. *Ibid.*
66. M. S. Robinson, "Nigerian Oil – Prospects and Perspectives", *Nigerian Journal of Economic and Social Studies*, Vol. VI, No. 2 (1969), p. 154.

government. An example of a political decision in its favour concerns the building of the petroleum pipelines from the oil-producing areas of the West to the terminal in the East where the shipment of the oil would take place. Ports in the West, notably Forcados in the Midwest, were closer to Europe, the destination of the oil, than those in East. Too, the port facilities at Bonny were inadequate. It took a considerable investment of capital to transform it into a port capable of taking tankers of 60,000 tons. Forcados, on the other hand, could handle tankers of over 200,000 tons. Also after independence, there was a gradual shift in the location of industries from the West to both the North and the East. This is reflected in increases in electricity consumption. Of the regions, the East had experienced an increase of about 230 per cent between 1958–1959 and 1964–1965, the North 182 per cent and the West 50 per cent.[67]

By far the most important and persistent struggle among the ethnic groups for federal resources was carried on over revenue allocation. The federal government is the principal revenue earner in the country. Therefore, the central government has always controlled more resources than its component units. Prior to the Richards Constitution of 1946, the central government controlled most of the sources of revenue in the nation, except the direct or poll taxes which the local administrations levied and collected. Often the central government aided the provincial administrations financially. But at times, the latter aided the former. For example, during the depression of the 1930s, the revenue of the central government, which depended essentially on customs duties, was badly depleted, whereas the revenues of the native administrations accruing mainly from direct taxes were not so badly affected. The governor, Sir Donald Cameron, sought financial aid from the native administrations. Again, as a result of the difficulties of the World War II, the governor, Sir Bernard Bourdillon, appropriated the reserves of the native administrations at the outset of the war promising to refund the money at the end of the war. He discontinued the practice during the fiscal year 1940–1941 and refunded the appropriated fund in 1942.[68]

67. A. Bamishaiye, "Ethnic Politics as An Instrument of Unequal Socioeconomic Development in Nigeria's First Republic" in A. O. Sanda, ed.) *Ethnic Relations in Nigeria* (Ibadan: Ibadan University Press, 1976), pp. 87–89.

68. Nigeria, *Report of the Fiscal Commissioner on the Financial Effects of the Proposed New Constitutional Arrangements* Comnd. 9026 (London: H.M.S.O., 1953), p.2.

Following the Richard's Constitution, certain sources of revenues were regionalised. Regional revenues were derived from licenses for, and taxes on, hunting, liquor, motor vehicles, and driving, forestry, rents on mining rights and leases, court fees, water supply projects, direct and income taxes, reimbursements and miscellaneous sources. Obviously, money collected from these sources were much less than that accruing to the federal government essentially from customs duties, interest, posts and telegraphs, railways, direct tax, fees, excise duties, export duties, company tax, corporation tax, mining royalties, and the profits of public corporations. The Hicks-Phillipson Commission, arising from the Ibadan Constitutional Conference in 1950, recommended that regional revenues should be augmented by taxes on petrol which should be placed under regional control. But the federal government postponed the decision, pending a study of the practical difficulties of implementing it.

Since only a fraction of this central government's revenue was required for the running of the central governmental institutions and agencies, the excess fund was available for allocation to the various governmental units in the country. With the politicisation of ethnicity, regionalisation of politics, and domination of the regions by ethnically-based political parties, interethnic struggle for the national wealth found an expression in the interregional struggle for this revenue. Competition among the regional leaders was very bitter. They badly needed this money to supplement that accruing from the regionalisation of the funds of the marketing boards. In the struggle, factions of the privileged classes in one region virtually ignored the fortunes of the rival factions in the other regions.

Various revenue allocation commissions were appointed as referees in this competition. The first of these was the Phillipson Commission of 1946. This commission recommended the principles of derivation and even progress as the fair basis for allocating federal revenues to the regions. By derivation is meant the principle by which revenues originating from within a region are allocated to it. The notion of even progress required that in the interest of an even development of the country, a relatively poor region should receive a relatively disproportionate share of federal revenues. Difficulties arose in the implementation of the Phillipson formula, with the North arguing that the money that was due to it had gone to the East, while the latter and the West charged that the North had received an unfairly large allocation.

The dispute came to a head at the Ibadan Constitutional Conference of 1950. The Northern delegates argued for the distribution of central revenues to the region on a per capita basis, those from the West called for the unalloyed adoption of the principle of derivation in view of its overwhelming contribution to such revenue, while the Eastern delegates pleaded on behalf of the principle of need which was more beneficial to their relatively poor region. The resultant Hicks-Phillipson Commission recommended the principles of independent revenue, need, national interest, and special grant. In accordance with the notion of independent revenue the regional governments would exercise clear control over tax rates on taxable regional revenue matters, and decide how much of the direct taxes would be administered by the native administrations. Population was used as a vague criterion of need, to be satisfied by a capitation grant based on the number of adult tax payers in the region. The commission recommended a special grant of ₦4 million to the North to help it cover deficiencies in equipment. National interest was left undefined but on the basis of it the Commission recommended: (a) a grant to each region equal to its educational grants-in-aid to the local areas (b) a refund to each region of all regional expenditures on the Nigerian Police force, minus those for staff buildings, (c) a refund of regional expenditures on the maintenance and equipment of the native administration police force, minus those for buildings, and (d) the establishment of a loan commission for the formulation of loan policies.

Nevertheless, central government's expendable revenue continued to be allocated arbitrarily on the basis of derivation with some regard to the principle of even progress. However, the period 1952–1954 saw the gradual introduction of the principle of independent revenues and tax jurisdiction for regional governments. Some regional leaders even demanded that large firms be required to reorganise their administration to facilitate the regionalisation of import duties. Other extreme views included a suggestion that the federal government should be just a little more than the agent of regional governments, and that it should derive its funds from a levy on regional governments.

In 1954, Sir Louis Chick was appointed to review the system of revenue allocation. His report was unequivocal in its emphasis on the principle of derivation. In his terms of reference he had been enjoined to ensure that "the principle of Derivation is followed to the fullest degree compatible with meeting the reasonable needs of the Centre and each of the Regions."[44] However, he also recommended that the federal government should have discretionary power to make grants to the regions when they are in serious difficulties. Following the government's acceptance and implementation of the report in 1954, the federal government had a surplus of ₦8.32 million, the North ₦3.08 million, the West ₦8.98 million, while the East had a deficit of ₦0.92 million. It was, therefore, recommended that the East be relieved of expenditure on Southern Cameroons, be allowed to impose a sales tax, and be granted ₦1.0 million that year to help it overcome its financial difficulties. In the division of the uncommitted reserves, the North received ₦6 million, the West ₦4 million and the East ₦4 million.[69]

The Yoruba faction of the privileged classes stood to benefit most from the application of the principle of derivation. Although there was a boom in the sellers' markets for the products of the West and North, cocoa and columbite respectively, the revenue from the sale of cocoa far outstripped that of any other product. Hence, in 1956, in a budget speech, the Premier of the Western Region publicly rejoiced over the benefits his government received from the application of the principle of derivation in the allocation of revenues. But even the leaders of the East which benefited least accepted the principle in the hope that the imminent discovery of petroleum in the region would turn it to their advantage. Even then these leaders attacked it as discriminating against the East at a time when the former primary source of national revenue and the region's main source, palm produce, had declined in competition with other countries and other types of oil.

By 1957 the application of the principle of derivation had "poisoned intergovernmental relationship and had exacerbated interregional rivalry and conflict. Perhaps more than any other single factor, it had hampered the development of a sense of national unity or common citizenship in Nigeria."[70] It soon became clear that, in relation to its size and needs, the North suffered most from the application of the principle. Northern opposition to it became vehement. At the same time slumps in the cocoa trade of the West and the columbite trade of the North whittled away the earlier advantages to the West of the principle.

In response to these and other criticisms and developments the

69. E. O. Awa, op. cit., p. 200.
70. A. Adedeji, Nigerian Federal Finance (London: Hutchinson, 1969) p. 254.

Raisman Commission on revenue allocation, approved by the 1957 Constitutional Conference, played down the principle of derivation. Instead it took account of (a) population, (b) the basic responsibilities of each regional government, (c) the need for continuity in regional public services, and (d) the need for a balanced development of the country. The excess federal revenue to be allocated to the regions was referred to as the distributable pool. Out of this pool, 40 per cent would go to the North, 24 per cent to the West, 31 per cent to the East, and 5 per cent to the Southern Cameroons. In addition, mining rents and royalties should be allocated as follows: 50 per cent to the region of origin, 20 per cent to the federal government, and 30 per cent to the "distributable pool." The General Import Revenue should be allocated as follows: 70 per cent to the federal government, and 30 per cent to the "distributable pool.[71]

Although, by and large, Nigerians welcomed the recommendations of the Raisman Commission, the regional governments agreed that the federal government should appoint, from time to time, a Fiscal Review Commission. Before the end of party politics in 1966, only one such commission had been appointed. In 1965, the Binn's Commission was appointed. This commission accepted, among other things, arguments of the various regional governments for a substantial increase in the "distributable pool," and the payment to the regions of a block annual grant on the basis of 53.3 per cent to the North, 21.3 per cent to the East, 16 per cent to the West, and 9.3 per cent to the newly created Midwest. The aim was to place each region in a comparable financial position such that, after making due allowance for differences in financial policies, it can make an equivalent contribution from its recurrent budget towards the financing of its capital development programme.[72]

In spite of these various recommendations and their implementation, the problem of revenue allocation still plagues the country. It has remained an emotional, sensitive, and highly politicised issue. The regional factions of the privileged classes have continued to manoeuvre and scheme for greater advantages in the

71. Federation of Nigeria, *Preliminary Report of the Fiscal Commission* Cmnd. 481 (London: H.M.S.O., 1958).
72. I. O. Dina, "Fiscal Measures" in A. A. Ayida and H. M. A. Onitiri, *Reconstruction and Development in Nigeria* (Ibadan: Oxford University Press, 1971), pp. 381–383.

division of the common cake. Only in this manner can they improve their benefits from society.

Rivalry in the Provision of Amenities

Interethnic socioeconomic competition was also expressed in the rivalry of the various regional governments for the provision of welfare services to populations under their control. Mention has been made of the socioeconomic basis of the emergence of ethnicity; that for the individual ethnic group associations largely performed the function of widening opportunities for employment, education and the enjoyment of good medical services and other forms of social security. It is to be expected, therefore, that with the politicisation of ethnicity, ruling parties, identified with the various ethnic groups and commanding much vaster resources than the ethnic unions, would take over most of the functions of the latter. Essentially their legitimacy and, therefore, the continued support of the members of the ethnic group depended on the party's ability to deliver the social welfare goods.

One example can be seen in fact that the initial difficulties of the Action Group to make good its promise of free universal primary education cost it the 1954 federal elections in the West. In 1953, the AG government of the region imposed an education and health levy of ₦1.50 per taxpayer towards the cost of the region's welfare plans. In spite of the strenuous effort of the government to justify this tax, it was deeply and widely resented by the population. This resentment was exploited by the NCNC opposition which claimed that only 25K rather than ₦1.50 charged by the government was required, and that the surplus would be used by the Ministers to enrich themselves. In Oyo these anti-tax sentiments led to riots in which several people were killed. Since the new taxes were to be paid before the children began to enjoy the free education programme it was difficult to convince the people of the merit of the levy when no results could be shown.

Hence, the AG suffered badly in the November 1954 election to the Federal House of Representatives. It obtained only 35 per cent of the vote and 18 seats compared with the NCNC's 53 per cent of the vote and 23 seats. Anti-tax independent candidates obtained 12 per cent of the vote and one seat.[73] By contrast, in 1956 when the free education programme was working relatively

73. *Ibid.*

well, the AG fared much better in the regional elections than in the 1954 federal elections. It won about half the popular vote and 48 of the 70 seats.[74]

The Nigerian privileged classes could only expect to mobilise mass support, particularly in the villages, by promising more welfare services than the British or the chiefs could deliver. This was clearly the case in the South where their hold on the population was quite tenuous. It was more so for such parties as the Action Group which came later than the NCNC. The latter had already appropriated most of the support accruing from militant anticolonialism. For example, the first badge of the AG was the mosquito symbolising militant anticolonialism. Its first motto was "Freedom from British Rule". When the leaders realised that the masses hardly rallied behind these slogans they discarded them. In their stead, they adopted the palm tree as a badge, symbolising wealth and prosperity, and changed their motto to: "Freedom for All and Life More Abundant." Egbe Afenifere, the AG Yoruba name means "the society of the lovers of good things." The risk lay in the fact that, with limited resources, the inability to deliver the promised welfare would generate a hostile public reaction.

In the absence of conflicting anti-imperial or ideological platforms, the Southern political parties depended for their votes on promising to provide amenities for the populace. This emphasis on welfare in party politics was reinforced by the politicisation of ethnicity. Ethnic group loyalties are consolidated and the ruling parties' mass base strengthened when amenities are provided to the ethnic group as a whole without disrupting established social patterns. It is not surprising that more than any other ruling party, the AG emphasised the provision of welfare services. This was not unrelated to the schisms in Yoruba support for the party and the desire to overcome them.

Thus, in the absence of disagreements on the fundamentals of politics, the various ruling political parties competed with one another in promising the same thing such as hospitals, educational facilities, roads, and industries. With the politicisation of ethnicity, this competition was translated into interethnic rivalry in the provision of social welfare. Ethnic ascendancy in this competition promoted pride in the ingroup.

The level and rate of colonial socioeconomic attainments has become a basis for interethnic inferiorisation and the myth of

74. *Ibid.*

ethnic superiority.[75] For example, in 1947, Obafemi Awolowo asserted that,

"In embracing Western culture, the Yorubas take the lead, and have benefitted immensely as a result. The Efiks, the Ijaws, the Ibibios and the Ibos come next. The last four named are particularly ambitious, and are doing all they can to overtake the Yorubas. The Hausas and Fulanis on the other hand are extremely conservative, and take reluctantly to Western civilisation ... And if the race is to be swift, in spite of their lower cultural background, the Ibos or the Ibibios would certainly qualify for self-government, long before the Hausas.[76]

As a result of the close relationship between the racism of colonialism and this ethnic ideology of the colonised, the nationalist challenge to colonialism was accompanied by the struggle of the ethnic groups to move up the ladder of interethnic inequality and achieve a favourable position in the system of ethnic stratification. Associated with this was the desire for cultural self respect, assertiveness, and ascendancy in the interethnic scheme of things. In fact, much of the ethnic tension in African politics emanates from this struggle. The privileged ethnic groups are reluctant to make the necessary sacrifice for raising the socioeconomic standards of the underprivileged. And the latter are too impatient to tolerate a gradual long-drawn process of equalisation. Sooner or later competition turns to conflict. The consequence is interethnic acrimony which divides, undermines, and weakens the African nation.

Interethnic rivalry in the provision of amenities is significant for the interethnic struggle for federal resources. In the field of education, for example, an important initial goal was to prepare Nigerians for employment in the colonial administration, mines, and private firms. Nigerians were needed essentially as clerks and artisans in these institutions and as subordinates in the army and police force. Later, a small beginning was made in training them for higher positions in the technical services. Obviously, therefore, the share of the various ethnic groups in the Nigerianisation of the federal public service was dependent, in part, on the availability of qualified personnel from the ethnic groups. The provision of educational facilities in an ethnic homeland improved the

75. Aristide Zolberg, *Creating Political Order* (Chicago: Rand/McNally, 1966), p. 69.
76. Obafemi Awolowo, *Path to Nigerian Freedom* (London: Faber and Faber, 1947), p. 49.

chances of the relevant ethnic group in the struggle for positions in the federal service. The occupation of such positions generated other returns to the homeland because of the tendency of senior civil servants to divert federal contracts, projects, and other resources under their control to members of their ethnic group and to their ethnic homeland. Similarly, in the field of industrialisation, success in the competition increases the financial power, growth, and supremacy of the relevant regional faction of the business community.

Also, such rivalry is politically significant in efforts to woo support for the winning faction. This is particularly important in the minority areas. Since each ruling party seeks the support of minority elements in its rivals' regions, it presents them with bright prospects of welfare benefits and, consequently, wins their support if it can demonstrate its superiority in the provision of amenities to the population under its control. In addition, this superiority may help to fan the embers of minority agitation by providing an ideal with which the regional government may be assessed and criticised. The inability to provide amenities to the same level as in the ideal region becomes a basis for charging the regional government with neglect of the ethnic minorities. On the contrary, threat of withdrawal or non-provision of amenities and the consequent lowering of the ethnic group's status in the system of stratification may be used to intimidate minorities into supporting the regional government. Such thinking was important in the alliance between the Äkintola faction of the Western ruling circles and their Northern counterparts, the fear that the Yoruba privileged classes were being left out of the interethnic scheme of things.

This intergovernmental rivalry in the provision of amenities is pervasive. For example it is evident in the field of industrialisation. Although manufacturing has never represented a high proportion of the nation's total production, it occupies a special status in the minds and hearts of Nigerians as a symbol of modernity. Regional rivalry in all fields spurred industrial development but also led to the duplication of industries. By 1966, there were cement factories in the East, West and North; bicycle-assembly, bitumen-processing, and asbestos-cement plants were located in both the East and West; factories for bakery products, textiles, brewing, book-binding, cigarette manufacture, furniture metal fabrication, soft-drink bottling, industrial gas production, printing, tyre production, toilet preparations, and the assembly of umbrellas were located in all the regions, and industries for the manufacture of plastics, shoe, prestressed concrete, pharmaceuticals, paints, phonograph records, candy, bedding, dairying and enamelware were situated in one or more of the country's major political subdivisions.[77]

Interregional rivalry led the North to proclaim that it would have a cement mill well before the project had been proved feasible and justificable. More illustrative still was the establishment of a glass factory in the East.[78] On 22 June 1961, the Western Nigeria Development Corporation and the Amkor Corporation of New York were reported to have signed an agreement enabling the latter to construct a ₦4.2 million brewery and glass plant in the Region. The Eastern Region, which hitherto was conducting tests on its glass sands, reacted immediately by announcing the decision to set up a glass factory in the Region that would be completely owned by the Eastern Nigeria Development Corporation. This decision was taken even though two glass manufacturing factories in the country were not economically advisable in view of the limited market. Such excessive fragmentations of the national market constituted a threat to an intergrated industrial development.

Again, in the textile industry there was a similar regional "me-tooism." In 1954, the only spinning mill in the country was located in Mushin, Lagos. Eight years later there was an integrated textile mill in each region. The Ikeja mill, scheduled to go into production in 1962, decided to go straight into the manufacture of finished shirtings and prints unlike the Kaduna mill which took five years to achieve the same goal. However, the decision of the Ikeja mill was congruent with its immediate market which customarily purchased prints. This favorable market offset the difficulties and cost of embarking on printing. At about the same time, the Eastern Region, contrary to expert advise, decided that its projected integrated mill to be opened in Aba in 1962 should be reworked to include the capability for bleaching, finishing, dyeing, and printing.[79]

Such uneconomic and unadvisable emulation of one region by another caused inefficiencies in the use of the nation's resources.

77. Alan Sokolski, *The Establishment of Manufacturing in Nigeria* (New York: Praegu, 1965), pp. 266–267.
78. *Ibid.*, p. 276.
79. *Ibid.*, pp. 249–250.

The economic advantage of Nigeria's large population lies in its relationship to a large national market and the impact on economies of scale. The fragmentation of the economy into regional components caused unnecessary duplication of efforts and created market difficulties for some of the country's manufactured products.

One of the consequences of the colonially induced pattern of consumption and resource use in the dominant economy of the country was the limitation of the size of the national market because of the neglect of the consumption habits of the vast majority of the country's population. Since protected foreign markets are closed to Nigerian products, and the import-substitution manufacturing strategy of the nation dictates an emphasis on the domestic market, the fragmentation of the already limited domestic market would necessitate a corresponding decrease in the scale of industry. But for the privileged classes, such patriotic considerations were secondary to their class interests of enriching themselves in the short term and mobilising the political support of their ethnic followers through prestige projects.

By far the most glaring and politically significant rivalry between the regions for the provision of amenities was the competition over the free primary education schemes in the South. They were the most widely publicised, most expensive and most administratively demanding schemes launched during the 1950s. The Action Group leaders were the first to conceive the scheme. And they were motivated by their perception that their region of control lagged educationally behind the East controlled by their main rival the NCNC. Obafemi Awolowo claimed that, when the AG came to power in the West, primary school attendance rates in the East were 65 per cent but 35 per cent in the West. He also believed that there were 105 secondary schools in the East and only 25 in the West.[80] These claims were exaggerated in that, in fact, the West, including Lagos, actually exceeded the East in the number of secondary schools and secondary school enrollment. Nevertheless during the early 1950s the West was educationally behind the East because an estimated 33 per cent of the 5–13 age group in the West compared to 37 per cent in the East were enrolled in primary schools in 1952.[81]

80. Obafemi Awolowo, *Awo: The Autobiography of Chief Obafemi Awolowo* (Cambridge: Cambridge University Press, 1960), p. 262.
81. David Abernethy, *The Political Dilemma of Popular Education* (Stanford, Cal.: Stanford University Press, 1969), pp. 139–140.

The launching of the free primary education by the West was a deliberate attempt by the AG leaders to close this educational gap between the two regions. However, they soon ran into financial difficulties in the implementation of the plan. In response, the regional government decided in 1953 to impose an education and health levy of ₦1.50 per person primarily to finance the project. The ever-present competition with the East was reflected in Awolowo's speech in defence of this decision. He referred to education levies of ₦3.70 per capita imposed by communities in the East and wondered if that region was more desirous of education or richer than the West. He enjoined Westerners to emulate people in the East in order to avoid doing harm to their generation. When Nnamdi Azikiwe, the NCNC opposition leader in the Western House of Assembly, challenged the wisdom of the levy, arguing that it was unduly high and beyond the means of the average Westerner, an AG minister charged him with seeking to "lull the West into a sense of security so that the East where they are in power may go on forging further ahead in the race for education than the West".[82] Obviously, the regional government was determined not to lose this race. It went ahead with the levy in spite of its unpopularity, exorbitant cost, and its negative consequences for the ruling party at the 1954 federal elections.

In 1955 the Western Region introduced free primary education in the West. The political benefits were immediate. In the regional elections that year for the Western House of Assembly, the AG was much more successful than at the federal elections of 1954, winning almost half of the seats. This political success spurred the NCNC government of the East to introduce a similar scheme in its region of control. This regional "me-tooism" was clearly reflected in 1955 by the Eastern Minister of Education's admission that the example of the free primary education in the West and Lagos forced his government to follow suit: "We have heard that in the Federal Government (Lagos), universal primary education will be introduced in 1957. The West has already introduced this. I would just ask the Honourable Member: Where do you want us to go?"[83]

The importance of interregional rivalry in the Eastern Region's decision becomes clearer within the context of the relatively inferior financial capacity of the region to implement the prog-

82. Quoted in *ibid.*, p. 140.
83. Quoted in *ibid.*, p. 142.

ramme. The East was much poorer than the West at the time. Following the regionalisation of the assets of the marketing boards and the allocation of revenues on the basis of derivation it could not be otherwise. In addition, by 1956, the trend in the allocation of federal funds for education was shifting from the East to the West, and the capacity of the Eastern local government authorities to generate revenue was severely constrained by widespread corruption and the inadequacy of the machinery for tax collection. In 1956, the remedial attempt of passing a finance law substituting a regional income tax for local rates yielded less than half the revenue than had been anticipated. Instead the attempt became a political liability because it was popularly interpreted as a means of paying for the cost of the free education programme.

Thus interethnic struggle for resources was carried on essentially through the instrumentality of the regional governments controlled by the various ethnic groups. Although this rivalry led to the expansion of the public services and industrialization which increased employment for the population and vastly expanded the nature and scope of governmental welfare services to the people, it encouraged ethnic thinking and identity as well as the perception of Nigerian politics as the struggle for the division of the national cake among the various ethnic groups. More important still, it encouraged the thinking that, unless an ethnic group controlled some governmental apparatus, its ability to successfully compete with the others in the distribution of resources would be severely limited. It is not surprising, therefore, that in spite of the division of the country first into two constitutional units, then into three, four, twelve and now nineteen units the demand for the creation of more states has persisted.

The class character of this struggle, is also clear. It is illuminating that those policies such as the proliferation of regional governmental bureaucracies, the expansion of regional public industries, financial institutions, and opportunities for contract jobs, took place without the imposition of new taxes, and more importantly, at no cost to its beneficiaries, the various regional factions of the privileged class. On the other hand, the introduction of free primary education in the East and West necessitated the imposition of taxes to be borne essentially by the underprivileged classes, the unpopularity of these levels notwithstanding. The standard cliché about the unavailability of financial resources for the programme was pleaded in each case. The reality, however, concerned the unwillingness of the ruling classes to make sacrifices in the interest of redistributing resources to the advantage of policies in the broad public interest. Their class interests and privileges took priority over the basic needs of the broad masses of the society. Hence, the free education policy in the East was later abandoned and that in the West was watered down. Also, to the Nigerian ruling classes, patriotism or the pursuit of the national interest was a hollow propaganda intended to mask class selfishness. The fragmentation of the national market for industrial goods without adequate concern for an integrated national market or, in some cases, even for the economic viability of the industries, the regionalisation of national resources, the appropriation of the regionalised resources for the private use of the members of these classes, and the perpetuation and promotion of the colonially inherited economy are clearly illustrative.

The major danger of this interethnic socioeconomic competition to national unity, apart from its impact on the persistence and growth of ethnic identification and sensitivities, lies in its potential for the full transformation of ethnic divisions into class divisions, and, therefore, the conversion of the non-antagonistic contradictions among the masses of the various ethnic groups into antagonistic class contradictions of the type existing between the Africans and Asians in East Africa. Within a long period of time it is possible for a powerful regional faction of the ruling classes to appropriate enough of the national resources to transform the system of ethnic stratification into an essentially class system in which certain groups become proletarianised. In South Africa, Rhodesia, and the states of East Africa where such transformations have taken place, they have been the result of the domination of the governmental apparatus by an ethnic group. While peaceful means may succeed in the resolution of non-antagoniositic conflicts, violence is inevitable in the resolution of antagonistic contradictions. And in the course of violence the future is unpredictable.

Chapter 7

POLITICS AND THE GROWTH OF ETHNICITY

The Dynamics of Ethnic Hostility

Under conditions of the politicisation of ethnicity and the use of governmental powers for interethnic socioeconomic competition, ethnic hostility is inevitable. In his concept of antagonistic cooperation, W. G. Sumner notes the tendency for interhuman hostility to be aroused by competition for desired but scarce values, such as the satisfaction of economic needs, high status, political ambition, or sex partners.[1] Deprivation is the source of this hostility toward competitors. As John Dollard observes, the inability to recognise the existence of this factor accounts for the failure of many attempts to solve the ethnic problem.[2] Within the ingroup, and especially during competition with outgroups, hostility among individuals is usually met with a united hostile front by all the other members through the process of socialisation. If necessary, it is forcibly suppressed.[3] But as Kimball Young observes, the internal restraints against hostility are relaxed at times of intergroup rivalry which stresses economic competition. Such a relaxation permits hostility toward the outgroup.[4] According to Fred Brown such hostility is again socially legitimate against the outgroup where there is an actual threat to the dominance of the ingroup.[5] The ingroup accepts rivalry manifestations as legitimate modes of keeping the outsider in his place.

1. W. G. Sumner, *Folkways* (New York: Dover, 1959).
2. John Dollard, *Caste and Class in a Southern Town* (Garden City, New York: Doubleday, 1959), p. 00.
3. John Dollard, "Hostility and Fear in Social Life", *Social Forces*, Vol. XVII, No. 1 (October 1938), p. 16.
4. Kimball Young, *Social Psychology* (New York: Dover, 1930), p. 474.
5. Fred Brown, "A Social Psychological Analysis of Race Prejudice," *Journal of Abnormal and Social Psychology*, Vol. XXVII, No. 4 (1932–1933), pp. 365–367.

John Dollard is correct in identifying two types of hostility in ethnic relations: direct aggression and indirect aggression.[6] In indirect aggression, intense competition, and the resultant deprivation and frustration, lead to pervasive insecurity. This condition produces hostility and aggression which are designed to restore a balanced situation. The individual or group imposing the frustration and inciting the hostility is identified and the agressive response capable of controlling it is meted out. This phenomenon is illustrated by competition for white man's jobs in towns in Southern United States. Whites hostile to competing black workers use political and other measures to limit competition.[7] The riotous attacks against the invasion of the Northern employment facilities of East St. Louis and Chicago by Southern Afro-Americans reflects the same points.[8] A Nigerian example is the Northernisation policy of the NPC government of Northern Nigeria.

In the case of indirect aggression, the cause of the aggressive response is not the victim of hostility. The aggression cannot be directed at the individual or group that caused it because of the danger connected with this course of action or its remoteness to the aggressor. The latter finds a substitute. Hostility to an out-group is more fully actualised for direct than indirect aggression because of the lack of inhibitions and tender ties towards it.[9] Therefore, ethnic hostility would tend to be quite vehement even without the admixture of displaced aggression. Many times, however, the victim of direct and indirect aggression coincides to further exacerbate interethnic hostility. Difficulties within the ingroups caused by one of its members tend to be displaced onto the traditional rival or rivals.[10] Thus, it is clear that during periods of stress, ethnic hostility and aggression are the result of the rational motive of competition. In other social situations the irrational motive may play a more important role.[11]

Irrationality in interethnic antagonism is sometimes related to the emergence and escalation of an interethnic conflict spiral. Although the conflict spiral, characterised by the Richardson

6. John Dollard, "*Hostility and Fear in Social Life,*" *op. cit.*, pp. 18–19.
7. John Dollard, *Caste and Class in a Southern Town, op. cit.*
8. Chicago Commission on Race Relations, *The Negro in Chicago* (Chicago: 1922), especially pp. 1–71.
9. John Dollard, "Hostility and Fear in Social Life," *op. cit.*, pp. 19–21.
10. Fred Brown, *op. cit.*
11. Frantz Alexander's discussion of "Hostility and Fear in Social Life", *Social Forces*, Vol. XVII, No. 1 (October 1938) p. 27.

process,[12] has been applied essentially in the analysis of international conflicts, its principles apply to all forms of intergroup hostility. For example, as antagonism between two ethnic groups X and Y increases in intensity, the possibility grows for the emergence of an interethnic conflict spiral. This arises when, for example, X group correctly or incorrectly perceives itself threatened by group Y. There is a high probability that X will respond with a threat or hostile action which acts to elicit a hostile and "defensive" reaction from Y. Thereafter X's original perception of threat and danger would be confirmed and will further increase its "defensive" hostile activity. Soon the exchanges between the two are caught in an increasingly intense spiral of self-confirming hostile suspicions, actions, counteractions, and expectations virtually unrelated to the initial cause of the antagonism, and which opens the possibility for interethnic violence.

It is no longer a question of excluding outgroup members from jobs and the enjoyment of various social services but of ruthlessly eliminating them in violent presemptive actions. The history of interethnic tension in Nigeria between 1964 and 1967 is illustrative of the nature and consequences of this process of escalation. Similarly, in Kenya, the assassination of Tom Mboya in 1969 led to violence between the Luo and Kikuyu in Kisumu and Nairobi. During President Kenyatta's visit to Kisumu later in the year his escort opened fire on a hostile Luo crowd killing 11 and injuring 78. Thereafter, allegations of oath-taking ceremonies reminiscent of the Mau Mau uprising of the 1950s heightened interethnic tension in the country. The rise of General Amin to power in Uganda in 1971 was accompanied by a systematic liquidation of the Langi and Acholi ethnic groups within the Ugandan army and elsewhere in positions of authority and potential influence. In 1972, the unsuccessful attempt of the Hutu majority in Burundi to seize political power in June led to violent reprisals against them by the Tutsi ruling minority. Less than a month afterwards over 50,000 had died. In September the figure stood at 80,000 with no end in sight to the pogrom. The Hutu ruling majority of Rwanda, apparently reacting to events in neighbouring Burundi, descended with vengeance on their Tutsi minority.[13]

12. Lewis F. Richardson, *Arms and Insecurity* (Pittsburg: Boxwood, 1960); Lewis F. Richardson, *Statistics of Deadly Quarrels* (Chicago: Quadrangle Books, 1960); Robert North, Richard Brody and Ole Holsti; *Some Empirical Data on the Conflict Spiral*, Stanford University Monograph, October 1963.
13. Okwudiba Nnoli, "Socioeconomic Insecurity and Ethnic Politics in Africa," *The African Review*, Vol IV, No 1 (1974), pp. 1–2.

Decreasing Ethnic Imbalance and Increasing Ethnic Hostility

As a broad general factor, the dynamics of interethnic socio-economic imbalance accounts for the growth of ethnicity. Ethnic ideologues and intellectuals watch assiduously the pattern of distribution of resources in the society, often emphasising the neglect of their groups, thereby fanning the embers of interethnic prejudice and hostility. The interethnic struggle for socio-economic ascendency also inevitably leads to nepotism and its antisocial consequences. In order to promote his ethnic group, each gives preferences to its members wherever he can. Over a period of time, individuals begin to expect to give and receive ethnic preferences and to act on the basis of this expectation. But this outlook, which sanctions nepotism and thrives on it, sharply contradicts the bureaucratic and entrepreneural ideals of efficiency, meritocracy and universalism. It encourages the bureaucrat to devote his working hours more to the serious and lucrative business of watching who moves up in the hierarchy than to his responsibility to the society as a whole. In the process he exacerbates interethnic tensiom.

However, by far the most important and fundamental generator of increased ethnic tension associated with interethnic imbalance concerns the reduction of such imbalance. Contrary to the common expectation created by the propaganda of the ethnic ideologues and intellectuals of those ethnic groups low in the system of ethnic stratification, the reduction of interethnic socio-economic imbalance does not necessarily lead to increased interethnic harmony but may, instead, heighten interethnic tension. In fact, any solution to the ethnic problem that seeks mechanically to balance the socioeconomic attainments of the various ethnic groups while leaving intact the peripheral capitalist nature of the society, the regionalisation of the privileged classes, and the internecine struggle among the various factions of these classes for the division of the national cake would exacerbate interethnic tension. An adequate solution must be an integral aspect of an overall strategy to exorcise ethnicity from the body politic through a radical socioeconomic transformation of society.

Changes have taken place in the system of ethnic stratification in Nigeria. The early advantages enjoyed by some ethnic groups have been whittled away over time. Those who first made contact with colonialism, entered the colonial system of exploitation unrestrained by the local authority and/or had colonial projects located in their ethnic homelands, have seen the gap between them and some of the others considerably narrowed. For example, prior to 1930, the Yoruba enjoyed an educational advantage over the Igbo. Of the 26 secondary and teacher training institutions in the country at that time 17 were in Yorubaland and six in Igboland. Hausaland was relatively untouched by Western education. The 1921 census recorded 14,000 Yoruba and only 4,900 Igbo in the "educated" category.[14]

Since colonial education was geared toward jobs in the new colonial order, this higher level of education was reflected in the job positions held by members of the two ethnic groups. In 1921, the Yoruba held about 65 per cent of the jobs requiring the knowledge of the English language but constituted only 47 per cent of the total "educated" group and less than 16 per cent of the overall urban population. Although they accounted for 11 per cent of the "educated" group and about 10 per cent of the urban population the Igbo were not represented in the professional ranks.[15] At this stage, the latter were represented largely in the category of the educated who had completed primary school or less. Therefore, in the employment market they occupied essentially the positions of teachers, clerks and artisans.

However, by 1960, the socioeconomic gap between the Yoruba and Igbo had narrowed considerably. In fact, by the late 1940s the number of Igbo in British universities had at least equalled if not exceeded that of Yoruba. In any case, the number of Igbo with a secondary school education, a prerequisite of university training, had actually exceeded that of Yoruba with the same qualification.[16] Mention has already been made of the observations of Obafemi Awolowo that the East was ahead of the West in primary and secondary education, accounting for his introduction of the universal free primary education in 1955. In 1952, the number of Igbo enrolled at the University College, Ibadan was 115 compared with the figure of 118 Yoruba.[17] And, whereas in the early 1920s, there were 8 Yoruba physicians and no Igbo counterpart, in the early 1950s there were 76 Yoruba and 49 Igbo physicians.[18]

14. James Coleman, *Nigeria: Background to Nationalism* (Berkeley Cal: University of California Press, 1958), p. 152.
15. *Ibid.*, pp. 142–143.
16. *Ibid.*, p. 246.
17. *Ibid.*, p. 333.

This type of rapid rate of socioeconomic achievement of certain ethnic groups has been variously and incorrectly explained. For example, Igbo receptivity to change is viewed as central to the rapid change in the socioeconomic levels of the Igbo. But the precolonial Igbo are known not to have developed a high level of material culture or to have adapted so easily to the ways of life of their neighbours. It is unclear, therefore, why this assumed receptivity to change needed colonialism to express itself. And there are sections of the Igbo such as the Abakaliki people who have fiercely resisted Western influence.

Another viewpoint sees the answer in the similarity (culture synonym) between the culture of the advancing ethnic group and that of the colonialists. Of particular relevance here are the degree of individualism and the level of achievement motivation. Again this perspective is embarrassed by the empirical historical situation. Why was the precolonial Igbo society the least materially developed of the three major Nigerian ethnic groups despite its celebrated individualism and high achievement motivation, and the impact of these on the growth of production and the development of the productive forces? Similarly, the argument that the high rate of social mobility in the precolonial society explains the rate of contemporary socioeconomic achievements breaks down in the face of this question.

On the contrary, various other factors account for this rapid rate of socioeconomic achievements and the changes in the socioeconomic gap separating the various ethnic groups. Among them are those related to the differential rate of migration of members of the ethnic groups to the areas of colonial exploitation, previously mentioned, particularly the nature of the precolonial socioeconomic conditions. As pointed out earlier, in general, when the members of an ethnic group are unable to pay their taxes, school fees, and other costs by farming, fishing, or trading in accordance with precolonial norms and traditions, their rate of migration to colonial activity is high. Otherwise, their rate of migration is low. Thus the level of development of the precolonial productive forces is crucial for explaining the rate of socioeconomic achievement in the new order. Where it was low, the rate of progress has been high and where it was high the rate has been

18. Department of Labour, Nigeria, *Annual Report 1951–1952* (Lagos: Government Printer, 1953), pp. 37–39.

low. Therefore, the low level of precolonial productive forces in Igboland, together with the poor soil conditions and the high population density, have compelled the Igbo to migrate in ever increasing numbers to the new centres of gainful economic activities.

The rate of migration is significant for changes in ethnic stratification because migration correlates with upward mobility. R. Scudder and C. Anderson have found that a greater proportion of the sons of migrants than those of non-migrants have moved up in society, and that the former tend to depart markedly from their fathers' positions.[19] The man on the move is often a man trying to maintain or improve his socioeconomic position. In most cases, migration involves a risk that, to an extent, may strengthen self-reliance, adaptability, and enterprise, thereby positively affecting upward social mobility. The migrants embraced colonial life with less restraints than others.

The relationship between the rate of migration and changes in ethnic stratification is further illustrated by the Bamileke of the Cameroon. Among them, undivided inheritance of rights and property restricted the number of claimants on the land thereby forcing the younger siblings of the heir to found their own geneological lines or seek their fortunes outside the traditional homeland. The density of population in the Bamileke homeland is the highest in the country, reaching as high as 141 persons per square kilometre and averaging 103 per square kilometre compared to 17 per square kolometre for the Southern forest areas and 7 per square kilometer for the entire country.[20] This situation was often reinforced by the chief's abuse of his power in refusing to allocate usufructury rights over commercial lands which he holds in trust for the ethnic group. With respect to the availability of productive land, the Bamileke areas are over populated. Consequently, the rate of migration of the Bamileke to other areas of the Cameroon is very high. In 1963, of the total Bamileke population of 800,000, over 100,000 had migrated to other areas.[21] The largest number was found in the towns. In Yaounde, as in Douala, it is the Bamileke who, at the ethnic level, represent the principal

19. Richard Scudder and C. Arnold Anderson, "Migration and Vertical Occupational Mobility" *American Sociological Review*, Vol. XIX, No. 4 (1954), pp. 329–334.

20. Victor T. LeVine, *The Cameroon Federal Republic* (Ithaca: Cornell University Press, 1963), p. 48.

21. *Ibid.*

economic threat to the local Beti, and who have taken almost complete control of petty trading and transport.

The city of Douala was the site of the first European trading activity along the Cameroonian coast. In 1947 the Douala ethnic group constituted 46 per cent of the city's population and dominated its professions, trading and transport business as well as the upper echelons of the civil service. That year the Bamileke accounted for 16.3 per cent of the population. However, the 1955/56 census showed that only 20.4 per cent of the city's population were Douala while 26.2 per cent were Bamileke.[22] They had made significant in-roads into government service, mission work, and educational activities previously dominated by the Douala.[23] By 1964 the Bamileke had occupied 70 per cent of the professional positions and 30 per cent of the civil service jobs. They constituted 60 per cent of the traders, 80 per cent of the artisans, 40 per cent of the labourers, 12 per cent of the domestic workers.[24]

Another factor of change in ethnic stratification is related to the solidarity and organisational skills of the various ethnic groups. It is noteworthy that migrants, rather than the indigenous host population, took the initiative in forming ethnic associations. The socioeconomic insecurity of the "foreign" colonial enclaves presented them with challenges which they felt could be overcome through the solidarity and organisational framework of these associations.

The history of the Urhobo, Ibibio, Egbado and Igbo ethnic unions is illustrative. During the 1920s and 1930s, young men from these four previously underprivileged groups were migrating to the urban areas in large numbers in search of colonial socioeconomic amenities. The Urhobo, Egbado or Igbo in Lagos, for instance, were competitively at a disadvantage compared to the Lagos or Egba Yoruba. Igbo or Ibibio migrants to Calabar faced stiff Efik competition, the Urhobo in Warri with the Iteskiri, the Ibibio in Port Harcourt or Aba with the Onitsha Igbo. Faced with these handicaps, along with the contempt frequently shown them by the members of the economically and socially more priv-

22. *Ibid.*
23. *Ibid.*, pp. 50–52.
24. Willard R. Johnson, *The Cameroon Federation* (Princeton, New Jersey: Princeton University Press, 1970), p. 50.

ileged groups, the migrants began to band together and organise themselves to improve their lot. Hence, their hosts accused them of clannishness and aggressiveness but the lesson they learned about how to organise themselves, their homeland and their various activities contributed to changes in the system of ethnic stratification in their favour. Over time they were able to catch up with or even surpass groups with initial advantages.

Finally, changes in ethnic stratification may arise from changes in the international division of labour between the African countries and the advanced capitalist societies with which they are linked, and their consequences for the location of colonial and neocolonial socioeconomic projects in the various ethnic home-lands. After the second World War, African states became eco-nomically significant, no longer as reservoirs of cheap labour for the production of cash crops, but as the sources of cheap wage labour for foreign private capital in import-substitution manu-facturing industries, and mines for strategic minerals such as copper, uranium, and petroleum which are now critical for the new technological progress in the advanced capitalist nations. At the same time, synthetic substitutes for some of the raw materials such as rubber and sisal previously imported from Africa were discovered.

Therefore, as the old centres of production of cocoa, coffee, palm produce, sisal, rubber and groundnuts have declined in importance, new centres of migration into colonial and neo-colonial activities have developed. The flow of migrants is now in the direction of manufacturing industries and areas of produc-tion of strategic minerals. In some cases, such as in Lagos, the significance of the old urban centres has been reinforced by their use also for the more contemporary enterprises. The previous concentration of capitalist infrastructure in the city has attracted manufacturing enterprises to it. But such towns as Warri and Port Harcourt depend for their present status on the discovery and drilling of petroleum in the surrounding areas. Predictably, those ethnic groups whose homelands form the centres of the new economic activities have improved their relative position in the interethnic scheme of things. In fact, the phenomenal Igbo socio-economic advancement of the period 1960–1966 stems essentially from the importance of revenue from petroleum to the Eastern Region which they dominated. Mining royalties and rents were split among the regions on the basis of 50 per cent to the region of origin, 20 per cent to the Federal Government and 30 per cent to the other regions.[25]

Changes in the interethnic socioeconomic gap may lead to its being widened or narrowed. Of particular interest, however, is its narrowing. Most academicians and politicians have suggested, and based their solutions of ethnic discord on the assumption, that the wider the gap, the greater the interethnic tension. By implication, therefore, the narrower the gap the less the animosity. But the empirical experience of at least the Igbo of Nigeria, Bamileke of the Cameroons, and the Asian of East and Central Africa contradict this assumption.

By 1940, the Yoruba of Nigeria were socioeconomically far ahead of the Igbo and Hausa. On the other hand, the socioeconomic gap between the latter two groups was quite narrow. But interethnic hostility was only significant between the Igbo and Hausa and not between either of them and the Yoruba. In 1932, an Igbo-Hausa riot nearly erupted in Jos;[26] and in October 1945, hostility between them found a violent expression in a riot in which two people were killed and much property was damaged or destroyed. As a result of this history, the Igbo became such a traditional target of Hausa hostility that even when the socioeconomic gap between the two later widened, as in 1953, an incident provoked by the Yoruba led to renewed Hausa violence against the Igbo in Kano, a good example of indirect aggression.

Nevertheless, during the period 1946–1964, the pattern of interethnic animosity in Nigeria had shifted from the Igbo and Hausa to relations between the Igbo and Yoruba. This was precisely the period when the socioeconomic imbalance between the two ethnic groups had considerably narrowed. In fact, from 1946 to 1950 an interethnic cold was existed between the two groups, particularly in Lagos. It was waged in the press, at the work place, and, occasionally, in the streets. As previously mentioned, it was at this time that the Action Group emerged as the champion of Yoruba interests, using customary ethnic institutions and traditional instruments to organise that ethnic group, thereby forcing the NCNC to rely increasingly on the Igbo for its electoral support. The struggle for power between these two political parties

25. *West Africa*, August 14–21, 1965, pp. 899–929.
26. Leonard Plotnicov, "An Early Nigerian Civil Disturbance: the 1945 Hausa-Ibo Riot in Jos", *Journal of Modern African Studies*, Vol. V, No. 1 (1967), pp. 6–8.

in the early 1950s contributed immensely to the poisoning of the interethnic atmosphere.

This Nigerian experience is replicated in the Cameroon where, before 1930, hostility between the Bamileke and Douala was much less than in the 1950s. During the latter period the socioeconomic gap between the two groups had begun to narrow significantly. Then violence became salient in their relations. Hence, ever since 1958, first under the cloak of counter insurgency against guerrillas of the Union Progressiste Cameroonaise and later to curb Bamileke "aggressiveness", the Bamileke have become consistent victims of ethnic violence by the Douala and other ethnic groups. More convincing still is the situation in East and Central Africa. There, African hostility toward the Asian has always been more intense than toward the European even though the gap between the African and the Asian is much narrower than that separating the African and the European.

The view point that a reduction in the socioeconomic imbalance between ethnic groups would reduce tension is thus mistaken. It arises essentially from a static conception of the ethnic groups as innate primary units of actions, thereby neglecting the historical changes in the boundaries of the ethnic groups and deemphasising the role of class and individual factors in interethnic processes. This is because such a view neglects the role of peripheral capitalist production relations in creating market forces characterised by divisive socioeconomic competition among classes, as well as among individuals of the same class that makes them susceptible to the ethnic ideology and amenable to organisation and mobilisation along ethnic lines. Hence, interethnic hostility is a function of the size of the privileged classes and the number of individuals from different ethnic groups in competition for scarce socioeconomic resources. The larger the size and more the number the greater the hostility. The narrowing of the socioeconomic gap increases the size of the relevant classes and the number of individuals.

Before 1940 the comparatively narrow socioeconomic gap between the Hausa and Igbo meant that their members competed for similar resources: unskilled and semiskilled jobs, and petty trading. This intraclass competition among the under privileged classes took place at a time when the collective interests of the groups were focussed on such resources. Their collective interests were not directed at the resources that were important to the privileged classes. These resources were dominated by the Yoruba whose leaders emphasised them at the level of the collectivity. Therefore, hardly any violence ensued between either the Igbo or Hausa and the Yoruba over their competition for resources of interest to the underprivileged classes. Although the Igbo and Hausa also competed with the Yoruba for these resources the collective interests of the latter were focussed at the top echelons of the economy. The prestige and status of the group were determined by activities at these levels.

However, by 1954 when the socioeconomic gap between the Igbo and Yoruba was virtually closed, the Igbo were no longer only competing with the Hausa and Yoruba for the dominance of petty trading, menial jobs, and jobs in the lower and middle segments of the civil service and private firms, but also with the Yoruba for posts at the higher levels of the public and private sectors. The size of the Igbo petty bourgeoisie and comprador bourgeoisie had grown significantly and these Igbo privileged classes were seriously challenging the socioeconomic power and dominance of their Yoruba counterparts. As the scope of socio-economic competition widened the number of individuals who needed the solace of ethnic group identity increased. With such an increase, the effective sizes of the competing groups enlarged and their competitive power became more formidable. Inter-ethnic tension was exacerbated. Interethnic hostility expanded from the antagonism between the Hausa and Igbo to include that between the Igbo and Yoruba.

The ethnic scene became dominated by the rivalry and hostility between these two latter groups. These were reflected in attacks and recriminations in newspapers controlled by them, and in their struggle for the leadership of the labour unions, political parties, and professional organisations. Political campaigns were charac-terised by violence and fraudulent practices designed to secure advantages for the parties that represented their interests. The struggle for political power in Southern Nigeria degenerated into the strunggle for the ethnic ascendancy of one of them. The governments controlled by their respective political parties com-peted in\the fields of educational and welfare services. Their dis-putes over the census, elections, and constitutional changes aggravated interethnic tension and hostility. Each sponsored and supported .ethnic minorities in order to destabilise the areas dominated by the other, thereby promoting the proliferation of ethnic sentiments and demands, and the growth of ethnic tension throughout the country.

The Yoruba as a group felt insecure because of their loss of status arising from this rapid rise in the Igbo socioeconomic level. Progress by an ethnic group is usually interpreted by others to be at their expense. Therefore, as the previously "backward" Igbo overcame their disadvantages, the Yoruba felt threatened. As the Yoruba saw their socioeconomic dominance increasingly eroded by the rising rate of Igbo social mobility, they felt insecure and rallied round the phobia of "Igbo domination." This fear was grossly reflected in the 1965 University of Lagos crisis in which the politics of ethnic balancing, chauvinism, and self-aggradisement predominated. The resultant hostility toward the Igbo heightened the ethnic identification and solidarity of the two groups, as well as the level of tension between them, and throughout the country.

An increase in hostility as a result of the narrowing of the interethnic socioeconomic gap underlines the class character of ethnicity, and its function as a mask over class privileges. The leadership of the Igbo and Yoruba ethnic groups are essentially petty bourgeois and comprador bourgeois: lawyers, doctors, contractors, landlords, junior partners of foreign firms, importers and exporters, senior civil servants, school teachers and university lecturers. Their socioeconomic aspirations are directed at the top echelons of the economy. They neither suffer unemployment nor seek jobs at the lower levels. Hence, interethnic tension worsened when the socioeconomic gap between the Igbo and Yoruba narrowed because competition at the upper level had become significant. The men at the top manipulated ethnic sentiments for their own socioeconomic competitions. At the lower level, when the gap was wider, competition was not of interest to them and, therefore, they limited the intensity of ethnic hostility. At other times, when competition was in their interest and not those of the underprivileged classes, they encouraged it. Thus, for example, just prior to January 1966, the strong pro-Yoruba and anti-Igbo appeal of S. L. Akintola's Nigerian National Democratic Party (NNDP) found much more support among the well-educated and influential Yoruba than it did among the masses.

Therefore, no meaningful solution of the ethnic problems of Nigeria, including ethnic balancing or maintaining the "federal character" of the country, can succeed without (a) a fundamental change in the nature of the national leadership. The struggle against ethnic chauvinism cannot be waged under the leadership of that segment of the population that benefits most substantially and concretely from the prevailing interethnic situation. As a result of their success in ethnic politics, the privileged classes now occupy political and economic positions of power and status in the inherited colonial structures. Therefore, they have an objective interest in maintaining the ethnic pattern of activities and the imperialist structures both of which are inimical to interethnic harmony. (b) The elimination of the basic socioeconomic insecurity of the individual that causes ethnic group identification among members of the underprivileged classes who bear the brunt of the suffering generated by ethnic politics. This necessitates the elimination of socioeconomic scarcity and inequality, as well as the divisive competition for scarce resources characteristic of the peripheral capitalist market system. This latter requirement must result from the destruction of the inherited imperialist relations of production and distribution through structural disengagement from the world capitalist system which created this market, and the establishment of a new set of production relations in which the interests of the vast majority of Nigerians dominate those of foreign capitalists, and those of labour are dominant over those of capital. Thereafter reduction of ethnic imbalances will have a positive effect on interethnic harmony.

The Effects of Intemperate Utterances

Intemperate utterances of some Nigerian aspirants to leadership positions, arising from personal ambitions, have contributed significantly to the growth of interethnic hostility in Nigeria. In this regard, the early political activities of Nnamdi Azikiwe generated much of such virulent, chauvinistic and ethnically loaded remarks. He was deeply resented by some Yoruba and Hausa leaders, not only because they were threatened by his bourgeoning political fortunes, but also because he used his journalistic enterprises to portray them in very unfavourable light to the public. He scathingly referred to them as "misleaders" and their leadership as "Uncle Tom Misleadership" accusing them of being lackeys of imperialism who cringed to curry favours from their colonial masters.[27] His opponents were frightened about his power to ruin them not only politicially but also financially through branding them as stooges of imperialism.

This resentment against Azikiwe spilled over unto the other

27. J. S. Coleman, *op. cit.*, pp. 341–343.

members of his ethnic group, who happened also to be among his major supporters. His critics charged him with ethnic chauvinism and the glorification of the Igbo and their achievement to the neglect of the progress of other groups. In fact, some Yoruba leaders accused him of character assasination against prominent Yoruba.[28] Consequently, Igbo-Yoruba tension mounted leading to the formation of the Egbe Omo Oduduwa, and, thereafter, the inauguration of a period of cold war in Lagos between the two groups during which virulent and intemperate ethnic slurs and retaliatory remarks were freely and frequently made.

A press war of unprecedented violence was carried on between the *West African Pilot* representing Azikiwe, and the *Daily Service*, representing his Yoruba rivals. In 1948, at the height of this hostility Oluwole Alakija, a leading member of the Egbe, intemperately remarked that "we have tolerated enough from a class of Igbos and addle-brained Yorubas who have mortgaged their thinking caps to Azikiwe and his hirelings.[29] The *West African Pilot* countered by declaring war against the Egbe and its leaders at home and abroad, accusing it of being the main enemy of Nigeria. "There is no going back until the Fascist Organisation of Sir Adeyemo has been dismembered."[30] Between July and September, 1948, Igbo-Yoruba hostility assumed such high proportions that extremists on both sides bought up all available matchets in the Lagos markets in anticipation of ethnic violence. Although violence did not occur, growth in ethnic prejudice, identification, and sentiments had increased beyond a tolerable threshold.

The consequent spiralling of ethnic tension was reinforced by the introduction of ethnic machinations into the labour movement. On 29 November 1947, the General Council of the Trade Union Congress (TUC) voted to maintain its affiliation with the NCNC contrary to the wishes of the Yoruba-dominated NYM. *The Daily Service* blamed the decision on the Igbo in the TUC and embarked on a venomous campaign against Igbo trade union leaders of the Congress with such slogans as "Down with Ibos in the TUC," "TUC in Distress," and "They that have turned the

---

28. *Ibid.*
29. Oluwole Alakija, *Egbe Ome Oduduwa Monthly Bulletin*, (December 1948), p. 4, quoted in J. S. Coleman, *op. cit.*, p. 346.
30. *West African Pilot*, September 9, 1948, and quoted in J. S. Coleman, *op. cit.*, p. 346.

world upside-down have come hither unto us."[31] These attacks escalated after 17 June 1948 when Charles Daddy Onyeama, an Igbo lawyer and member of the Legislative Council, predicted that Igbo domination of Nigeria was only a matter of time. In response to this provocative statement, the newly formed Egbe Omo Oduduwa, among other things, infiltrated many trade unions and sought to remove their Igbo office holders. Their efforts were concentrated on important unions like the Railway Workers Union and the Amalgamated Union of UAC African Workers. The resultant internecine struggle for hegemony within the unions contributed to the growth of ethnicity.

The same effect was produced by the politicization of the panethnic unions of the Igbo and the Yoruba consequent to the cold war of 1948. Igbo solidarity behind Azikiwe led the Igbo of Lagos to decide that all personal attacks on him were attacks on the Igbo as a people because killing the leaders of a people exposed them to danger. In this frame of mind the Igbo Federal Union was converted into the Igbo State Union at a Pan-Igbo conference at Aba in 1948. Its goal was to defend the political interests of the Igbo. It united both the pro and anti NCNC Igbo leaders under the presidency of Azikiwe. Riding the crest of the new wave of ethnic chauvinism at the first Igbo State Conference in 1949, Azikiwe made a very dangerous ethnic remark:

"it would appear that the God of Africa has specially created the Ibo nation to lead the children of Africa from the bondage of the ages . . . The martial prowess of the Ibo nation at all stages of human history has enabled them not only to conquer others but also to adapt themselves to the role of preserver . . . The Igbo nation can not shirk its responsibility.[32]

More than any other factor, this ill-advised statement severely damaged Azikiwe's credibility as a pan-Nigerian leader, providing his critics with a ready-made weapon with which to promote fears of Igbo domination. In the light of this statement, his previous and subsequent opposition to ethnicity, his call for interethnic fellowship, his denunciation of separatism, and his efforts to present a multiethnic front within the NCNC could not be credible. Coming in the wake of a similar utterance by Onyeama it reinforced the increasingly widespread feeling in

31. Quoted in Wogu Ananaba, *The Trade Union Movement in Nigeria* (Benin: Ethiope, 1969), p. 92.
32. *West African Pilot*, 6 July, 1949, and quoted in J. S. Coleman, *op. cit.*, p. 347.

Southern Nigeria that Igbo nationalism was a cover for the pursuit of the goal of imposing the Igbo as a master race in the country, and relegating the other ethnic groups to servitude. Its inevitable consequence was the growth in the fears of Igbo domination on the part of the other ethnic groups created by the propaganda of their leaders that capitalised on the statement.

In the relations between the North and South of the country, a similar disregard for the social consequences of their utterances on the part of the Nigerian leaders has contributed to the growth of ethnicity. The attitude of the Western educated Southerners toward the less educated Northerner was usually and essentially negative and non-complimentary. The Southern Press ridiculed the Northerners and made disparaging remarks about their rulers. In Abubaker Imam's view of the relations "we despise each other . . . we call each other ignorant; the South is proud of Western knowledge and culture; we are proud of Eastern (culture) . . . To tell you the plain truth, the common people of the North put more confidence in the white man than in either their black Southern brothers or the educated Northerners."[33] A year earlier in 1942, the Sultan of Sokoto, in an ethnically provocative statement, urged the Southerners who desired a united Nigeria to embrace Islam.[34] More pungent still was Abubaker Tafawa Balewa's observation in 1948 that the Northerners looked upon the Southerners living in the North as invaders who do not mix with the Northern people.[35]

In his speech at the Nigerian Legislative Council of 24 March 1947, Balewa had made an even more dangerous remark: "I should like to make it clear to you that if the British quitted Nigeria now at this stage the Northern people would continue their interrupted conquest to the sea."[36] It is noteworthy that the British colonial government frequently cited the speech for which this quotation constituted the closing remark as evidence of the necessity of prolonged British suzerainty over Nigeria in order to foster the unity of a diverse people. In fact, Balewa was reported to have received a personal message of congratulations from his

33. Quoted in J. S. Coleman, *op. cit.*, p. 360.
34. *Ibid.*, p. 361.
35. Nigeria, *Legislative Council Debates, March 4, 1948* (Lagos; Government Printer 1948), p. 227.
36. Nigeria, *Legislative Council Debates, March 24, 1947* (Lagos: Government Printer, 1947), p. 212.

Governor, Sir Arthur Richard, an arch-opponent of self government for the country.[37]

These chauvinistic, provocative, and threatening remarks by
Northern political leaders were usually accompanied by expressions of genuine fears of Southern domination in a self-governing
Nigeria. They alleged that Southern clerks in the North discriminated against Northerners in government offices, in railroad
ticket offices, and in commercial firms, that Southerners tended
to take Northerners for granted and, therefore, to assume that in
a self-governing Nigeria the North would, in effect, be a backward
protectorate governed by Southerners, and that, in a united
Nigeria, the North would only furnish the labour. Such sentiments pervaded the speeches of most educated Northerners and
emirs both inside and outside the Legislative Council throughout
the immediate post World War II period. They were also frequently expressed in editorials in the Hausa weekly newspaper
Gaskiya Ta Fi Kwabo. Although such fears helped to stimulate
increased Northern participation in peripheral capitalist activities
in Nigeria they also contributed to the growth of ethnicity.

Such intemperate utterances affect the growth of ethnicity in
various ways. First, for those on behalf of whom they are made
the utterances create a feeling of pride and solidarity in their
membership of the ethnic group, and/or they create and reinforce
a feeling of injustice to the collectivity of which these people are
members thereby imbuing them with a missionary zeal on behalf
of their ethnic community. In either case, the ethnocentric component of ethnicity is reinforced, leading to a greater identification
with and exclusiveness of the ethnic groups. Second, with regard
to the victims of such remarks, the utterances inculcate a collective
sense of fear, danger and insecurity which, as during the formative
stages of ethnicity, are ameliorated by greater solidarity and identification with the ethnic ingroup. These fears in turn, lead to an
intensification of ethnicity. Third, such remarks provide the
various regional factions of the privileged classes with useful
opportunities for manipulating mass ethnic support on behalf
of their socioenconomic competition. The competition however,
lies at the roots of ethnicity. Finally, the remarks create possibili-
ties for the emergence of conflict spirals capable of escalating
interethnic hostility into violence. By their negative effects on the

37. Richard Sklar, *Nigerian Political Parties* (Princeton, New Jersey: Princeton
University Press, 1963), p. 98, footnote 25.

perceptions of ethnic opponents, such utterances create the opportunities for the emergence of an increasingly intense spiral of self-reconfirming, self-reinforcing, and self-perpetuating hostile suspicious, actions, and counteractions which fan the embers of ethnic antagonism and violence. The interethnic cold war of 1948 is illustrative. The inevitable effect is an increase in ethnicity.

Ethnic Violence

In their competition for national resources the various regional factions of the privileged classes employ both institutionalised and non-institutionalised means to limit competition in favour of one faction or a combination of factions. The Northernisation policy of the NPC was an institutionalised form. Nepotism is a non-institutionalised form. Violence is another non-institutionalised method of such competition and of changing interethnic stratification. For example, the pogroms of 1966 and the civil war of 1967–1970 have effectively curtailed the socioeconomic influence of the Igbo petty bourgeoisie and comprador bourgeoisie in Northern Nigeria and elsewhere outside Igboland.[38] Inevitably such violence leads to the growth of ethnicity.

The history of ethnic violence in Nigeria illustrates the basis of both the emergence of ethnicity and its growth. Leonard Plotnicov reports that, in 1932, an ethnic riot nearly erupted in Jos.[39] The town owed its existance to the tin-mining industry which was established in 1910 in its immediate surroundings. In fact, prior to the Second World War, jobs in the town were only available in the mines, government, and related activities. Yoruba and Hausa traders dominated petty trading. The Igbo came during the war.

The near riot was occasioned essentially by the scarcity of the Depression period. During the height of the Depression there was an exodus of European miners from the tin mines around the town. The exodus sparked off two pervasive rumors based on a general interpretation that it portended the end of colonial administration. One of the rumours alleged that the unemployed

---

38. On the effects of violence on the Ibo presence in northern Nigeria see Samir Amin, *Modern Migration in Western Africa* (London: Oxford University Press, 1947), pp. 72–85.

39. Leonard Plotnicov, "An Early Nigerian Civil Disturbance: The 1945 Hausa-Ibo Riot in Jos", *Journal of Modern African Studies*, Vol. IX No. 2 (August 1971), pp. 298–299.

Hausa, constituting mainly the Hausa who had migrated to the city following their retranchment elsewhere as a result of the Depression, were planning to take the property of all the departing Europeans, and drive all non-Northern Africans out of the town. The other rumour alleged that, instead, the indigenes of the Jos area were preparing to drive out the Hausa and revert to their precolonial forms of political administration. The nature of the rumours reflects the two patterns of ethnic conflict which coexisted in the middle belt region. Ethnicity arising from socio-economic competition within the colonial enclaves between Northerners and Southerners coexists with ethnicity arising from local resistance over the colonial administration's imposition of Hausa-Fulani emirate rule through the native administration of the area. Nevertheless, the anticipated end of colonial rule did not take place and the impending violence failed to materialise.

The outcome of a similar situation in the town in 1945 was quite different. By then Igbo traders had arrived in significant numbers. They lived in a section of the "Native Town" called Sarkin Arabs Ward or "Igbo Quarter." Before, this residential area, as well as the rest of the Native Town, had been occupied by the Hausa migrants who had cultivated a possessive attitude toward it. More importantly, 1945 was a year of acute socio-economic tensions. Although at one end of the Second World War there were high expectations that the socioeconomic hardships of the war years would disappear, the socioeconomic condition was characterised by pervasive scarcity, inflation and food rationing reminiscent of the years of war. The 1945 general strike adversely affected food supplies to the town by rail, causing a general feeling of anxiety and a severe shortage of food. Every morning the District Officer rationed out food to people in a long queue outside the market. Since the strike was a nationalistic outburst against the colonial administration, the British colonial officials siezed on the resultant hardships in the North to incite the Northerners against the strike and the Igbo. They blamed the strike and shortage on the Igbo led by Azikwe and manipulated Igbo-Hausa animosity over competition on trading and residential area to incite the Hausa against the Igbo.

At that time three conditions prevailed that were conducive to rioting between the two ethnic groups. First, there was increased interethnic contact particularly between the two groups under conditions of keen rivalry and competition in trade, job seeking, and residential quarters. They competed for the same scarce economic resources. The socioeconomic gap between them was quite narrow but the Igbo were beginning to surge ahead. Second, 1945 was a year of great expectations and frustrations. These were reflected in the general strike which, in turn, further adversly affected the livelihood of the people, creating intense socioeconomic insecurity. Third, in the rivalry between the privileged classes, the Igbo upsurge in the nationalistic activities and the prominance of Azikiwe caused the Hausa leaders to feel politically insecure. It is noteworthy that Northerners virtually boycotted the general strike. Therefore, contact, individual competition, frustration and the status insecurity of a regional faction of the privileged classes were critical for the rioting that occurred in October.

The actual incident that sparked off the rioting took place in the market for potatoes, chicken, eggs, timber, and planks. It concerned a dispute over the sale of one of these, probably potatoes. The Hausa and Igbo fought for two days. In the fighting two people were killed and many others injured, and considerable property was destroyed or damaged. It took the combined operations of the police and army sent from Kaduna to restore public order. As in Kano in 1953, but unlike the situation in Jos in 1966 when the indigenous populations joined the Hausa in attacking the Igbo, in 1945 only the Hausa were involved. The shock of the riot compelled the Igbo to move from the Native Town to the Township where their number rose from 6,213 in 1953 to 12,708 in 1959. They also sought representation in the Jos Township Advisory Council and the Native Town Council, and counselled their members against provoking further hostility.[40]

Again in 1953, violence erupted between the Hausa and Igbo in Kano. The genesis of this crisis was essentially political, the self-government crisis at the House of Representatives. Inter-party rivalry between the NCNC and the AG over supremacy in the drive for independance led them to fix 1956 as the date for self-government in Nigeria. On 31 March 1953, Anthony Enahoro moved a motion in the House of Representatives to implement this policy. However, the NPC had not officially adopted such a policy and, therefore, its members were reluctant to be precipitated into a binding decision without a mandate. Hence, the Northern leader Ahmadu Bello, the Sardauna of Sokoto, sought, through an ammendment, to replace the 1956

40. *Ibid.*, pp. 300–305.

date with the phrase "as soon as practicable."[41] The argument about a mandate nothwithstanding, the NPC was unwilling to support the motion because it felt that the North was so far behind the South socioeconomically that it would be a junior partner to it in an independent Nigeria. In essence, the Northern privileged classes would be worst off in the three concerned intraclass struggle for the national wealth.

The Southern leaders rejected the ammendment and, faced with a defeat on the issue, violently attacked the Northern leaders accusing them of colluding with the Britishers to perpetuate colonial rule. In response the Northerners were equally bitter and tempestuous. They accused the Southerners of being motivated merely by a partisan desire to outdo each other rather than by any genuine intention for the good of the country. The bitterness and acrimony continued outside the House. The AG and NCNC had, by this time, negotiated an alliance to press the issue of self-government in 1956. In the event of failure, they planned to summon a constituent assembly of Southern Nigerians, draft a constitution, and declare the independence of Southern Nigeria. Their supporters in Lagos hauled insults and abuses at the Northern delegates. Their newspapers subjected the Northerners to vitriolic criticism, and ridicule. These attacks exacerbated the anger of the Northerners, making them determined not to be subjected to such indignities again. Consequently, they adopted an eight-point programme which, in effect, would have meant Northern secession.

This action, in turn, led to harsher criticisms by the NCNC, AG and their newspapers. The NPC leaders were not only vilified as imperialist stooges who had no minds of their own; they were also accused of being unrepresentative of their people. The Southern leaders' strong belief in the latter accusation caused them to send their party delegations to Northern cities to campaign for self-government in 1956.

The AG delegation was led by S. L. Akintola. At his Kano meeting during the height of this North-South tension, rioting commenced. Although the AG supporters in the city were Yoruba settlers, once violence erupted, it involved mainly the Hausa on one side and the Igbo on the other. Among the Southern groups, the Igbo, who supported the NCNC, were the most numerous

41. Nigeria, *House of Representatives Debates Second Session March 3 – April 1, 1953* (Lagos: Government Printer, 1953), p. 992.

and, over the years, had become the traditional victim of Northern hostility because they were the major socioeconomic competitors of the Hausa. This example of indirect aggression arising from a conflict spiral lasted for four days, 16–19 May 1953, claiming 36 dead, 15 Northerners and 21 Southerners, and 241 wounded.[42]

As a result of this uprising the 1951 constitution was scrapped in favour of another which provided for a much looser federal arrangement, giving the regions greater autonomy. In addition, the growth of ethnicity was inevitable as the insecurity of socioeconomic competition was compounded by the fear for physical survival of Southern ethnic groups living in the North. Also, the memories of the near violence in Jos in 1932 and the violence in that city in 1945 were reinforced by events in Kano in 1953. The image of the Igbo as the traditional and "natural" victims of Northern hostility and violence was increasingly perpetuated, and the use of violence in interethnic trasactions had received a historical boost.

These ominous developments have proved to be mere dress rehearsals for the violent eruptions of the 1960s. In this regard the Kano violence was epitomatic: conflict among various factions of the privileged classes led essentially to the death and injury of the members of the underprivileged strata. Similarly, the Tiv riots of 1960 and 1964 were the results of the struggle for power between the ruling Hausa-Fulani aristocracy in the North and the emergent Tiv petty bourgeoisie. The victims were essentially the underprivileged workers and farmers of Tivland. In 1947, the Tiv had rioted over the imposition on Makurdi, a stranger town in Tivland, of a muslim Yoruba chief. In 1952 they rose up again over a boundary dispute with a neighbouring ethnic group. But the uprisings of the 1960s were on a much larger scale and had a much clearer political and ethnic character.

By the 1959 federal elections, two major political parties vied for Tiv support, the NPC and the United Middle Belt Congress (UMBC) led by Joseph Tarka and linked in an alliance with the AG. Tarka's support was based essentially on appeals to Tiv ethnic chauvinism and hostility against the Hausa-Fulani. His major campaign promise was a Middle Belt State in which the Tiv would be free of Hausa-Fulani control. He pointed to the lower status of the chief of the Tiv, the Tor Tiv, relative to the Hausa-Fulani

---

42. The Northern Region of Nigeria, *Report on the Kano Disturbances, 16th, 17th, 18th and 19th May 1953* (Kaduna: Government Printer, 1953).

emirs, and blamed the Northern rulers for the comparative absence of the Tiv in the public service of the region. He denounced those Tiv who supported the NPC as not being truly Tiv but Hausa, vowing to drive all Hausa out of Tivland. The NPC retaliated by referring to the UMBC supporters not as Tiv but Yoruba, a reference to the alliance between that party and the Action Group, a Yoruba party. In addition the ruling party, acting through the Tor Tiv and the local native authority system, mounted a campaign of harassment, intimidation and victimisation of its opponents. Tension mounted in the area.

The situation worsened after the election in 1959 which was decisively won by theUMBC. Tarka obtained the largest majority in the whole country. A similar landslide victory took place in all of the seven Tiv constituences where the UMBC candidates won over 85% of the Tiv votes. The NPC won just under 10 per cent of the votes, of which perhaps a half were from the Hausa living in Tivland, and a half were salaried native authority (NA) chiefs and tax collectors.[43] This result sharply contradicted the pattern elsewhere in the North where the emirs easily persuaded the voters to cast their ballots for the NPC. In Tivland the utmost efforts of the Tor Tiv and the NA had failed even to save the NPC candidates from losing their deposits.

The NPC reacted by seaking scapegoats. A number of NA staff were dismissed or declared redundant, including the personal secretary to the Tor Tiv who was accused of UMBC sympathy. Also the prison clerk who was suspected of advising the District Officer about some unfair sentences passed on UMBC supporters was dismissed. The bicycle hirers who, like the lorry touts, were UMBC supporters were penalized by being ejected from their central location in Gboko and forced into a less favourable one in the market. The local chiefs, including the Tor Tiv, were given more powers much of which they used oppressively against the opposition party supporters.

The latter reacted by attacking NA policemen, disobeying court summonses, abusing chiefs from political platforms, and refusing to pay taxes. The state of political tension increased steadily, causing the number of prisoners in Gboko to double its normal level of 400. Tarka's supporters who made up 85 per cent of the

---

43. J. M. Dent, "A Minority Party – The United Middle Belt Congress," in J. P. Mackintosh, *Nigerian Government and Politics* (London: Allen and Unwin, 1966), p. 486.

population perceived themselves as destined for a long period of ever increasing pressure and harassment from the NA with hardly any hope that the regional government would intervene on their behalf. Under these circumstances serious riots broke out in 1960 which required the intervention of the Army.[44]

The most serious incidents of the rioting occurred between August and November 1960. Initially, it consisted of attacks and ambushes against the police, court officials, NA personnel, and tax collectors by large numbers of armed men who collected in various villages frequently shouting "Tarka." Later they began to burn the houses of NPC supporters, Hausa-Fulani settlers, the chiefs and the officials of the native administration. During the course of the riots some 50,000 people were involved in the burning and over 30,000 houses were burnt. Some 20 burners were killed by householders defending their property and by police fire. The scale of the burning was so great that the Police force was rendered impotent to maintain law and order, in spite of the large numbers of prisoners it had taken and the participation of over 500 policemen. About 5,000 people were arrested, and property worth over ₦1 million was damaged.[45]

These riots were followed by a three-year period of peace among the contending political parties. However, in 1964 new riots broke out. Although they were not as extensive as those of 1960 and did not involve arson on a large scale, they were characterised by deliberate murder and a great loss of life before the Army was able to bring the situation under some control. Even then, this control remained tenuous until the military coup of January 1966. On the whole, during the 1964 riots, about 2,000 people died, much property was destroyed and thousands of people were imprisoned.[46] Again, as in the 1960 riots, the 1964 uprising was preceded by a general election which was won by the UMBC, and the consequent unleashing of oppressive rule through the NA system.

Next, the use of violence to limit ethnic competition again intruded into Nigerian politics with the coup of 15 January 1966. By this time, ethnicity had become militarised. This militarisation under conditions in which ethnicity had been politicised contri-

44. *Ibid.*, pp. 488–491.
45. *Ibid.*, pp. 461, 493–500.
46. J. I. Tseayo, *Conflict and Incorporation in Nigeria* (Zaria: Gaskiya Corporation, 1974), p. 221.

buted significantly to the politicisation of the military. As was the case with the public service, the intrusion of ethnic politics into the armed forces came with the Nigerianisation of the military institution. At the time of independence in 1960, the only major national instituion free from the ethnic political virus was the army. This ultimate instrument of state power was dominated by the colonialists until the end of colonial rule. It was, therefore, the last to be Nigerianised. For example, in 1960 only 17 per cent of its officer corps were Nigerians; and the British dominated the top command.[47]

With the end of colonial rule, a programme of indigenisation of the armed forces was embarked upon. The politicians who formulated and implemented the programme were, of course, steeped in ethnicity and ethnic politics. They were also quite conscious of the army's critical role in the political process as the final instrument of coercion. This consciousness is reflected in the efforts of the various ethnic political leaders to encourage members of their respective ethnic groups to join the army, as well as their desire to maintain communications with those of them already in the institution. For example, W. F. Gutteridge reports a case in which an emir in his campaign for his subjects to join the army ordered all the males in the appropriate age group to enlist irrespective of their physical conditions.[48] He also notes the intimate relationship which existed between Aguiyi Ironsi and Emeka Ojukwu of the army and Igbo political leaders.[49] At the 1963 treason trial, the AG was not only accused of seeking to infiltrate the army with some of its party agents, it was shown to have attempted to suborn army personnel.[50]

One of the reasons for these political interests in the military and the contacts with military personnel was the fear that if the social composition of the institution was not ethnically favourable to the politicians, they would lose power in the event that the army proved unreliable. Political leaders felt that only by ensuring

47. B. J. Dudley, *Politics and Crisis in Nigeria* (Ibadan: Ibadan University Press, 1973), p. 90.
48. W. F. Gutteridge, *The Military in African Politics* (London: Methuen, 1969), pp. 64–65, reported in *Ibid.*, p. 97.
49. *Ibid.*
50. R. L. Sklar, "Nigerian Politics: The Ordeal of Chief Awolowo 1960–65" in G. Carter, ed., *Politics in Africa: Seven Cases* (New York: Harcourt, Brace and World, 1966); L. K. Jakande, *The Trial of Obafemi Awolowo* (London & Lagos: John West, 1966).

the same ethnic balance within the army as existed in the political arena could they be confident that the interests of the various regional factions of the privilieged classes would be guaranteed if the army were to take political power. Their intention was, if need be, to continue the intraclass regional struggle for wealth by using the military instrument. This was only possible through the introduction of ethnic politics into the army, and the forging of alliances among the respective regional factions of the ruling classes and the petty bourgeoisie of the military bureaucracy.

Thus, in 1962, a quota system for recruitment into the armed forces was inaugurated. Rather than relate the proportions to the populations of the various federal units or regions the system related them to the structure of representation in the federal legislature which obtained during the period 1951–1958. Consequently, 50 per cent of the recruitment into the armed forces would come from the North, 25 per cent from the East and 25 per cent from the West. Consequently, while in 1962 two-thirds of all commissioned officers were from the East, in contrast, of the 163 commissioned in 1963/64 and who were Second Lieutenants by 1965, 25 per cent were from the East, 19 per cent from the West, 42 per cent from the North, and 14 per cent from the Midwest.[51]

Therefore, it is not surprising that the military coups of 1966 had an ethnic character. Much argument has been made on both sides about the ethnic or nationalistic motives of the plotters of the January coup. It is clear, however, that their true motives cannot be ascertained from what they indicate them to be. There is no way of determining whether what they say corresponds to their real motives. Therefore, as in all cases of social analysis, one must look beyond what the actors say they are doing to the objective facts of the situation. When this is done the coup presents itself as ethnic in character.

First, the plotters had no intentions, either stated or implied, to transform the inherited pattern of activities in such a way as to enthrone the interests of the underprivileged. Their emphasis was on the reformation of the system, in other words, to achieve the interests of the privileged classes without imposing undue strains on the system. None of the "ten proclamations in the extraordinary order of the day" broadcast by the coup leader Major Nzeogwu concerned the restructuring of the society. They merely sought to

51. B. J. Dudley, *op. cit.*, p. 92.

remove abuses.[52] There was even talk of installing Obafemi Awolowo in power. Under the circumstances their success would have ensured the continued hegemony of the privileged classes whose intraclass struggle for wealth and power was essentially responsible for the emergence and persistence of ethnic politics. Therefore, their actions objectively serviced the interests of certain regional-ethnic factions of these classes.

Second, the pattern of killing during the coup had a definite ethnic character. Twenty-seven people were known to have died in the coup. Among the civilians killed none was Igbo or from the East. They included the Premier of the North, the controversial Premier of the West, and the Federal Prime minister. No harm came to M. I. Okpara and D. C. Osadebe the Igbo Premiers of the East and Midwest respectively. Within the military, 4 out of 5 Northern officers of the ranks of Lt. Colonel and above were killed, 2 out of 5 from the West, none out of 7 from the East and 1 out of 4 from the Midwest. Only one of such officers of Northern origin who were in Nigeria at the time survived, two from the West, one from the Midwest and seven from the East.[53] The picture that emerges from this objective empirical situation is clear: an attempt to limit ethnic competition through the use of preemptive violence. Six of the seven majors and nineteen out of the other twenty-three who actively participated in plotting and executing the coup came from the same ethnic group.

Ethnic violence again occurred in May 1966. Smarting under its loss of political influence at the centre consequent to the January coup, the Northern faction of the privileged classes, the alliance of the traditional aristocracy with the petty bourgeoisie, the comprador bourgeosie, and the capitalist farmers, was apprehensive of the negative economic consequences of this loss, and the likelihood that it would lead to its loss of political and economic influence in the North as well. It seized on the unification of the country implicit in military rule and explicit in Decree no. 34 of 24 May 1966, to unleash a pogrom against the Easterners, particularly the Igbo resident in Northern Nigeria, as a preemptive measure against their increased dominance of economic life in the region.

Under the supervision and coordination of the local merchants,

---

52. For the ten proclamations see *ibid.*, pp. 112–113.
53. Robin Luckham, *The Nigerian Military* (Cambridge: Cambridge University Press, 1971), p. 43, Table 3.

contractors, and other men who enjoyed close links with the Native Authorities and the defunct NPC, were indebted by political patronage to the Northern Nigeria Marketing Board or the Northern Nigeria Development Corporation, were likely to be asked to pay arrears accumulated during the civilian era, and were in intense socioeconomic competition with the Igbo and other Southern groups for the control of petty contracting and merchandising, Igbo lives and property were attacked on a massive scale on 29 and 30 May 1966. It began with the demonstration in Zaria of the students of the Institute of Administration and the Ahmadu Bello University against the unification decree which they feared would adversely affect their competition for jobs by throwing open the relatively closed job market of the North to Southerners. They were later replaced by nonstudents who took violent actions against the Igbo. News of events in Zaria quickly spread to other Northern cities where the same pattern of killing, maiming, and destruction of property was carried out largely unhindered by the Native Authority police forces charged largely with the responsibility of maintaining law and order.

At the end of the second day of violence, calm began to return to the cities following the intervention of the federally controlled Nigeria Police Force. It is noteworthy that no cases of attacks on the Igbo were reported in the rural areas where intraclass rivalry among the various regional factions of the privileged classes was negligible. At the end of the debacle over 3,000 Igbo had been killed or wounded. As a reaction, large numbers of them returned to their ethnic homeland or sent their families back there. However, the majority remained in the North and some of those who left were subsequently persuaded to return following a series of appeals and assurances of their safety given by the religious, traditional, and military leaders.

Following closely in the wake of these May killings came the July massacre of the Igbo within the armed forces. With the dominant form of the intraclass struggle of the regional factions of the privileged classes now transferred into the armed forces, the Northern soldiers were determined to end Igbo supremacy in the military and the Federation. On 29 July 1966, they descended with ethnic vengeance on the Igbo officers and men, eliminating them in large numbers, and forcing the others to go into hiding. By August 9, when the killing virtually ceased, 27 Igbo officers, 12 non-Igbo officers, 154 men of "other ranks" from the East, and 17 from the West and Midwest had been killed and many others injured.[54] And Yakubu Gowon had replaced Aguyi-Ironsi as the Head of State. The coup and massacre succeeded, in part, because of the solidarity displayed by the Hausa and Middle Belt officers and men. This solidarity was essentially the result of the humiliating spurning of Tarka and his objective of a Middle Belt State by Aguyi-Ironsi. In fact, the latter refused to recognise the 500 or more Tiv in prison after the 1964 disturbances as political prisoners.[55]

One of the major consequences of this massacre was the regionalisation of the army. Igbo soldiers in hiding outside the Eastern region were allowed to return to their ethnic homeland in exchange for Northern soldiers in the East to return to the North. With the exception of the Northern troops who remained in the West and Lagos, the regions had become militarily homogeneous and exclusive similar to their previously acquired political, economic and bureaucratic homogeneity and exclusiveness. In theory, the country remained a federation of four regions. In practice, it consisted of two units which were culturally, socially and militarily impermeable, the East on the one hand and the rest on the other. Even outside the East, only the presence of Northern troops in Lagos and the West provided any semblance of unity. In reality the West, North and Midwest were virtually independent of one another. Only a tenuous tradition of association held the country together.

Even before the country could recover from the devastating effects of the July massacre a most destructive pogrom ensued in the North against Igbo residents there. Unhappy about the discussions at the Lagos Ad Hoc Constitutional Conference called after the July coup, particularly with regard to a possible loss of autonomy by the North and a possible division of the region into smaller constitutional units, the privileged classes of the North this time unleashed harrowing waves of killing against the Igbo in the North and elsewhere where Northern soldiers were stationed. Between 29 September and the end of November 1966 over 50,000 Igbo were gruesomely murdered, usually under inhuman conditions, maimed, or horribly mutilated, and over 2 million others who survived the killing and maiming became refugees in their ethnic homeland. The scale and spread of the violence, together with the participation of mutinous soldiers, was unprecedented.

54. *Ibid.*, pp. 76–77.
55. *Ibid.*, pp. 269–270.

The sad and morally painful fact about the killings was the rank indifference of non-Easterners. None of the other groups saw the massacres as posing a serious national problem, or if they did, were courageous enough to say so. Each ethnic group retreated into a womb-like isolation as if indifference and the passage of time would make the whole problem go away. At the time, Nigeria seemed morally anesthesized. The few non-Eastern intellectuals who dared to appeal to the nation's conscience were either jailed or driven into exile. The federal military regime rendered no apology for failing to protect lives, took no concrete steps to reassure the Igbo of their security, and gave no meaningful assistance to the massive refugee problem. The Aburi Agreements which were designed to correct this state of poor statesmanship were later disregarded by the Lagos regime.

Under these circumstances, the social fabric of the federation was destroyed as the return of the Igbo to the East on a massive scale and in a volatile and increasingly xenophobic state compelled the military governor of the region to expel non-Easterners from the East. The interhuman network that cut across regional boundaries was severed, and with it, the lingering sense and feeling of unity between the Igbo and the rest of Nigerians. In fact, only in the North, Lagos, and parts of the Midwest was there any support for the Federal Government. In the West the leaders demanded, in no uncertain terms, the withdrawal of Northern troops to their region of origin. They regarded these soldiers as an army of occupation. In both the East and the West strong sentiments were expressed in favour of the secessions of the respective regions. However, as a result of the continued presence of Northern troops in Yorubaland, the most serious threat of secession came from the East.

The Eastern military governor Lt. Colonel Odumegwu Ojukwu refused to accept the authority of the new Head of State and Commander in Chief of the Armed Forces, Lt. Colonel Gowon. Acrimonious exchanges ensued between the Eastern leaders on the one hand and the leaders of the North and the federal government on the other over such issues as the overall control of the armed forces, the leadership of the armed forces, the nature of the relationship to be forged between the regions, the place of meeting of the various military leaders of government, the resumption of the constitutional talks which had broken down in the wake of the September–November massacres, the responsibility for resettling the millions of persons displaced by the massacres and the after effects, the property left behind by the displaced persons, and the payment of the salaries of federal civil servants who had fled to the East. The agreement reached over most of these issues at Aburi in Ghana were later unilaterarilly abrogated by the Federal Government and therefore not implemented.

Under the circumstance of this governmental stalemate, the relations between the East on the one hand and the North and the federal government on the other were caught in an increasingly intense spiral of self-confirming hostile, suspicious expectations and actions. For example, the East illegally confiscated produce worth ₦412,000 belonging to the Northern Nigeria Marketing Board, impounded one-third of the entire rolling stock of the Nigerian Railways including 115 oil tankers, forbade the supply of oil products from the Port Harcourt refinery first to the North and later to the rest of the federation. Also, after March 31 the East began to keep all revenues collected in the region which were payable to the federal government, took over a number of federal statutory bodies such as the Nigerian Coal, Railway, Electricity and Broadcasting Corporations, authorised its Marketing Board to buy and sell produce outside Nigeria directly instead of through the Nigeria Produce Marketing Company, and set up its own Court of Appeal. On its part, the federal government imposed strict controls on foreign exchange transactions by and for the East, terminated all Nigeria Airways flights to the region, imposed a state of emergency in the region and elsewhere in the country, and divided the region arbitrarily into three states.

The inevitable end of this runaway conflict spiral was the secession of the East on 30 May 1967 and the disastrous civil war of 6 June 1967 – 10 January 1970. The resultant human and material loss is yet to be fully and precisely reported but the estimates are staggering. Its net effect was the defeat of secession along with the consequent elimination of the Igbo influence in the interethnic scheme of things. Thus, for example, between the end of the war and July 1977, no major federal project was sited in Igboland. The area has become notorious for bad roads and the issue of Igbo property abandoned during the war was resolved politically to the detriment of the Igbo and with utter disregard for the basic principles of citizenship and the sensitivities of the Igbo. The overall effect of the war is the intensification of ethnicity.

Interethnic violence is a pernicious contributor to the growth of ethnicity. First, it is a very important agency of socialisation into the ethnic scheme of things. In the internecine struggle to destroy or protect lives and property, the ethnic lines are very sharply demarcated. The individual's identity and exclusiveness are vividly circumscribed as each act of violence reinforces his feeling of being different, and of his being able to count only on members of his group for action, security, and welfare. Such violence, more than any other factor, leaves behind the longest lasting bitter memories of interethnic relations. This is essentially because it touches those aspects of man's existence which are dearest to him, life and death, the provision of shelter, and the making of a living. Also, its message is clear and unambiguous. Violent activities are easily empirically observable by the population at large and, therefore, cannot easily be mystified. Successive acts of violence such as the killing of the Igbo by the Hausa in 1945, 1953, May 1966, July 1966, September–November 1966, and June 1967– January 1970 build on each other to heighten the feeling of ethnic exclusiveness, insecurity, and hostility.

Second, apart from its function of passing on ethnic sentiments from generation to generation, interethnic violence also leads to the growth of ethnic group solidarity. On the part of both the perpetrators and their victims alike, a certain collectivism characterises such violence. Involved on both sides are a collective sense of belonging, mission, self-realization and self-affirmation within the collectivity, and a feeling of seizing the individual's and the group's destiny in one's hands akin to the dynamics of mob action. Under the unifying force of ethnicity, the inevitable consequence of such attributes is a greater inward orientation to the ethnic ingroup, with a consequent growth in ethnic identification. A shared history of achievement on the part of the perpetrators, and of suffering on the part of the victims becomes an important component of the ethnic situation. Such a history increases the exclusiveness, feeling of uniqueness and, therefore, the solidarity of the group. The antagonism of the two histories leads to the intensification of ethnic tension and, therefore, the growth of ethnicity.

Inherent in violence are escalating conflict and tension. Both reflect a growth in the factors which characterise the previolence situation or phenomenon. Since violence leaves behind a lingering taste of bitterness, it is very difficult for tension to return to its original level at the end of the violent activities. Instead, equilibrium is achieved at a different but higher level of hostility between the perpetrators and their victims. Such upward shifting of the equilibrium of interethnic tension accounts for the continual growth in ethnicity with interethnic violence. This is particularly so when successive conflicts reinforce memories of previous ones. In such cases, growth in tension and, therefore, ethnicity becomes greater than otherwise. Thus, as a result of the violence which has characterised interethnic relations in Nigeria, the growth of ethnicity over time has taken place.

Growth in Socioeconomic Competition

Growth in ethnicity has been inevitable under conditions in which the objective factors which gave rise to the phenomenon in the first place have grown in intensity. The persistence of the peripheral capitalist structure of society, the expansion of the petty bourgeoisie and comprador bourgeoisie which, together with the traditional aristocracy and the capitalist farmers, constitute the priveleged classes, the intensification of the intraclass struggles for resources among these classes, and the growth of scarcity and inequality in spite of the new-found oil wealth, have contributed substantially to the increase in ethnicity in the country during the post-colonial period.

The persistence of the inherited pattern of socioeconomic and political activities foisted on the country by the financial oligarchies of Europe is most glaringly reflected in the attitude of the majority of the Constitutional Drafting Committee (CDC) of 1976 to the social transformation of the country. Consisting exclusvely of members of the privileged classes, they made no attempt to question the continuation of the inherited import-export economy. Therefore, they neglected the consequences of such an economy for the marginalisation of the vast majority of the Nigerian population, distortion of the consumption pattern, restriction of the capitalist mode of production from disintegrating the precapitalist modes and increasing production in accordance with its own internal dynamics, predominance of tertiary activities (trade, banking, insurance, consultancy services, public service, etc.) over the more productive primary (agriculture) and secondary (manufacturing) sectors, the expatriation of profits and, therefore, the loss of the benefits accruing from investments made with them, the high propensity to import and, consequently, the loss of the benefits that would accrue from the use of the relevant income to purchase goods and services within the country, and the confinement of the nation to the realm of immitative, rather than innovative, technology. Social formations arising from the colonial and neocolonial modes of production were not tampered with; they were hardly ever mentioned.

The inherited pattern of activities has not only persisted, it has been reinforced and intensified through the greater integration of the country into the world capitalist system. With the increased activities in the fields of manufacturing, importation, and construction, occasioned by the growth in the oil wealth, Western and Japanese capitalist firms have been flooding the country in increasing numbers. The West Germans, the Japanese, the French, and the Americans have joined the British as major exploiters of Nigeria's resources, and the major instruments in its integration into the global capitalist system. The growth in economic transactions between the country and these advanced non-Commonwealth capitalist nations has been so phenomenal that Nigeria and the U.S., as recently as June 1977, proudly warned the South African government that Nigeria had overtaken South Africa as the major trading partner of the U.S. on the African continent.[56]

As a result of this persistence and intensification of peripheral capitalism the inherited social formations together with the dominant sociopolitical and economic process have persisted and intensified. More than ever before, the petty bourgeoisie and comprador bourgeoisie have remained oriented toward the distribution of national wealth to the utter neglect of production. The tendency to exploit public resources for private capital accumulation has intensified. Hence, the malpractices and malfeasance of public officers, revealed by the numerous public inquiries which came in the wake of the coup of July 1975, have been more widespread, brazen, and callous than those revealed by the Foster-Sutton Tribunal and the Coker Inquiries which preceded them.

Just as the advent of military rule forced the ex-politicians to turn into very successful businessmen, the retirement exercises of 1975–1977 have led to a new crop of successful businessmen constituted by the ex-public servants. An increasingly important method of sequestering public funds for private use has been the practice by the compradors of inviting and joining foreign firms and business interests in the looting of the national treasury. This practice reached its perfidious extremes in the cement scandal at the end of the Gowon regime in 1975 when Nigerian businessmen colluded with foreigners to exploit the port congestion for the purposes of defrauding the country of large sums of money. But

56. This claim was first made by Andrew Young, the U.S. ambassador at the United Nations. It was later repeated by the Nigerian ambassador to the U.N., Leslie Harriman.

on a much lesser scale, through the receipt of commissions and the acceptance of position in foreign firms, Nigerian compradors are carrying on the same practice, and legitimately too.

Similarly, intraclass competition among the privileged classes has intensified. Rather than reduce, through satisfaction, the demands of these classes for upward mobility, the increased wealth of the country, arising from the exploitation of petroleum, has merely whetted their appetite for more and more capital accumulation. Consequently, instead of intraclass competition diminishing, it has been increasing in intensity. In their unending search for more and more wealth, members of these classes have stopped at nothing. They have invaded the public sector turning it virtually into the private sector through the practice, whereby, public enterprises operate essentially through the activitieis of private contracting firms. With the Nigerianisation of the public services virtually complete, these classes have turned their efforts toward the indigenisation of foreign economic activities under the cloak of economic nationalism.

However, it is clear that the privileged classes have no abiding and overriding interest in ending national dependence on the activities of the foreign firms. Even where full implementation of the indigenization decree has taken place, foreign influence has persisted because the indigenized enterprises' ethoes, symbols, values, life style, relations of production, and modes of operation have all continued to derive from the imperative of exploiting local resources for the benefit of metropolitan capital. These factors constitute strong built in-pressures on local persons to conform to the wishes of the new territorially absent foreign interests. Consequently, instead of the enterprises becoming more and more national in the use of local resources and the satisfaction of the needs of the vast majority of the local population, it is, in fact, the new local owners of the enterprises who become more an extension of the enterprises. It is they who become denationalised. This gives the indigenised firms a national image and protection without seriously endangering their foreign character. In addition, as long as the indigenised companies carry on the same pattern of activities as before, so long will they be effectively controlled by foreigners without ownership participation. The latter's greater bargaining skills, control of technology, and dominance over the enterprises' imported raw materials and exports give them a decided superiority and power over the new local owners of these firms.

On the contrary, the interest of the privileged classes in indigenisation lies merely in their share of the profits of the enterprises. They want to participate in the distribution of these profits. This fact is reflected in their attitude to landed property as a form of lucrative investment even though it is not investment in the directly productive primary and secondary sectors. In the assessment of the CDC majority,

"Land in this country is a vital and critical asset. Until recently investment opportunities in company shares were so few as to be almost non-existent for the vast majority of the population with capital to invest. Happily, the Indigenisation Decree has altered the position somewhat by bringing into the stock market the shares of numerous industrial and commercial companies. Even so, the shares available for sale are so small relative to the demand, with the result that most of the applicants for them get disappointed. For this reason landed property remains unquestionably the most accessible and dependable avenue of investment in this country. It is an investment that traditionally carries with it both prestige and status, a quality lacking in company shares, and which therefore makes it highly prized and sought after."[57]

This view of the CDC majority also contains the perception by the members of the privileged classes that the resources available for them to share are limited and insufficient to go round. Such thinking during the colonial period had led to the factionalization of these classes along regional and ethnic lines so crucial for the emergence of ethnicity. Its presence during the post-colonial period has acted to reinforce ethnicity. It is not surprising, therefore, that factionalism and regionalism within these classes has reached such heights that the advocacy of separate statehood has increased manyfold. Such advocacy has been articulated, organized, and directed by members of these classes. For example, where as in 1958 demands for statehood were confined to minority ethnic groups in regions dominated by the majority ethnic groups, in 1975–1976 there were demands for statehood from even within the same ethnic group. The increased competition for petty bourgeois and comprador bourgeois fortunes has generated ethnic-like antagonism within the same ethnic formation. Although the number of new states created in 1967

57. Federal Republic of Nigeria, *Report of the Constitution Drafting Committee Containing the Draft Constitution* (Lagos: Federal Ministry of Information, 1976), Vol. I, p. xi.

more than doubled that demanded in 1958, the number demanded in 1975–1976 more than doubled that created in 1967. And today intraethnic rivalry and hostility are as pervasive and pernicious as interethnic antagonism.

Part of the reason for the scarcity of the resources available to the privileged classes to share, in spite of the increasing national wealth, is the growth in the size of these classes. Over the years, increased urbanization, greater opportunities for education, particularly at the post-secondary level, and increased industrialisation have produced an increasing number of people who have joined the ranks of the petty bourgeoisie and the comprador bourgeoisie. Many more people now than before have joined the public service at the senior service level; there are many more indigenous contractors, lawyers, doctors, engineers and members of the other professions than before; the number of people in petty trading, small scale industries, import export trade, whole-sale trade, and in the teaching and nursing professions has grown tremendously. Although their numbers are still less than adequate for the needs of the country, nevertheless, they are high enough to engender a vicious and destructive competition for the growing national wealth.

More important, however, is the fact that growth in the national wealth has been growth without development.[58] Hence, it has been accompanied by growth in scarcity and inequality, and, therefore, the socioeconomic insecurity of the individual, the original basis for the successful mobilization of the under-privileged classes along ethnic lines by the privileged classes. The uncaring attitudes of the political leaders to the interests of the workers and farmers which led to the disastrous general strike of 1964 that paralysed the country and the Agbekoya revolt of 1968 respectively, and the numerous strikes precipitated by the

58. On growth without development see Osvaldo Sunkel, "Some Notes on Development, Underdevelopment and the International Capitalist Economy," paper sponsored by the World Law fund as part of the World Order Models Project; Clive Thomas, *Dependence and Transformation: The Transition to Socialism* (New York: Monthly Review, 1974); Colin Leys, *Underdevelopment in Kenya* (London: Hienemann, 1975); T. Szentes, *The Political Economy of Underdevelopment* (Budapest: Akademia Kidao, 1971); Walter Rodney, *How Europe Underdeveloped Africa* (Dares Salaam: Tanzania Publishing House, 1972), Frantz Fanon, *The Wretched of the Earth* (Hammondsworth: Penguin, 1967); P. Baran, *The Political Economy of Growth* (New York: Monthly Review, 1968); and A. G. Frank, *Capitalism and Underdevelopment in Latin America* (New York: Monthly Review, 1969).

report of the Udoji Salary Review Commission in 1975, the widening gap between the rich and the poor, the rapidly deteriorating conditions of the rural areas and the quality of life of the rural population, the worsening food situation, the accompanying high rate of inflation, the uncontrollable hoarding of essential goods and services, and armed robbery are symptoms of the same malaise of scarcity and inequality. In turn, these elements heighten socioeconomic insecurity. Until 1976, education was still conceived as a scarce commodity to be sold to the population. The same is true of medical services. Even today, education at the non-technical secondary and university levels is not free, and is tied to employment.

The growth in urban unemployment after 1959 has continued to pose serious problems. Although the creation of new jobs was an explicit goal of the Six Year Plan, 1962–1968, "Nigerian industry faced with the familiar conflict between employment and output objectives, to date has opted clearly for the latter, leaving employment to be taken up, if at all, in small industry and services."[59] Emphasis has continued to be placed on projects that employ a few people rather than on those with backward linkages to the traditional and transitional sectors of the economy. Largely ignored have been efforts to upgrade the typical rural farm, small indigenous businesses and the apprenticeship system. The preference for highly visible symbols of modernity is continually reinforced by foreign investors whose interests lie in the export of "up-to-date" products and techniques irrespective of their relevance to Nigeria's needs and resource capacity.

Hence, and coupled with the insertion of a very lucrative petroleum enclave, the migration from the rural to the urban areas has increased, despite the obvious fact that hundreds of thousands of migrants were already unemployed or severely underemployed in the cities. The migrants have kept coming because the certainty of poverty, hopelessness and powerlessness in the villages is outweighed by the possibility, even if very slim, of employment and wealth in the urban area. In the absence of the transformation of the structure of incentives in favour of the rural areas, the present massive outflow of population from the rural to the urban areas will continue along with its adverse consequences. Given the existing emphasis on import-substitution

59. G. K. Helleiner, *Peasant Agriculture, Government, and Economic Growth in Nigeria* (Homewood, Illinois: Irwin., 1966), p. 330.

industrialization and capital-intensive technology, the migrants that can be absorbed into gainful employment over a long period of time will continue to diminish.

Under these conditions of intensified scarcity of essential goods and services, the existence side by side of the most conspicuous extravagant affluence and squalid poverty, the most sophisticated scientific education and stark illiteracy, which reflect a deep and fundamental inequality in social relations, and an increasing threat to physical life posed by armed robbery, communal groups have become more salient for the amelioration of the individual's insecurity than before. The government's apparent abdication of its responsibilities, and the consequent disenchantment of the population, have created a large vacuum filled by the communal groups. In many parts of the country self help projects, organized along communal lines, have become the major agency for the social and economic progress of the people, as well as the only means of ensuring their physical security. In the process, the communal factor in national life has been reinforced.

The same effect has been produced by the Muritala-Obasanjo return to the discredited system of indirect rule. Apparently afraid of the direct participation of the people in the governmental process, of a direct interaction between the people and their national leaders, they have sought intermediaries to mediate between the people and their government. This evident lack of confidence by the government in the ability of the masses to take care of their own affairs is clearly colonialist in design and inspiration. And, like the colonial regime, the military leadership relies on the exceedingly reactionary institutions of chieftancy as the major intermediary. Hence, traditional chieftaincy institutions have been reinvested with greater powers and mystical aura than is warranted by the socioeconomic changes that have taken place since the precolonial times. Unable or unwilling to learn from their colonial predecessors, however, the military regime has even ignored history and concrete conditions in its effort to refeudalise the society. Contractor chiefs, using their inexorable financial powers, are now imposing themselves on the people in areas where chieftaincy has not been a significant institution in the lives of the people. The resultant return to and refurbishing of cultural norms and values, most of which are irrelevant for contemporary living merely serve to reinforce the communal factor in relations within the country at large. Under these circumstances, growth in ethnicity is assured.

Thus, singly and in combination with one another, various factors have contributed to the growth of ethnicity in Nigeria. Obviously this escalation creates serious difficulties for the social order and the political process in the country. For example, it is not accidental that the 1973–1974 census created a great deal of tension. The figure of 79 million was reported for the whole country. Out of this 60 per cent was purported to have been contributed by the Northern states. Ethnic ideologues and politicians from the South became immediately apprehensive of the consequences of these figures for the Northern domination of the political process. On his assumption of power, Muritala Mohammed cancelled the census. But without an accurate census figure, effective socioeconomic and political planning for the country, or parts of it, is severely hampered. Similarly, it is becoming more and more difficult to agree on a formula for revenue allocation. It is noteworthy that the Constitutional Drafting Committee found itself unable to suggest one. Instead, it recommended a panel of experts to tackle the problem. The intensified polarisation of the society into subnational ethnic and subethnic cultures, widely separated in terms of identity and loyalty, is encouraging further hostility rather than greater cooperation in the relations among communal groups in the country. Therefore, the necessity to find a solution to the ethnic problem has become even more urgent.

Chapter 8

TOWARD INTERETHNIC HARMONY

Ethnicity and the Creation of States

Much has been written about the need or otherwise for the creation of states in Nigeria. The debate goes as far back as 1942–1943 when Nnamdi Azikiwe published a series of articles in the *West African Pilot*, which were subsequently revised and published as a booklet. He suggested that the country's twenty-five provinces be regrouped into eight states.[1] In 1947, Obafemi Awolowo argued for a federal constitution based on the ethnic factor, in which each ethnic group, irrespective of size, is autonomous in regard to its internal affairs.[2] In the same year, the NCNC, led by Azikiwe, launched the Freedom Charter in opposition to the Richard's Constitution. This Charter suggested, among other things, the creation of ethnic-linguistic states in the country as a means of allaying the fears of minority cultural-linguistic groups. Again in 1953, Awolowo suggested the creation of nine states as a recognition of the ethnic factor. Ever since then, these two leaders of the nationalist movements have advocated the creation of states or of new states as a means of ensuring national unity and stability. James Coleman correctly perceives their position on this question as essentially similar.[3]

As a result of their arguments and those of many others who share similar views on the subject, the impression that has been fostered and is daily being reinforced is that the creation of states is indispensable for the unity and good government of Nigeria. Hence, it is now merely a question of deciding the appropriate number of states as well as their relations to one another and to the central authority. On the contrary, however, the foregone analysis of the ethnic question in the country

1. Nnamdi Azikiwe, "Creation of More States in Nigeria," in *The Senator*, Vol. I, No. 1 p. 25.
2. Obafemi Awolowo, *Path to Nigerian Freedom* (London: Faber, 1947) p. 54.
3. James Coleman, *Nigeria: Background to Nationalism* (Berkeley and Los Angeles: University of California Press, 1958), pp. 388–389.

clearly indicates that, far from solving the nation's socioeconomic and political problems, the creation of states is more likely to reinforce and aggravate them, or at best encapsulate them, preventing them from being solved in the near future.

The ostensible central motivating force of those who support the creation of states is the desire to ameliorate, if not eliminate, interethnic tension which undermines national unity. Various views exist about how this subversion of national unity takes place. Some contend that unless the various ethnic groups have a certain political and economic freedom they cannot maintain their identity. The result is alienation from the national unit and consequently a desire to break away. And, of course, the larger they are as constitutional units, the easier it is to do so. Others suggest that unless the various ethnic groups have a direct access to decisions about the resources allocated to their population the national wealth will not be equitably distributed. The resultant social frustration will yield conflict among ethnic groups which will destroy the social fabric of the nation. Also, by providing a forum for local participation in national activity, the creation of states promotes social mobilization toward the national effort, thereby overcoming disenchantment which is often blamed on the activities of other ethnic groups.

A fundamental and erroneous assumption seems to underly this central motive: that whenever different linguistic or cultural groups exist in the same political unit, conflict between them is inevitable unless each controls most of its own affairs. As has been indicated in the course of this analysis, this assumption is not supported by historical or other empirical evidence. A more important deficiency of the arguments for the creation of states is the tendency to move rapidly from this fundamental assumption to conclusions and recommendations without any intervening concrete scientific historical analysis of the interethnic situation in Nigeria which clearly and systematically exposes its objective and subjective characteristics, its interconnection with various other phenomena in the society, and its rate and direction of change. All that is offered is a mere description of a succession of events in which the ethnic factor is involved. Usually, such descriptions are highly subjective and, in most cases, ethnically motivated. It is no wonder, therefore, that in spite of the constitutional changes from two protectorates to three and then four regions, followed by twelve states, and nineteen states, it has not been possible to ameliorate interethnic tension. Diagnosis must precede and inform prescription. The latter must flow clearly, strictly and systematically from the former.

The subjective nature of the suggestions for the creation of new states was observed by the Willink Commission appointed in 1958 to look into the matter. It found that "except to a limited degree in the case of the Ijaws, the representatives of the minorities who came before us saw in a separate state the remedy for the dangers they feared; most, when questioned, replied emphatically that nothing else but a separate state would serve their purpose."[4] In the view of the Commission, however, there were other and better alternatives than the creation of states. These included the entrenchment of fundamental human rights, the establishment of special development authorities, and the successful implementation of democratic practices. Hence, the Commissin recommended against the creation of states.[5]

In 1976, the Federal Government White Paper on the Report of the Panel on the Creation of States accepted that part of the agitation for the creation of states resulted from bad government. "Even if the Government established 'one family, one state', there would continue to be agitation for more states whenever there was a vacillating and purposeless government. But with the right leadership and good government committed to balanced development, it will be possible to contain states agitation arising from neglect, discrimination and minority fears."[6]

Therefore, it is necessary to explain why advocates of the creation of states have been unwilling to entertain other solutions to the minority problem; why they remained adamant to the recommendations of the Willink Commission, and have continued to press for more states after the creation of the present nineteen state structure and the federal government's plea for emphasis to be shifted to the search for good government and leadership. The foregone analysis of ethnic politics suggests that the relevant explanation lies in the class character of Nigerian ethnicity, particularly the desire of the various regional factions of the privileged classes to carve out their own spheres of economic domination. Such interest cannot be satisfied by the recommenda-

---

4. Nigeria, *Report of the Commission Appointed to Enquire into the Fears of Minorities and the Means of Allaying them* (London: HMSO, 1958), p. 28.
5. *Ibid.*, pp. 88–106.
6. Federal Republic of Nigeria, *Federal Military Government Views on the Report of the Panel on Creation of States* (Lagos: Federal Ministry of Information, 1976), p. 9.

tions of the Willink Commission or the call by the Irikefe Commission for good government. It can only be achieved by the creation of states in which these factions reign supreme. Hence, the creation of states is advocated even within the same linguistic-ethnic groups. This class interest is rationalized and mystified by claims of ethnic domination of minorities.

However, it is clear that for domination to be inherently and uniquely ethnic it must take place along those characteristics which are inherent to and characteristic of ethnicity. These are language and culture. Otherwise, it becomes difficult to distinguish it from domination within the same ethnic group or the domination of one class by another. But both the Willink and Irikefe Commissions found that the grievances of those who wanted new states were mostly socioeconomic and political rather than linguistic-cultural in nature. These grievances concerned the ethnic composition of various public Boards and Corporations such as the Scholarship Board, Marketing Board, Production Development Board, Finance Corporation, the Civil Service. There were also fears regarding the maintenance of public order, with the ethnic minorities complaining that the instruments of law and order were and would be arbitrarily used against them by governments controlled by the majority group. This fear was particularly strongly expressed by the minorities in the North during the 1950s and early sixties when the law enforcement instruments were under the control of the native authorities in which the influence of the traditional emirs was pervasive.

Also, fears have been expressed about the distribution of public services. In fact, it is this fear that prompted B. J. Dudley to warn that the splitting of ethnic homelands such as Igboland and Yorubaland into more states, created the danger of encouraging new growth points in areas which, relative to the rest of the country, are already overdeveloped.[7] Other fears include the rigging of elections in minority areas by the governing party, the manipulation of the chiefs to support the government, and the distribution of government patronage. Obviously, there is nothing particularly ethnic about these concerns. They exist in relations within the same ethnic group, within the same class, and across classes.

On those matters which are particularly ethnic in content,

---

7. B. J. Dudley, "Implications of the 19 – State System," in *Business Times*, Lagos, 2 March 1976, p. 9.

hardly any significant fears were expressed outside of the North. In the North in 1958, some non-Muslim areas particularly the southern parts of Zaria and Ilorin complained that District Heads appointed by the Emir carried out their functions contrary to the traditions of the people who had been accustomed to the rule of traditional chiefs of their own. Similar complaints were made that the teaching of Hausa in schools was compulsory and, therefore, that the minorities were in danger of losing their mother tongue and that this was part of a deliberate plan to strengthen Hausa and Fulani influence throughout the Region. There were other fears too regarding the position of women in non-Muslim areas, particularly with regard to the institution of the purdah, and fears about abstenance from the eating of pork and the drinking of beer as well as the imposition of the sharia court system. Minorities argued that unless they controlled their own states, these alien cultural practices would be extended to them.[8] However, these practices had existed prior to the demand for states and nothing had happened to suggest that the situation would change for the worse. Fears of cultural domination, although well founded in these areas, cannot fully account for the desire for separate states.

In fact, in the Eastern Region such fears were never expressed by the minorities. Their insistence was on the dangers of political domination. "Faced with the prospect of being perpetually in opposition, the minorities were prepared even to reject the hope of independence, asserting that colonial dependence had been preferable to what was now before them."[9] They suggested that there was never any hope of anything but a solid Igbo majority behind the NCNC. In the Western Region, minorities made only a very weak case for Yoruba cultural domination. They charged that the actions of the Regional Government pointed to a deliberate intention of obliterating the separate language, culture and institutions of the Midwest or, at least, of fostering tendencies which would have this result. However, their concrete examples were limited to the Government's association of the Region's parliamentary mace with four ceremonial swords symbolic of the authority of Yoruba chiefs, and the complaint that the Yoruba used derogatory epithets in reference to the non-Yoruba of the

8. *Report of the Commission Appointed to Enquire into the Fears of Minorities and Means of Allaying Them, op. cit.*, pp. 58–59.
9. *Ibid.*, p. 38.

Region.[10] Otherwise, the fear most generally expressed was that the people of the Midwest would always be dominated socio-economically and politically by the Yoruba majority of the rest of the Region.

Clearly the agitation for states in 1958 and 1975–1976 had socioeconomic and political rather ethnic foundations. They were not genuinely motivated by fears of domination of the minor ethnic groups as people were made to believe. Further proof of this is evident in the policies of the various governments both prior to and after the creation of states. Neither the regional governments nor those of the states that succeeded them embarked on any clear-cut cultural policies such as the institutionalisation of language or cultural traditions. In the North where the fear of cultural-linguistic domination was most intense, the new regional and state governments merely continued the practices which they inherited from the colonialists. One would have expected the various state governments created in 1967 and 1976 to formulate aggressive cultural and linguistic policies designed to ensure ethnic self-assertiveness and identity. But most of their policies have been confined to the socioeconomic and political realms. In any case, these states were welcomed by the inhabitants of the former minorities even when they were not ethnically homogeneous. The Federal Government was correct in viewing the demand in terms of political stability,[11] provided that such stability is conceived only in terms of the satisfaction of the significant demands of the various factions of the privileged classes.

Various other reasons, not necessarily connected with the ethnic factor, have been advanced for the creation of states.[12] However, like those based on ethnicity, they merely serve to rationalise and mystify the interests of the privileged classes rather than justify separate states. First, there is the argument that a very strong movement existed which demanded the creation of states, and, therefore, that political stability cannot be guaranteed without it. Many questions are left unanswered by this argument. For example, stability for whom and why? Is the creation of states a more important factor of stability than the

10. *Ibid.*, p. 12.
11. *Federal Military Government Views on the Report of the Panel on Creation of States, op. cit.*, p. 10.
12. These are enumerated in *ibid.*, p. 10.

rapidly deteriorating food situation, the high rate of inflation, and the worsening housing situation of the urban poor? Or is it more important than the interests of the trade unions, the working class and the vast army of unemployed? How have countries with much larger population than Nigeria such as China and Brazil, and such countries with as large an area and as many linguistic groups as Tanzania, been able to maintain stability without the creation of states? In the light of the continuing agitation for more states in spite of the increase in number from two to nineteen has political stability been guaranteed with their creation? How many such states are necessary to guarantee such stability? An honest attempt to answer these questions will expose this argument as essentially a mask over class interests. Since the privileged classes, the major beneficiaries of the creation of states, constitute the ruling classes, they have accorded this question a greater priority than the food question which is of most concern to the underprivileged classes.

Second, it is argued that the creation of states allows for the greatest possible diffusion of economic and political power which, in itself, guarantees the maintenance of the freedom of the individual; therefore it is the only alternative to the development of an arbitrary despotism. Again, the argument is highly abstract. It is not clear what the freedom referred to is for and whom it is for. Is it the freedom of the poor majority to eat more and better food, drink purer water and make the major decisions affecting their lives, or is it the freedom of the rich minority to get promoted to higher senior posts in the public services, procure government contracts to the exclusion of their counterparts from other states, prevent children from other states from attending primary and secondary schools in their states of control, and exclude people from other states from participating actively and meaningfully in the political processes of their states? In what way and to whom does the creation of states diffuse economic and political power? Certainly, it is not diffused to the underprivileged classes.

Third, another argument suggests that the creation of states brings the government nearer to the people by making it more democratic and more efficient, thereby providing a permanent indefeasible devolution of state affairs. This argument is clearly belied by the necessity for the coup of July 29, 1975. In spite of the creation of the twelve state structure from the four regional system in 1967, the country witnessed an unprecedented period of undemocratic and inefficient government, particularly at the state levels until the coup toppled the Gowon clique. Only arbitrary arrests and internment, floggings of political opponents, paper projects, badly maintained roads, scarcity of essential commodities, embezzlement of public funds, conspicuous official consumption, and utter disregard for the welfare of the underprivileged classes were devolved to the people. Indeed, the 1976 Federal Government White Paper on the creation of states points out that part of the agitation for more states resulted from "bad government especially at the state level."[13] Judging from the precipitous increase in the number of demands for separate states between the Willink Commission in 1958 and the Irikefe Commission in 1975 (Table 8.1) the vast increase in bad government with the proliferation of states becomes obvious. In any case, is the creation of states the only, or even the best, instrument for democratising the governmental process or making this process more efficient? Would an efficient democratic local government system run by an egalitarian democratic party motivated by the objective interests of the underprivileged classes, dominated and guided by various political and economic organisations of these classes and devoted to the implementation of progressive policies not be a better instrument for achieving this purpose?

Fourth, it is also argued that the creation of states quickens the pace of development. Unfortunately the concept of development that is involved is that of a checklist of artifacts such as roads, hospitals, schools, postal services, electricity, cars, refrigerators, and televisions. However, development is a dialectical phenomenon in which the individual and the society interact with their physical, biological, and human environments, transforming them for their own betterment and for humanity at large. It ceases to be development for them if others do these things and merely provide them with the resultant artifacts or products. The major engines of development are primary economic activities such as agriculture and, especially, manufacturing. There is clearly no link between the creation of states and the improvement of agriculture and manufacturing in Nigeria or elsewhere. In fact, the agricultural situation has worsened since the creation of states. In the peripheral capitalism of Nigerian-type societies, gainful economic activities tend to concentrate in the tertiary sector of the economy, import-export trade, insurance, banking, whole sale and retail trade, contract and professional work, and

13. *Ibid.*, p. 9.

TABLE 8.1   *Changes in demands for the creation of new states 1958–1975*

Regions in 1958	Demands in 1958	No.	States in 1967	No.	Demands in 1975	No.	States in 1976	No
WEST	Midwest	1	Western Midwestern **Lagos	3	Oyo Ondo Ogun Ijebu South W.	9	Oyo Ondo Ogun Bendel Lagos	5
					Delta Warri Niger Lagos			
EAST*	Ogoja Cross River Rivers	3	E. Central S. Eastern Rivers	3	Wawa Imo E. Central Abakaliki	8	Anambra Imo C. River	4
					C. River Qua-Iboe			
					Rivers P.H.		Rivers	
NORTH	Middle Belt	1	B. Plateau North East N. Central Kwara North West Kano	6	Plateau Benue Adamawa Bauchi Borno Sarduana	14	Plateau Benue Borno Bauchi Gongola	10
					Katsina Zaira Nasarawa		Kaduna Kwara	
					Kabba Kwara		Sokoto	
					Sokoto Niger		Niger Kano	
					Kano			
TOTAL NO.	3	5		12		31		19

* Calabar-Ogoja- Rivers state was also advocated but since it includes the three states listed it has not been included as a separate new state.

** Lagos became a federal territory separated from the West in 1958, but it did not have the status of a state. It is grouped under the West for convenience.

Sources: Federal Republic of Nigeria. *Report of the Panel Appointed by the Federal Military Government to Investigate the Creation of More States and Boundary Adjustments in Nigeria* (Lagos: Federal Government Printer, December 1975), pp. 53–114; Nigeria, *Report of the Commission Appointed to Enquire into the Fears of Minorities and Means of Allaying Them* (London: HMSO, 1958).

public administration. The contribution of this sector to development is relatively insignificant. If anything the creation of states has contributed to the proliferation of the activities of the tertiary sector through the expansion of public administration with the creation of more state bureaucracies.

By focussing on the distributive side of the production process to the neglect of the production aspects, the creation of States militates against the mobilisation of the creative energies of the population toward growth in production through the transformation of the productive forces. Development is inconceivable without growth in the productive forces of the society. It is necessary to reiterate here that this emphasis on distribution is characteristic of the petty bourgeoisie and the comprador bourgeoisie. Unable historically to increase production because of their remoteness from the directly productive functions, they rely on the manipulation of the distributive forces for whatever benefits they derive from the production process. Consequently, they have not been known to build any material civilisation, this has been the historical role of the bourgeoisie proper and the working class.

Fifth, another argument links the creation of states with a balanced federation through the former's impact on the equitable distribution of resources. Again this argument is embarrassed by the empirical situation which it presumes to explain but for which it cannot account. Mention has already been made of Dudley's observation that the creation of states in 1976 led to new growth points in already relatively overdeveloped areas. Even then, the question of balance and imbalance in development is often presented in abstraction and only along regional ethnic lines. For example, the increasing imbalance between the urban and rural areas in reflected in the widening income differentials between the two areas.

Teriba has observed that, contrary to what would have been expected from the general situation of excess labour supply in the urban areas due to high unemployment, urban wages are not only higher but are rising faster than rural incomes.[14] In addition, he notes that while producer prices have been unstable and tended to decline over the years, the prices of locally manufactured goods,

14. O. Teriba, "Quantitative Indicators of Inequality in Africa: Nigeria as a case Study", a paper presented at a conference organised by the Joint Committee on African Studies of the United States Social Science Research Council in Inequality in Africa, held at Mt. KisCo, New York, 6–9 October 1976, p. 34.

and prices applicable to the distributive sector have been rising. In other words the rural-urban terms of trade have been moving against the rural areas. He further contends that, in addition to the higher wages enjoyed by the urban dwellers relative to their rural counterparts, the former also enjoy a greater implicit wage supplements in the form of relatively greater government social overhead expenditure. Similarly, urban-oriented activities attract the bulk of the commercial bank loans in the country. For example, by December 1973 the share of total bank loans to rural activities such as agriculture, forestry, and fishing amounted to a mere 2.9 per cent while the equivalent for urban enterprises such as manufacturing, general commerce, transportation and communication was more than 67.5 per cent of the total.[15]

There has also been a higher concentration of commercial banks, an indicator of accessibility to the capital market, in the urban areas. Out of a total of 329 banks in Nigeria about 278 were located in urban areas. This means that only 20 per cent of the total banking offices in the country serve over 80 per cent of the country's total population, the rural inhabitants.[16] The obvious imbalance between the rural and urban areas in the field of banking is clear. But such imbalances are of no interest to the privileged classes, most of whose members are urban dwellers. They are only interested in the imbalance between the various urban enclaves where they reside. The creation of states is expected to correct such imbalances.

Even in this regard the evidence is not supportive. In spite of the creation of twelve states in 1967, manufacturing has continued to be disproportionately concentrated in the Lagos metropolitan area. In fact, by 1971 the East Central State, West, and Lagos states dominated the distribution of manufacturing industries. In the peripheral capitalist society of the type inherited by Nigeria, development takes place in areas of concentration of foreign private investment in manufacturing industries. The latter is attracted to areas of high buying power and concentration of capitalist infrastructure such as banking, insurance and shipping. As more states have been created these attractions have increasingly been more disproportionately located in Lagos and, to some extent, Kano.

Also, there are glaring imbalances in the accessibility of the

15. *Ibid.*, p. 36.
16. *Ibid.*

various states to credit in Nigeria. This is reflected in the distribution of banking services in the country. By 1974 the branches of the various commercial banks were concentrated in a few states with the two top states, Lagos and the West, accounting for about 42 per cent of the total. The six Southern states accounted for about 72 per cent of the bank branches in the country even though these states contained only 46.4 per cent of the total population. Of all the 16 commercial banking houses operating in the country at the time, only three did not have offices in Lagos while the Northern states were served by only five of them and a state like the South Eastern State had only four.[17]

Thus, most of the arguments proferred for the creation of states either leave too many questions unanswered to be taken very seriously or are clearly unconvincing. They are, therefore, mere rationalisations of the interests of certain segments of the population which cannot be as openly and publicly advocated. The foregone analysis indicates that the objective interests served by ethnicity are those of the privileged classes. These interests tend to run along lines of geographically contiguous enclaves, regions,

TABLE 8.2   *Distribution of industries by state, 1971*

State	Percentage of total population	No. of industries	Industries as percentage of total	Percentage of industrial employment
South Eastern	8.3	28	3.2	3.5
North Eastern	14.0	14	1.6	0.7
Mid West	4.5	64	7.4	5.9
Benue Plateau	7.2	48	5.5	2.3
North Western	10.3	16	2.8	1.5
East Central	11.2	149	17.13	5.8
Kano	10.4	41	4.7	6.3
North Central	7.3	37	4.3	13.1
Rivers	2.8	11	1.3	1.0
Kwara	4.3	21	2.4	3.7
Lagos	2.6	273	32.0	46.7
West	17.0	163	13.7	9.5
Total Nigeria		870	100.0	100.0

Source: O. Teriba, "Quantitative Indicators of Inequality in Africa: Nigeria as a Case Study", Paper presented at a Conference on African Studies, organised by the United States Social Science Research Council and held at Mt. Kisco, New York, 6–9 October 1976, p. 30. Table 13.

17. *Ibid.*, p. 31.

or states which correspond with ethnic homelands. But such interests are not fully manifested when ethnicity is propagated. Arguments for the creation of states, and even those against it, serve as a mask for the pursuit of these class interests. They are used because of their high propaganda value.

For those who see sociopolitical progress as inconceivable outside a solution of the ethnic and other problems through the creation of states, it is pertinent to ask the question; who benefits from the establishment of these states? Certainly it is not the farmer or low or middle income worker but the bureaucrats who become permanent secretaries overnight, the university dons who achieve professorial status irrespective of merit because of new universities located in their states, the university dons, lawyers, and doctors who become commissioners, chairmen of public corporations and various institutes and broadcasting services, and the contractors and businessmen who monopolise official contracts in their states of origin. The rest, the poor workers and peasants, are told that the exercise will bring development. But they wait in vain. They witness the changes from two to three to four regions, and then to twelve and nineteen states without noticing any improvement in their living conditions. If anything, their situation has worsened. The truth, of course, is that they must wait in vain for this development. The logic of development in Nigerian-type societies has nothing whatsoever to do with the creation of states which has nothing to contribute to the improvement of the productive forces and relations of production.

Politics and the Reflection of a Federal Character

Apart from the creation of states, other recommendations abound for solving the ethnic problem. Among them are those designed to reflect what the Constitutional Drafting Committee (CDC) refers to as the "federal character" of the country. Underlying this concept is the assumption that the various linguistic groups in the country are essentially significant in their differences rather than in their similarities. The increasingly pervasive belief is that there is ethnic diversity of such magnitude that the country has a "federal character". In its official report, the CDC says nothing about the symbols, values, norms, customs, histories and experiences which are common to the various linguistic ethnic groups. Those common sociocultural and economic-historical attributes usually associated with the

African personality, some and even more of which can be cultivated in a Nigerian personality that transcends linguistic boundaries are utterly neglected. In fact, in its definition of the concept
"federal character" the CDC majority refers to

"the distinctive desire of the peoples of Nigeria to promote national
unity, foster national loyalty and give every citizen of Nigeria a sense
of belonging to the nation *notwithstanding the diversities of ethnic origin,
culture, language or religion which may exist* and which it is their desire to
nourish and harness to the enrichment of the Federal Republic of
Nigeria".[18]

Hence, the CDC makes provisions for bridging these differences:

"The composition of the Federal Government or any of its agencies and
the conduct of their affairs shall be carried out in such manners as to
recognize the federal character of Nigeria and the need to promote
national unity and to command national loyalty. Accordingly, the
predominance in that Government or in its agencies of persons from a
few states, or from a few ethnic or other sectional group shall be
avoided. The composition of a government other than the federal
government or any of the agencies of such government and the conduct
of their affairs shall be carried out in such manner as to recognise the
diversity of the peoples within their area of authority and the need to
promote a sense of belonging and loyalty among all the peoples of
Nigeria."[19]

In order to ensure the effectiveness of this provision, the
Draft further provided in Article 123 that "at least one minister
of the government of the Federation shall be appointed from
among Nigerian citizens who belong to each of the states comprising the Federation"[20] Also, Article 173 insists that "the
members of the executive committee or other governing body of
a political party shall be deemed to reflect the federal character of
Nigeria only if the members belong to different states, not being
less in number than two-thirds of all the states comprising the
federation".[21]

18. *Underliving is* mine. Federal Republic of Nigeria, *Report of the Constitution
    Drafting Committee Containing the Draft Constitution* (Lagos: Federal Ministry
    of Information, 1976), Vol. I, p. X. It is also contained in Article 8 of the
    Draft Constitution.
19. *Ibid.*, p. 11, Article 8 (2 and 3).
20. *Ibid.*, p. 49, Article 123 (2).
21. *Ibid.*, p. 71, Article 173 (26).

The methodological difficulties of implementing these provisions indicate their inadequacy as a solution to the current problem of national cohesion. As Yusufu Bala Usman has aptly observed, their crucial words, "belong to a state", are quite problematic.[22] These are defined in Article 210 which states that "'belong to' when used with reference to a state refers to a person either of whose parents was a member of a community indigenous to that state".[23] Usman continues his critique of these provisions by correctly pointing out that it is quite difficult in Nigeria to decide what exactly constitutes "a community indigenous to a state." It is not clear the number of generations a family is expected to stay in a state before its members become indigenous. "Who are the indigenes of Gongola State, for example? Is it the Bachama who somebody will say claim to come from Gobia? Or the Jukun who somebody will claim to come from Egypt? Or the Fulani who somebody will say claim to come from Senegal?"[24]

As an illustration of some of the difficulties involved Usman envisages a political situation in which a minister of the government, chairman of a public corporation, or director of a broadcasting service on appointment would have to publish his geneology with some commentary. And a court action may follow to prove he is not an indigene.

"Everytime a political party publishes the name of the members of its executive council they would have to attach their geneologies and probably court action will follow, not only on the origin of the individuals and their parents and grand parents but on the indigeneity or not of particular communities they claim to belong to. There shall be very lucrative business for us in history, fabricating and exposing geneologies"[25].

As Usman contends, such an exercise would make indigeneity a permanent political issue. It would also grossly contradict provisions of the constitution regarding residence rights, and completely undermine the development of a national citizenry, a

22. Yusufu Bala Usman, "Democracy and National Cohesion: The Bankruptcy of the C. D. C. Majority Draft, "a text of a public lecture for the National Union of Gongola Students at the Murtala Muhammed College, Yola, Saturday 1 January 1977, p. 8.
23. Quoted in *ibid.*, p. 8.
24. *Ibid.*, pp. 8–9.
25. *Ibid.*, pp. 8–9.

basic requirement for national cohesion.[26] One of the consequences of these provisions would be the creation of three types of Nigerian citizens arranged in an hierarchy of superiority and inferiority. The first class citizens would be the residents of states who are able to prove that they belong to indigenous communities of such states. Those citizens who are able to show that they belong to communities indigenous to some states but are themselves resident in other states would become second class citizens. In order to fully participate in the political process they have to move back and forth to their "states of origin." Finally, the third class citizens would be those people who are unable to prove that they belong to a community indigenous to any of the states but are nevertheless full-fledged Nigerian citizens.[27]

Such a discriminatory system of citizenship is highly confusing, divisive, and destabilising. Its negative consequences will be pervasive. They will not be confined

"to the people of Igbo, Hausa, Efik or Nupe origin living in Lagos, Ibadan or Port Harcourt or just to the people of Yoruba origin in Kaduna, Jos, Kano or Makurdi. It is going to extend to the Kanuri, Sakhwatawa and Nupe here in Jimeta. It is going to extend to the Jassawa of Kano origin, the inhabitants of Ibadan of Igbirra, Igala, Hausa, Ijebu or Benin origin, to the Fulani of Bida and Ilorin, the people of Marghi origin in Gongola, and to millions of Nigerian citizens the movements of whose parents and grandparents over centuries has woven the real fabric on which national citizenship and cohesion may be forged".[28]

Therefore, rather than contribute to national cohesion these provisions are more likely to lead the country farther away from that goal. Their objective purpose is to exclude Nigerian members of the privileged classes of other states from enjoying the perquisites of public office in a state. They are merely part of a number of devices and tactics deployed in the intraclass struggles of the various regional factions of the privileged classes. Their only relationship to unity is their pretension to establish some order in the struggle of these factions for the division of the national cake.

Furthermore, the CDC draft constitution enjoins states to

26. *Ibid.*, p. 9.
27. *Ibid.*, p. 10.
28. *Report of the Constitution Drafting Committee, op. cit.*, Article 9 (2), p. 11.

"encourage inter-marriage among persons from different places of origin, or of different religions, ethnic or linguistic associations or ties; and promote or encourage the formation of associations that cut across ethnic, linguistic, religious or other sectional barriers;"[29] and "foster a feeling of belongingness and of involvement among the various peoples of the country, to the end that loyalty to the nation shall override sectional loyalties."[30] However, it is not clear whether the authors of the document are suggesting that the ethnic problem is the result of the absence of interethnic marriages and the inability of the various Nigerian governments to foster a feeling of belongingness and involvement in the country. In any case the word "government" is used in abstraction, without any class content. And it is hardly suggested that it may be in the objective interests of the classes that control the government to encourage ethnic sectionalism, or indeed that such sectionalism is the inevitable consequence of the economic activities of these classes. Finally, no guidelines are given for the practical implementation of these injunctions, confining them therefore to the level of impracticable rhetoric.

This obsessive and abstract rhetorical concern with the constitutional aspects of the ethnic question, typical of the major beneficiaries and the victims of the ethnic ideology, is also encountered in the CDC draft constitution's provisions for the election of the executive President. He is deemed elected, if "(i)(a) he has the highest number of votes cast at the election; and (b) he has not less than one quarter of all the votes cast at the election in each of at least two-thirds of all the states within the Federation; or (ii) where there are only two candidates for the election, he has a majority of all the votes cast at the election and wins a majority of votes in more than half of the states within the Federation; or (iii) in default of a candidate who is duly elected in accordance with paragraph (i) of subsection (4) of this section, there shall be a second election at which the only candidates shall be the candidate who secured the highest votes at the first election and that one among the remaining candidates who has a majority of votes in the largest number of states : Provided that if there are more than one candidate with a majority of votes in the highest number of states the one with the higher total of votes cast at the election shall be the second candidate for the election; (iv)(a) in default of a

29. *Ibid*., Article 9 (3).
30. *Ibid*., Article 9 (3).

candidate who is duly elected in accordance with paragraph (ii) or (iii) of this subsection, the Electoral Commission shall within seven days of the result of the second election hold an election in each House of the National Assembly and in each of the Houses of Assembly of every state in the Federation to determine which of the two candidates shall be elected as President; (b) the election mentioned in this subsection shall be held simultaneously in every state and the person who has simple majority of the votes cast at such election shall be deemed to have been duly elected as President."[31]

The views of the CDC on the ethnic question along with Yusufu Bala Usman's excellent critique of them have been discussed in detail because the CDC majority represent the privileged classes whose thinking is very influential in shaping the attitudes and beliefs of the rest of the population on various national and local issues. Since their deliberations are recent, they reflect the most up-to-date kinds of solutions envisaged in the society for the ethnic problem. However, the CDC majority obviously represent the interests of the petty bourgeois and comprador bourgeois classes, the major local beneficiaries of the neocolonial economic activities organised by the financial aligarichies of Europe, America and Japan together with the accompanying ethnic phenomenon.

First, the CDC members display an obvious desire and strength of will to maintain the existing pattern of economic activities foisted on the country by the foreign financial oligarchies. There is no attempt to question the continuation of the inherited import-export economy. Therefore, the draft constitution neglects the adverse consequences of such an economy. Second, they maintain the inherited separation of the activities of the superstructure (politics) from those of the infrastructure (relations of production). Social formations arising from the colonial and neocolonial modes of production are not tampered with; they are hardly ever mentioned. Therefore, it is deemed more important for the political process for parliamentary constituencies to run along geographical lines rather than along lines of the relations of production, the roles that individuals play in the production process. It is also deemed more important that the President represents the majority of the various ethnic groups than that he is not in any way dependent on the multinational cor-

31. *Ibid.*, Article 111 (4) pp. 44–45.

porations owned by the financial oligarchies of Europe, America, and Japan.

This very conservative attitude of the document which is characteristic of the local privileged classes is again most glaringly reflected in its discussion of the allocation of state land. To the suggestion of one of its subcommittees that no person "shall own or occupy more than one plot of state land throughout the country,"[32] the majority of the CDC countered with the argument that it is "obnoxious, immoral, unethical and wholly unjustifiable to take away through the Constitution by ways of mandatory provisions vested rights of a citizen which he lawfully acquired and for which there is no state necessity or need. This is confiscatory in concept though dressed in a different garb.[33] In defence of their vested interests, they are willing to use extremist and radical language. Also by limiting themselves to the allocation of state land[34] they ignore the increasingly explosive question of the rapidly emerging landless peasantry in the rural areas as a result of farmers losing their land to petty bourgeois and comprador bourgeois elements through their mortgaging, pledging and leasing of land.[35]

Another evidence of the unwillingness of the CDC majority to change the inherited economy is seen in their opposition to such economic and social rights as the rights to full employment, education, and medical services. They mystify and rationalize this opposition with the flimsy argument that such rights require certain facilities for their implementation.[36] Obviously, they are reluctant to create these facilities if it means a reduction in the privileges presently enjoyed by the petty bourgeois and comprador bourgeois classes. It is quite illuminating that they did not think it fit to impose a time limit for the establishment of these facilities. They are probably afraid that the implementation of these rights would require a radical reorganisation of social and economic life which may undermine their class privileges. They concern themselves with abstract rights such as the freedom of speech and association which have no economic content. Their interest does not lie in seriously challenging the foreign monopoly of production in the country.

32. *Ibid.*, p. x.
33. *Ibid.*, p. xi.
34. *Ibid.*, pp. x-xii.
35. T. C. Mbagwu, "Oil Palm Economy in Ngwaland (Eastern Nigeria,)" Ph.D. thesis, University of Ibadan, Nigeria, 1971.
36. *Report of the Constitution Drafting Committee, op. cit.*, pp. xv-xvi.

Similarly, other suggestions which would mean a radical change of the inherited pattern of social and economic activities have not been included in the draft. For example, on the code of conduct for political leaders the relevant sub-committee of the CDC was specific in recommending that

"A leader shall not put himself in a position where his personal interest conflicts with his responsibilities as a leader, or which enables him to exploit others ... a leader shall not (a) hold more than one public office (b) engage in any private business, trade or profession (c) receive any remmuneration, gain or profit other than the emolument payable to him in respect of the specified office held by him."[37]

The CDC majority emasculated this recommendation by merely providing that

"A public officer shall not put himself in a position where his personal interest conflicts with his duties and responsibilities ... a public officer shall not (a) (i) accept or be required to undertake additional public functions which would make it impracticable or difficult for him to perform the duties and responsibilities of a specified office adequately or (ii) receive or be paid the emoluments of such office at the same time as he receives or is paid the emoluments of another public office. OR (b) engage or participate in the management or running of any private business, profession or trade to such extent as to make it impracticable or difficult for him to perform the duties and responsibilities of a specified office adequately or in such a manner as would enable him to advance the interest of such business, profession or trade through his position as a public officer.'[38]

Similarly, the subcommittee recommended that "A leader shall not be a member of, belong to or take part in the organisation or management of the Ogboni or Owegbe Societies or any other secret society of a similar nature."[39] And the CDC decided on a watered down version: "A public officer shall not be a member of, belong to, or take part in any society the membership of which is incompatible with the functions or dignity of his office."[40]

Similar class interests are also reflected in the draft constitution by expressions of attitudes on private investment, the profit

---

37. *Report of the Constitution Drafting Committee* (Lagos: Federal Ministry of Information, 1976) Vol. II, p. 42.
38. *Ibid.*, pp. 56–57.
39. *Ibid.*, p. 43 (12)
40. *Ibid.*, 58 (12)

motive, individualism and the public sector. On the question of the control of the economy the CDC rejected the recommendations of its relevant subcommittee for socialism and opted for a system in which "The State shall within the context of the ideals and objectives provided for in this Constitution, control and operate the major sectors of the economy while individual and group rights to operate the means of production, distribution and exchange shall be protected by law."[41] Underlying this provision are among others, the following arguments (a) "It is through (private) investment and effort that we can increase the accummulation of the foods to distribute to all."[42] "Do we allow for the role of incentives, private profit, and larger reward for the more effective worker or manager in bringing forth the maximum efforts from the people?"[43] Even the subcommittee which recommended a socialist form of social organisation could not escape some of the clutches of these inherited ideological elements. Following its examination of the leadership codes of Tanzania and Zambia it rhetorically asked "Is the restriction on the individual freedom of enterprise and of acquisition severe? What is to be the reasonable balance between the need for individual initiative and the prevention of exploitation? Is the loss to the nation resulting from the exclusion of "leaders" from entrepreneurial initiative a reasonable price to pay for the prevention of exploitation?"[44] Its members are thus willing to accept some degree of slavery for the purposes of protecting the value of individualism.

On the question of the public sector, the attitude of the CDC is at best contradictory. On the one hand, its members provided for a mixed economy in which the public sector plays a large and leading role and able to determine basic prices and to mitigate the harsher effect of private competition."[45] On the other hand they liquidate the Marketing Board system, exposing the farmers to a more direct and intense exploitation as well as the whims and caprices of middlemen and their private companies.[46] In any case, no thought is given to changing the relations of production in the public enterprises in favour of labour over capital, or

41. *Report of the Constitution Drafting Committee, op. cit.*, Vol. I, p. xiv.
42. *Ibid.*
43. *Ibid.*
44. *Report of the Constitution Drafting Committee, op. cit.*, Vol. II, p. 41.
45. *Report of the Constitution Drafting Committee, op. cit.*, Vol. I p. xiv.
46. *Ibid.*, pp. xxiii-xxv.

operating them under socialist norms, symbols and values. Not even the practice whereby public enterprises operate essentially through the activities of private contracting firms is discussed. In short, no major change in the conception, role, and manner of operation of the public sector is envisaged despite the rhetoric about the state control of the major sectors of the economy.

In fact, in the words of the CDC

"The term 'major sectors of the economy' shall be construed for the purpose of this section to refer to any economic activity as may from time to time be declared by the resolution of each of the Houses of the National Assembly as one to be managed and operated exclusively by the Federal Government. Until a resolution to the contrary is made by the National Assembly the economic activities being operated exclusively by the Federal Government on the date immediately preceding the day when this section comes into force whether directly or through the agencies of a statutory or other corporation or company shall be deemed to be major sectors of the economy."[47]

By this provision the committee maintains without change the inherited pattern of activities of the non-profitable public enterprises designed to serve the needs of the private sector dominated by the foreign finance oligarchies for profit maximization and capital accumulation through the exploitation of wage labour, and financially sustained by the local taxpaying population. Nothing is said about extending the public enterprises into the vital agricultural and manufacturing sectors.

Ethnic Mask Over the Class Struggle

If thus, the Nigerian privileged and ruling classes are very desirous of perpetuating the inherited socioeconomic organisation of the society, with its accompanying interethnic situation because of the benefits they derive from it, then their appeals to ethnic sentiments and the rhetorical solutions which they proffer for the ethnic problem constitute a mask over their class privileges, the struggles among them for the sharing of these privileges, and the struggle of the oppressed classes against such privileges. Mention has already been made of how the struggle of the various regional factions of the petty bourgeoisie and comprador bourgeoisie for the division of the national wealth contributed to the emergence of contemporary ethnic identity, feeds on it, and is

47. *Ibid.*, p. 12, Article 10(2).

masked by it. Similarly we have exposed the origin of the ethnic ideology in colonial racism and the function of that ideology in masking the foreign exploitation of local resources, including labour. This function of ethnicity has persisted. In addition, ethnicity masks struggles which have not contributed to its emergence and do not feed on it but which are crucial for the motion of the society, particularly the direction of this motion.

Among these is the struggle between the remnants of the pre-colonial aristocracy, essentially of the feudal and tributary modes of production, and the emergent petty bourgeoisie, comprador bourgeoisie and more recently local independent bourgeoisie. This struggle has had several strands. One of these was the struggle in the North between the feudal aristocracy represented by the NPC and the petty bourgois populism of the NEPU. The former was an alliance of the precolonial ruling class and the emergent Hausa wealthy businessmen, particularly the compradors and and the commercial bourgeoisie. The alliance was under the domination of the former. Its major policies were designed to protect the main basis of the power of the emirate system and, therefore, of the precolonial aristocracy, notably the control of land by this class, the dominant role in administration of the native authority dominated by it, the perpetuation of the Islamic religion and the social and legal systems based on it, and control of the rate of embourgeoisement of the Northern population by colonialism and neocolonialism, especially through the isolation of the Northern population from its Southern counterparts who had caught the peripheral capitalist virus. The alliance made a token response to the interest of the junior partner for business and jobs in the public and private service through the Northern-isation policy and appointments to federal posts.

Essentially the dominant interests of this alliance severely contradicted those of the petty bourgeoisie being pursued by the NEPU. This was the party of the non-aristocratic elements, mainly intellectuals, independent traders, and a few rich businessmen, in addition to a large number of small traders, craftsmen, and shop-keepers. The party preyed on the predisposition of the urban tala-kawa to oppose traditional aristocratic authority, in order to pursue its goal of eliminating those traditional devices which constrain the embourgeoisement of the local population, that prevent the Northern petty bourgeoise from transforming itself into the bourgeoisie proper. Hence, it waged a relentless struggle against the native authority system which was used by the emirs to keep their subjects in their traditional places, against the legal limitations of political liberties in the North and in favour of Western education for males and females alike. It is only within this context that the party could be regarded as progressive, it wanted the destruction of the prevailing feudal system as a prelude to the growth of a benevolent capitalism.

The failure of the party to achieve its progressive intention lay significantly in its alliance with the NCNC. The NPC propaganda seized this opportunity to portray the party as an extension of the NCNC which it referred to as a Southern party. This constant appeal to ethnic and regional sentiments succeeded in diverting attention from and masking the relatively popular policies of the party. It put the party constantly on the defensive, obliged to rebut the damaging allegation that it was Southern-dominated and therefore anti-Muslim. This latter factor accounted, in part, for the precipitous decline of NEPU influence in the largely Christian lower North. In fact, by 1959, its influence among the non-Hausa ethnic groups of the North had virtually disappeared except in the kilba group of Adamawa.[48]

A similar struggle was also waged in the Western Region between the AG and the traditional ruling aristocracy. In the words of Obafemi Awolowo, there is "a mutual distrust verging on antagonism between the educated few and the Chiefs."[49] The latter feared that the former were out to remove them from their privileged positions. And the educated leaders charged that the excessive power of the chiefs was the major source of tension within Yorubaland. They argued that, as a fundamental principle, the chiefs should not be permitted to dominate the people, emphasising that the sole legitimate foundation of government must be the consent of the people freely and democratically expressed. Hence, the AG became a champion of universal adult suffrage. Historically, such arguments have often been used in the struggle of the emergent bourgeoisie and petty bourgeoisie against the dominant inherited aristocracy. They were first popularized during the French revolution of 1789. Emphasis is on political rather than economic freedoms and rights.

This struggle which was dramatically illustrated by the celeb-

---

48. B. J. Dudley, *Parties and Politics in Northern Nigeria* (London: Frank Cass, 1968), p. 297.
49. Obafemi Awolowo, *Path to Nigerian Freedom* (London: Faber, 1947), pp. 31–32.

rated case of the Alafin of Oyo, 1952–1954, culminated in the victory and ascendancy of the emergent privileged classes. In 1952, the Alafin had clashed with the AG over supremacy in the Oyo Divisional council. In reprisal the AG controlled government of the West reduced his salary and suspended it entirely in 1954 for alleged collusion with agitators against a regional levy. Thereafter, the conflict between the two parties was caught in a self-confirming conflict spiral which led to violence and the death of six people on 5 September 1954. The governing party blamed the incident on the Alafin and used it as a pretext for suspending him from office and banishing him from his domain. Eventually he was deposed contrary to the recommendations of the government-appointed inquiry into the allegations against him.[50]

This test case created the impression that no chief in the West could oppose the AG and survive. Legislation had been introduced empowering the regional government to suspend or depose any chief in the interest of peace, order or good government. Moreover specified local government councils under the political parties were empowered to determine succession to traditional offices in their areas of jurisdiction. For example, at Oyo, the succession to the deposed Alafin fell to the Oyo Divisional Council controlled by the AG. Hence an AG supporter was elected. Since the deposition of the Alafin of Oyo, few chiefs in the Western Region have dared to assert their opposition to the government in power. They could neither oppose the AG nor be politically netural. In 1958, only one of the 54 members of the Western House of Chiefs was identified as not being a supporter of the party.[51]

At the same time, there has also been class struggle between these traditional aristocracies of Hausaland and Yorubaland on the one hand and the common people of these areas respectively, the peasants, artisans, handicraftsmen and workers. The Aristocrats' control over land and their demand for tributes lead to the economic exploitation of the masses. In addition, the former's denial of political and human rights to the latter in local affairs, together with the absence of the right to the due process of the law

50. The Western Regional Government, *Report of a Commission of Inquiry into Disturbances at Oyo by Mr. R. D. Lloyd* (Ibadan: Government Printer, 1958).
51. Richard Sklar, *Nigerian Political Parties* (Princeton, New Jersey: Princeton University Press, 1963), p. 457.

in Hausa and Yoruba customary and Muslim courts, constitute different forms of repression of the masses by these aristocracies. They offset the appeals of radicalism to the lower classes by invoking the communal values, customs and traditions of the indigenous people.

By far the most decisive class struggle in the political history of Nigeria has been the conflict between the Northern aristocracy and the Sourthern petty bourgeoisie, comprador bourgeoise and to a much lesser extent commercial bourgeoisie. It is reflected in the contradictory interests of the NPC on the one hand and the AG and NCNC on the other. The major political goal of the Hausa-Fulani aristocracy is to maintain its social, relgious, economic and political domination of the emirates of Northern Nigeria. In order to do this, it is objectively in this aristocracy's interest to limit and control the rate of penetration of peripheral capitalist structures and values into the Hausa-Fulani feudal realms. Hence, Northern rulers have limited the acquisition of Western education, the separation of religious and secular matters, the granting of political rights to the populace, the introduction of the Western legal system, and above all the socioeconomic penetration of the area by Southerners. The emirs encourage non-traditional enterprises only under the conditions of the traditional system of clientage.

In order to achieve these purposes it is objectively necessary first to control state power in the North. Hence the NPC put more premium on its control of the Northern Regional Government than on its control of the Federal Government. This is reflected by the fact that its leader, Ahmadu Bello, persistently remained as regional Premier even when he had the option of becoming the federal Prime Minister. But control at the federal level was necessary to ensure effective control at the regions. This is clearly illustrated by the creation of the Midwest and the AG leadership crises of 1962–1965. Therefore, it was also imperative for the NPC to control the federal government if the Northern feudal aristocracy would control social and economic transformations of the emirates in the way they wished. In this regard, it is noteworthy that the NPC was not as interested in the economic rewards of controlling the federal government as the NCNC and the AG. Although they made some responses to the Northern petty bourgeoisie through federal appointments, this was also necessary to ensure Northern participation in the formulation and implementation of federal policies which may affect the North.

These interests of the Northern feudal aristocracy sharply contradicted those of the emergent privileged classes of the South who saw their ambitions to make more money and get better jobs by moving to the North effectively blocked by the policy of Northernisation. In order to dislodge this aristocratic hold on the area it was necessary to expose the injustices of the emirate system, mobilize the majority oppressed by it, and bring them into political power in the area through democratic processes. Hence the NCNC and AG consistently attacked the Native Authority system of the North, its courts, and law enforcement agencies. In addition, they called for mass education and the democratisation of the political process.

Any ambition on the part of the Southern leaders to control the Northern government was unrealistic. Hence they concentrated their attention on using federal power to effect the necessary changes in the North. But first the Southerners had to win political power at the federal level. They failed. Although their policies were, in general, relatively more progressive than the backward-looking programmes of the feudal aristocrats, these programmes were drowned in the sea of ethnicity and regionalism which the Southerners themselves did much to generate. First, the Southern strength was so effectively divided and sapped by ethnicity that not only did the NCNC and AG fail to unite against the NPC but, in fact, the NCNC entered an alliance with the latter after the 1959 federal elections. This fact, together with the knowledge that the AG also sought an alliance with the NPC following that election illustrates the importance which the Southern petty bourgeoisie and comprador bourgeoisie attached to the economic rewards of office. Of course, they rationalized their behaviour on the illogical grounds that it was the only way to guarantee the impending independence of the country.

Second, the NPC successfully appealed to the ethnic and regional sentiments of the Northerners who constituted the majority of the electorate. In the atmosphere of ethnic identity and chauvinism that prevailed at the time the effect was predictable. In fact, the Southern parties concentrated their efforts and made their major electoral gains in the North in the minority areas.

Finally, there is the class struggle between the privileged classes and the underprivileged classes. This is reflected by the conflict between the NPC, AG, NCNC and NEPU on the one hand, and the organisations of the workers and peasants on the other.

Mention has already been made of the disastrous general strike of 1964 which paralysed the country for two weeks. In 1968, a similar struggle by the military counterpart of these parties and the representative of the peasantry in the West was reflected in the Agbekoya rebellion. The peasants rose against the repressive and exploitative machinery of the privileged classes.[52]

It is further reflected today in the efforts of the Obasanjo regime to muzzle and emasculate the country's trade union movement. The Trade Disputes Decree No. 7 of 1976 was designed to provide stringent measures against the activities of the trade unions. Among other things it consolidated the obnoxious Trade Disputes (Emergency Provisions) Decree No. 21 of 1969. Also it provided for the establishment of a National Industrial Court to exercise appellate jurisdiction over the awards of the Industrial Arbitration panel, to be dominated by the privileged classes. The decisions of the court would be binding and final. Strikes and lockouts prior to the decisions of the court were prohibited. Nevertheless, and in spite of the severe penalties prescribed for a breach of the decree, the trade unions virtually ignored it and threats of strike mounted. Consequently, barely three months afterwards, the Trade Dispute (Essential Services) Decree No. 23 of 1976 was promulgated which provided for the proscription of recalcitrant unions, and the detention of their leaders. Predictably, the decree was silent on recalcitrant employers. More important still, that regime has taken upon itself to purge the leadership of the unions, a curious case of an enemy purging the camp of its major adversary. But the struggle has continued.

The conflict between the privileged and underprivileged classes has also been waged in the area of the appropriation of the society's surplus from production. It is reflected in the findings of the various tribunals and commissions which have inquired into the cases of bribery and corruption in the country. The most celebrated of these have been the Foster-Sutton Tribunal report, the report of the Coker Commission and the findings of the numerous probes and inquiries instituted by the Murtala-Obasanjo regime. Obviously undertaken to expose one faction or the other of the privileged class by another or other factions, their

---

52. Gavin Williams, "Class Relations in a Neo-colony: the case of Nigeria," in Peter C. Gutkind and Peter Waterman, eds., *African Social Studies* (London: Heinemann, 1977), p. 286.

findings illustrate the unabashed and brazen appropriation of public funds by members of the privileged classes to the exclusion and detriment of the underprivileged classes. And, what is more, the culprits, far from being punished by the law, have continued to assume positions of social, economic, and political leadership. Those found corrupt in one area of the economy have been allowed conveniently to transfer to other areas. Some have been given bigger and more rewarding jobs. Those in the private sector are not even touched in any adverse manner. The untenable rationalization is that otherwise the economy would collapse. Objectively, however, the exercise reflects class solidarity of the privileged classes in their confrontation with the underprivileged classes.

These various class struggles have persisted and intensified, occasionally surfacing above their ethnic mask. They are conditioned by a determinate development of the country's productive forces as well the restrictions on this transformation, and the intercourse which correspond to these forces. Social praxis and, therefore, the nature and direction of motion of society are governed by the dynamics of the conditions of this development. They are the only basis for a change in the reality of social-material existence. Ethnic consciousness can only be significant in the social process to the degree to which it is congruent with the production relations and the class struggles which form the basis of social praxis. Otherwise, ethnicity plays a largely obscurantist role. Solutions to it which are not an integral part of solutions to the general problem of the transformation of the productive forces and production relations will be bogged down in the realm of rhetoric.

Recommendations

Adequate solutions for the ethnic problem of Nigeria must stem logically from a rigorous scientific analysis of the causes of the emergence, persistence, and growth of ethnicity in the country. On the basis of the preceding analysis the following are the major causes:

1. Colonial-type socioeconomic scarcity and inequality. These are the consequences of the peripheral capitalist system of economic organisation imposed by colonialism and inherited from colonial times. They have no relationship whatever to the creation of states or the existence of a federal character. They can only be

overcome by a reorganisation of the nation's economic life away from peripheral capitalism, and the private ownership of the means of production, distribution and exchange which lies at the heart of the structure of the inequality in capitalist societies. The new system must be designed to ensure a rapid growth of the productive forces and a salutary transformation of the consequent relations of production.

2. The intraclass competition for the division of national wealth arising partly from the organisation of the economy in isolated regional enclaves linked to the advanced capitalist societies but not to one another, and partly by the class character of the privileged classes which orients them essentially to distribution. An adequate remedy lies only in the creation of a nationally integrated economy and the removal from positions of power and national leadership of the present privileged classes together with their replacement in power by the working class that is oriented essentially toward relations of production and which has no vested interests in the present interethnic scheme of things.

3. The absence of class consciousness.

4. The internalization of ethnic sentiments.

5. The use of the ethnic base for political competition.

6. The use of regional governmental apparatus for ethnic competition

7. Political, social and economic policy differences which run along communal lines.

8. Differences in the traditional way of life and

9. The emergence of a section of the population which benefits from the allocation of resources along ethnic lines. Therefore, any programme for the creation of national unity should be judged by its effectiveness in eliminating or at least ameliorating the impact of these factors.

It soon becomes clear that the creation of states cannot overcome the difficulties posed by these factors. Instead, it will aggravate the interethnic situation by hampering the emergence of class consciousness in favour of state consciousness, permitting the use of regional governmental resources for ethnic competition, reinforcing the internalisation of ethnic sentiments, continuing the emphasis on the division of the national cake rather than the baking of such a cake, and whetting the appetite of those who stand to gain from the allocation of resources along ethnic lines. The energy and attention dissipated and focussed on the question of states should instead be deployed in favour of activities which ameliorate the impact of these factors.

Thus, emphasis should be placed on a drastic reduction of colonial-type, scarcity and inequality through a revolutionary development programme which, among other things, satisfies the demands of each citizen for a minimum of biologically and socially reasonable standards of nutrition, drinking water, free education, free health services, employment, housing, clothing, care of the old, entertainment and effective participation at all levels in national activities to which he is entitled as a matter of social policy; and by a revolutionary onslaught on the structure of private ownership in the country. By combating socioeconomic insecurity which arises from scarcity and inequality such a programme will pull the rug from under the feet of ethnic identification. Otherwise, the vast majority of the population will remain an easy prey to the machinations of the self-appointed champions of ethnic interests.

Both the internalisation of ethnic sentiments and the absence of class consciousness can be counteracted by a concerted governmental effort to ensure that all references to ethnic, state or other communal ties are exorcised from the news media and other national instruments of propaganda by law or through governmental ownership. A simultaneous effort should be made to create a new set of references which explains the basis of our present deplorable situation and can form the foci for a new set of identifications. In this regard, there is no substitute for a propaganda which emanates from the distinction between progressive and reactionary forces, exploiters and exploited, neocolonial and nationalist elements, and imperialist stooges versus anti-imperialist forces. In addition, all official references to individuals in official forms and other documents should emphasize their occupation and should not be extended to their ethnic origin.

The use of the ethnic homeland as a political base may be discouraged by the sponsorship of a political process based on the role of individuals in production. Representatives will be drawn from occupational rather than geographical constitutiences. Politicians will have their bases in the poor peasants, petty traders or similar interest groups. Similarly, the use of governmental instruments for ethnic competition can be avoided by such a political process, as well as by a reduction in the status of the present states from constitutional to merely administrative units.

The problem of the present material base of national unity should be tackled urgently and forcefully. A new base whose dominant economic sector integrates the various geographical sections one with the others should replace the present one which integrates them with Britain and the other advanced capitalist nations. It is necessary that the center of innovation be transferred into the country so that primary, secondary and tertiary economic activities will take place within the nation with each receiving the full complement of the others. Also, it is important that these activities be based on the satisfaction of local needs through the use of local resources. The overwhelming desire to catch up with the advanced nations should give way to an overriding wish to meet the most basic needs of the vast majority of our population. In the pursuit of this wish, the comparative advantages of the various geographical regions in the production of local necessities should be maximised.

Political, social, and economic policy differences and imbalances across communal lines should be remedied by the formulation, as well as strict application of identical rules, norms and regulations throughout the country, together with a definite and special revolutionary effort to remedy the present imbalances in the socioeconomic attainments of various areas of the country. Differences in the traditional cultures of the people should be deemphasised and similarities emphasised. In this regard, the strong emphasis on the role of the traditional rulers by the present military regime is misplaced. The role of the traditional chiefs in national and local life should be abolished and replaced by the direct democratic participation of the masses in all spheres of life. Similarly, festivals of the arts which tend to portray differences in art forms should be played down at this juncture and, instead, a conscious effort made to encourage cultural shows which display more similarities than differences across communal groups.

The unfortunate orientation of the national population to the division of the national cake should be shifted to an emphasis on the production of the national cake. It is when the national cake (creative production as opposed to mere extraction of petroleum) is not increasing at a rate commensurate with the social and economic expectations of the people that destructive competition for the existing resources ensues. But without a strong orientation to production, the growth of the productive forces is stunted. A new system of incentive and social rewards based on the success of production units to meet their targets should be propagated throughout the nation. At the same time, wealth should be de-emphasized as the basis for social status and replaced by the level of creative production of goods, services and ideas.

Finally, the struggle against ethnic chauvinism should not be waged under the leadership of that segment of the population which benefits from the contemporary interethnic situation. Such leadership includes the Nigerian businessmen, big and small, rural notables, the top echelons of the civil and military bureaucracy, landlords, and university lecturers. They are the major beneficiaries of the present nineteen state structure, as they were of the regional system, and as they will be of any constitutional set up composed of units with different Civil Service, Government and control over important contract jobs. Also, together with the top achelons of the military bureaucracy, the advanced capitalist nations, notably Britain, and foreign capitalists, the Nigerian petty bourgeoise and comprador bourgeoise are the major beneficiaries of the inherited colonial ceremony.

Opposed to the existing conditions are the vast majority of Nigerians who have remained largely silent, remote from the political and economic seats of power and merely marginal to the realm of income distribution. They consist of the middle and lower echelons of the working population, the semi-skilled and unskilled workers, the unemployed, petty traders, and the middle and poor farmers. While it is the privileged classes that hold political and economic power in the inherited colonial order, it is these underprivileged groups who must assume political and economic power if the country is to pull itself out of its present interethnic quagmire and out of the rot of its socioeconomic underdevelopment. Progress toward a shift in the balance of power from the former to the latter must, therefore, remain the major criterion for deciding whether any Nigerian regime is revolutionary or reactionary; it must also determine the extent to which it is making a positive contribution to the political and social development of the country, whether a revolution is taking place or not. Arguments which plead the pragmatic necessities of politics or the need to be realistic can no longer suffice as an excuse for not doing what must be done. Rather, such arguments should be seen as an expression of the bankruptcy of the programmes of the regime that subscribes to them. And the colonialist and fascist myth that the masses cannot effectively take the reins of their government in their own hands should be answered in a manner reminiscent of the nationalist struggle for flag independence, namely, that the masses have the right and should be granted the power to manage or mismanage their own affairs. All they have witnessed ever since the outset of colonization has been a mismanagement of their affairs by others.

A progressive or revolutionary regime should cultivate and strengthen an alliance between it and the rural and urban poor majority. It should divert funds and energy from the creation and consolidation of states to the formation of viable associations of poor peasants, workers, petty traders and the underemployed and unemployed. This should be done through the instrumentality of a political movement motivated by their interests, dominated and guided by their organisations, devoted to the implementation of progressive policies, and protected by an army that would have transformed itself from an inherited colonial institution designed to protect foreign capital to a veritable people's defence force.

The peasants, workers, petty traders and artisans, and the underemployed and unemployed are the only true and dependable ally in the struggle against ethnic sectionalism and the inherited colonial system. In the past, their devotion to the interests of the nation as a whole has been unparalleled. During the pre-petroleum days they held the foreign exchange fort. Today they hold the anti-hunger fort. And by bearing in silence the major brunt of the consequences of the distorted taste pattern, the high prices of goods and services, and the loss of benefits from programmes that might have been undertaken in a broad public interest, they hold the stability fort. But the drums of their silence are beating louder than ever.

INDEX

aphic-visual production: Editora Ática S.A. - São Paulo - Brazil — Printed in Brazil by W. Roth Ltd.